1. Dimensions

THE DIMENSIONS OF THE PRIESTHOOD

the
DIMENSIONS
of the Priesthood

THEOLOGICAL
CHRISTOLOGICAL
LITURGICAL
ECCLESIAL
APOSTOLIC
MARIAN

Compiled by the

Daughters of St. Paul

Second printing.

ST. PAUL EDITIONS

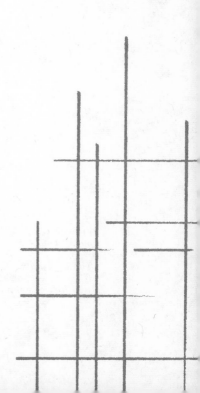

Grateful acknowledgment is made to the following
for use of translations in this book:

NC News Service
1312 Massachusetts Ave., N.W.
Washington, D.C. 20005

L'Osservatore Romano
English Weekly Edition
Vatican City

and official Vatican texts.

Library of Congress Catalog Card Number: 73-76310

The Daughters of St. Paul are an international
religious congregation serving the Church
with the communications media.

FOREWORD

The radical and rapid social and moral changes in contemporary life affect the lives of many human beings, including the lives of those dedicated to the service of God through the service of His people.

The Catholic priest experiences the difficulties of normal human beings and reflects in his life the problems of the general population. Additionally, he encounters the problems of constantly striving for perfection and measuring up to the transscendental demands of his vocation. He strives to be a man of God among men; to be in the world, but not of the world; to conform the world to Christ, and not to be conformed to the world; to exercise a changeless ministry rooted in Christ and preach the timeless truths of the gospel amid the changing conditions and circumstances of life and to be a witness and a dispenser of a life other than this earthly life.

The priest must preserve continuity amid continued change. He must promote authentic renewal, but he must also resist the whimsical and arbitrary changes which impoverish or distort the word of God. He must guard against those who would

9

bury God and who attempt to construct a godless Christian religion committed to serve men in this life only and to liberate and deliver man from everything except from sin to a life of grace. Such views often lead to social action which ignores the direct relationship of men to God and seeks to reconstruct the secular universe on its own terms, thereby creating a kingdom in the world, instead of the kingdom of God. Such views contradict the teaching of Jesus that love of God and love of neighbor are one single reality. Such views not only engender confusion about the ministerial priesthood, but also imply that it is meaningless and serves no purpose.

Since the Second Vatican Council, priestly life and ministry has been the subject of a great deal of discussion and of a great deal of writing. The flow of literature on the priesthood has been constant. Some of the literature, written in a scholarly scriptural, theological, historical fashion, is a significant contribution toward theological development. Some of the literature has a great inspirational and devotional value. Some of the literature seems at best to be in the form of tracts, manifestoes and blast-offs. As often happens, such literature, which has minimal intrinsic value, receives maximum publicity and circulation.

The nature and dimensions of the problems of priestly life and ministry have also been the subject of studies and of sociological and psychological surveys. Such surveys, recommended by at least three conciliar documents, are not a means of determining what the ministerial priesthood is, or what its purpose is. This was determined by Christ. The surveys, however, do present the nature and dimensions of current problems, in themselves and in the manner in which they are perceived. Such information is valuable and even necessary to give proper direction to the adaptation of the priestly ministry to current needs. "Scientific" surveys are designed to highlight problems—not to solve them. Not all the surveys on the ministerial priesthood are of equal value. Some were excellent. Many were mediocre. Some were spotty and biased and at times geared to a predetermined conclusion to serve as instruments of propaganda. Some were the work of lobbyists rather than scholars.

Granting the unquestionable value of truly scholarly studies and scientific surveys, the fact is that the priestly ministry cannot be interpreted only in sociological terms. The ministerial priesthood is not a chairmanship democratically delegated by constituents. The priestly ministry is essentially different from all other ministries. It was established by our Lord, and it is conferred by the sacrament of Orders. Surveys can tell us much about the ministerial priesthood, but only Jesus Christ, who established such a priesthood, can tell us what its nature and functions are. As the Synod of 1971 tells us, "By the laying on of hands, there is communicated a gift of the Holy Spirit which cannot be lost (cf. 2 Tm 1:6). This reality configures the ordained minister to Christ the Priest, consecrates him and makes him a sharer in Christ's mission under its two aspects of authority and service."

Theological discussion and study can be an invaluable contribution to a better understanding and appreciation of the ministerial priesthood. However, we can never ignore the fact that the guarantee of the truth of the Faith, and the truth of the nature and function of the ministerial priesthood is not the chair of the professor of theology, but the Chair of St. Peter. It is to this Chair of St. Peter that the Daughters of St. Paul have recourse in presenting: **The Dimensions of the Priesthood.**

This volume is a compilation of 325 selected passages from the documents of Vatican II; from post-conciliar documents; from the writings and addresses of Popes Pius XII, John XXIII, Paul VI, and the 1971 World Synod of Bishops. This treasury of selected passages is presented on six main tracks: Theological, Christological, Liturgical, Ecclesial, Apostolic and Marian.

My best recommendation of this volume cannot possibly match the merit of its contents. Every seminarian and every priest will find in this volume an incomparable treasure of the Church's authentic teaching on the ministerial priesthood. **The Dimensions of the Priesthood** is an indispensable book in the library of every cleric. It is a source book, a book of meditations, and a book of prayer and of spiritual reading. A studied reading of the book will help the priest to achieve a greater union with Christ and His Church and to be conformed to Christ in carrying out His mission.

John Card. Krol

JOHN CARDINAL KROL
Archbishop of Philadelphia

Key to Abbreviations

AA   —*Apostolicam actuositatem,* Decree on the Apostolate of the Laity, Vatican II.

AG   —*Ad gentes,* Decree on the Mission Activity of the Church, Vatican II.

APC   —*Ad Petri cathedram,* Encyclical Letter, Near the Chair of Peter, Pope John XXIII.

CD   —*Christus Dominus,* Decree Concerning the Pastoral Office of Bishops in the Church, Vatican II.

DAS   —*Divino Afflante Spiritu,* Encyclical Letter, Promotion of Biblical Studies, Pope Pius XII.

DH   —*Dignitatis humanae,* Declaration on Religious Freedom, Vatican II.

DV   —*Dei Verbum,* Dogmatic Constitution on Divine Revelation, Vatican II.

EcS   —*Ecclesiam Suam,* Encyclical Letter, Paths of the Church, Pope Paul VI.

EM   —*Eucharisticum Mysterium,* Instruction on the Eucharistic Mystery, Sacred Congregation of Rites.

GS   —*Gaudium et spes,* Pastoral Constitution on the Church in the Modern World, Vatican II.

IOE   —*Inter oecumenici,* First Instruction on the Liturgy, Sacred Congregation of Rites.

LG   —*Lumen gentium,* Dogmatic Constitution on the Church, Vatican II.

MC   —*Mystici corporis,* Encyclical Letter, Mystical Body of Christ, Pope Pius XII.

MD   — *Munificentissimus Deus*, Apostolic Constitution on the Assumption of the Blessed Virgin Mary, Pope Pius XII.

MF   — *Mysterium fidei*, Encyclical Letter, Mystery of Faith, Pope Paul VI.

MM   — *Mater et Magistra*, Encyclical Letter, On Christianity and Social Progress, Pope John XXIII.

OT   — *Optatam totius*, Decree on Priestly Training, Vatican II.

PC   — *Perfectae caritatis*, Decree on the Adaptation and Renewal of Religious Life, Vatican II.

PO   — *Presbyterorum ordinis*, Decree on the Ministry and Life of Priests, Vatican II.

PP   — *Populorum progressio*, Encyclical Letter, On the Development of Peoples, Pope Paul VI.

PT   — *Pacem in terris*, Encyclical Letter, Peace on Earth, Pope John XXIII.

RF   — *Ratio Fundamentalis Institutionis Sacerdotalis*, A Basic Scheme for Priestly Training, Sacred Congregation for Catholic Education.

SC   — *Sacrosanctum concilium*, Constitution on the Sacred Liturgy, Vatican II.

SCl   — *Sacerdotalis coelibatus*, Encyclical Letter, On Priestly Celibacy, Pope Paul VI.

SNP   — *Sacerdotii nostri primordia*, Encyclical Letter, From the Beginning of Our Priesthood, Pope John XXIII.

SP   — *Summi pontificatus*, Encyclical Letter, Function of the State in the Modern World, Pope Pius XII.

SV   — *Sancta virginitas*, Encyclical Letter, Holy Virginity, Pope Pius XII.

UR   — *Unitatis redintegratio*, Decree on Ecumenism, Vatican II.

The above documents are available in pamphlet form from the Daughters of St. Paul, 50 St. Paul's Avenue, Jamaica Plain, Boston, Ma., 02130.

Contents

Theological Dimension

> Called and Chosen - Transmission of Charism
> - Who Is the Priest?

> To Serve the Lord - To Serve Our Brothers

Christological Dimension

> In the Priesthood of Christ - Other Christs -
> Discipleship - Holiness: The Force Behind the
> Ministry - Perfect Manhood in Christ - Witness
> Value

Liturgical Dimension

Ecclesial Dimension

INTRODUCTION

The heart of a priest: I think
that your hearts too are at times uneasy and disturbed by
the many questions and problems that have arisen since
the Council even in our ordinarily tranquil minds. What
has happened? The exploration of the causes and the
examination of the phenomenon of this state of mind which
is unusual for a priest precisely because of what he is and
what he does, have given rise, as you know, to much study,
writing, discussion, and certainly also to many personal
reflections on your part. The aggressive tide brought by
the critical period that we are going through has reached
us too. From some points of view it is providential, from
others it is dangerous and negative. It has obliged us to
rethink our priesthood in all its elements: biblical, theological, canonical, ascetical, and operative. The fact that
this rethinking has been taking place face to face with the
challenges of the whirlwind of changes in modern life,
both in the field of ideas and above all in the practical,
active, and social field, has made us too ask whether the
traditional life of the priest should not be studied in a
new historical and spiritual context.

The world is changing, and are we standing there
motionless, as though we were canonically mummified in
our crystalized outlook and in our traditional customs,
the meaning and value of some of which are no longer

understood by many, neither by the society that surrounds us, nor at times by ourselves? Trust in a certain type of renewal is given us not only by this formidable pressure from outside but also by the Council, which was authoritative and good, and which spoke to us of "aggiornamento." Some have interpreted this "aggiornamento" as a justification, indeed as an apologia for an extremely delicate criterion, that of historical relativism, of adaptation to the times, to the famous "signs of the times" (as though these were capable of being interpreted intuitively by all), of conforming, in other words, to the world—that world in which we find ourselves and from which the Council urged the Church no longer to separate herself as a matter of principle, but to immerse herself in it in order to fulfill her mission.

The onslaught of this thrust towards novelty has often given us ecclesiastics too, a certain feeling of dizziness (cf. Is 19:14), a lack of confidence in tradition, a certain low estimation of ourselves, a mania for change, a capricious need for "creative spontaneity," and so on. Intentions which are without doubt subjectively upright and generous have also found a place in this vast and complex attempt at transforming ecclesiastical life. We shall point out two of them to show you how We follow these phenomena with loving attentiveness. First, there is the intention, deeply and painfully felt, of escaping from the state of what is now called frustration, that is, from a sense, experienced by some, of the uselessness of one's being paralyzed in the discipline of the ecclesiastical organization. What is the use, they ask, of being a priest?

It is a bitter and anguished question in places where the community to which these priests belonged has profoundly changed in numbers and life-style and where the priest's ministry, tied to a fixed place and fixed customs, seems to have become either superfluous or ineffective. The objection that one's life is useless is, especially today, when we are so conscious of utilitarian efficiency, a very tormenting one. It deserves at the least loving understanding, even if an adequate remedy is not possible. The other intention, which is likewise certainly inspired by a good desire, is that of those who would like to remove every clerical or religious distinction of a sociological nature, of dress, profession, or state, in order to identify with the ordinary people and to conform to the life-style of others — in short, to laicize themselves, in order thus to penetrate society more easily. This is, if you will, a missionary intention, but what a dangerous and injurious one it is, if it ends up with the loss of that specific power of reacting on society that is included in Our definition of "the salt of the earth," and if it reduces the priest to a uselessness worse than that to which We have already referred. This is what the Lord says: "What is the good of salt that has become tasteless?" (cf. Mt 5:13)

Dear brothers, read the introductory part of the document on the ministerial priesthood discussed in the recent Synod of Bishops. There, in a brief but comprehensive and vigorous synthesis, is described the priest's situation today, with all its problems. You will see with what an attentive eye, and with what an affectionate heart the Church is considering the present condition of the clergy. Realism and love have shaped this serious, but at the same time considerate and optimistic, study.

We now draw your attention to this important matter. Throughout this situation with its internal and external problems, one question concerning our priesthood stands out above the others. In a certain sense it sums them all up. It is that question which has become a common one in the complex discussion concerning us; the question is about the so-called identity of the priest: who is he? ...Once the meaning and sacramental value of our ministry, that is, our apostolate, is understood, a whole set of other elements can give shape to the spiritual, ecclesial, and even the social figure of the Catholic priest, so as to identify him as unique among all, whether inside or outside the ecclesiastical society. The priest is not just a presbyter presiding over the community on religious occasions. He is truly the indispensable and exclusive minister of official worship, performed in the person of Christ and at the same time in the name of the people; he is the man of prayer, the only one who brings about the Eucharistic Sacrifice, the man who gives life to dead souls, the dispenser of grace, the man of blessing. The apostle-priest is the witness of the faith, the missionary of the gospel, the prophet of hope, the center of the community. From him it goes outward and to him it returns. He builds up the Church of Christ, which is founded on Peter.

And here we come to that title which is properly his, a title both lowly and sublime: he is the shepherd of God's People. He is the worker of charity, the guardian of orphans and little ones, the advocate of the poor, the consoler of the suffering, the father of souls, the confidant, the counselor, the guide, the friend of all, the man for others, and, if need be, the willing and silent hero. If you look closely at the anonymous countenance of this solitary man with no home of his own, you will see one who can no longer love just humanly, because he has given all his heart, without withholding any portion of it, to that Christ who gave Himself for him even to the cross (cf. Gal 2:20) and to that neighbor whom he has resolved to love to the extent that Christ does (cf. Jn 13:15). This is in fact the meaning of his intense, happy sacrifice in celibacy. To put it in a single phrase, he is another Christ.

This in the final analysis is the priest's identity: as we have so often heard repeated, he is another Christ.

Well, then, what ground is there for doubt or fear?
—Pope Paul VI, to Lenten preachers, 2-17-72.

22

THEOLOGICAL DIMENSION

Priests by sacred ordination and mission which they receive from the bishops are promoted to the service of Christ the Teacher, Priest and King. They share in His ministry, a ministry whereby the Church here on earth is unceasingly built up into the People of God, the Body of Christ and the Temple of the Holy Spirit. —PO 1.

The Priestly Identity

CALLED AND CHOSEN

TRANSMISSION OF CHARISM

WHO IS THE PRIEST?

CALLED AND CHOSEN

God, who alone is holy and who alone bestows holiness, willed to take as His companions and helpers men who would humbly dedicate themselves to the work of sanctification. Hence, through the ministry of the bishop, God consecrates priests, that being made sharers by special title in the priesthood of Christ, they might act as His ministers in performing sacred functions. — PO 5.

These ministers in the society of the faithful are able by the sacred power of Orders to offer Sacrifice and to forgive sins,[1] and they perform their priestly office publicly for men in the name of Christ. Therefore, having sent the apostles just as He Himself had been sent by the Father,[2] Christ, through the apostles themselves, made their successors, the bishops,[3] sharers in His consecration and mission. The office of their ministry has been handed down, in a lesser degree indeed, to the priests.[4] Established in the order of the priesthood they can be co-workers of the episcopal order for the proper fulfillment of the apostolic mission entrusted to priests by Christ.[5] — PO 2.

In the same way, actually, that Baptism is the distinctive mark of all Christians,... the sacrament of Holy Orders sets the priest apart from the rest of the faithful who have not received this consecration.

...For they alone, in answer to an inward supernatural call have entered the august ministry, where they are assigned to service in the sanctuary and become, as it were, the instruments God uses to communicate supernatural life from on high to the Mystical Body of Jesus Christ. Add to this, as We have noted above, the fact that they alone have been consecrated "in order that whatever they bless may be blessed, whatever they consecrate may become sacred and holy, in the name of Our Lord Jesus Christ."[6] —MD.

Priests, who are taken from among men and ordained for men in the things that belong to God in order to offer gifts and sacrifices for sins (cf. Heb 5:1), nevertheless live on earth with other men as brothers. The Lord Jesus, the Son of God, a Man sent by the Father to men, dwelt among us and willed to become like His brethren in all things except sin (cf. Heb 2:17; 4:15). The holy apostles imitated Him. Blessed Paul, the doctor of the Gentiles, "set apart for the Gospel of God" (Rom 1:1) declares that he became all things to all men that he might save all (cf. 1 Cor 9:19-23). Priests of the New Testament, by their vocation and ordination, are in a certain sense set apart in the bosom of the People of God. However, they are not to be separated from the People of God or from any person; but they are to be totally dedicated to the work for which the Lord has chosen them (cf. Acts 13:2). —PO 3.

All priestly power and ministry in the Catholic Church derives its origin from the unique and eternal priesthood of Christ, who was sanctified by the Father and sent into the world (cf. Jn 10:36), and made His apostles in the first place, and their successors, the bishops, sharers in the same priesthood. In different ways the various members of the Church share in that one same priesthood of Christ: the general, or common, priesthood of the faithful constitutes a certain simple degree of this sharing, the faithful who through baptism and the anointing of the Holy Spirit "receive consecration as a spiritual house, a holy priesthood. It is their task, in every employment, to offer the spiritual sacrifices of a Christian man."[7]

Priests share in the priesthood of Christ in a different way: they "do not possess the high dignity of the Pontificate; they are dependent on bishops for the exercise of their power. They are nevertheless united to them in priestly honor. In virtue of the sacrament of Orders, they are consecrated in the likeness of Christ, high and eternal priest (cf. Heb 5:1-10; 7:24; 9:11-28), as genuine priests of the New Testament, for the work of preaching the gospel, tending the faithful, and celebrating divine worship."[8] For this reason, therefore, the *ministerial priesthood* of priests surpasses the general priesthood of the faithful, since through it some in the body of the Church are assimilated to Christ the Head, and are promoted "to serve Christ, their Master, Priest and King, and to share His ministry. Thus the Church on earth is constantly built up into the People of God, the Body of Christ and Temple of the Holy Spirit."[9]

"There is an essential difference between the faithful's priesthood in common and the priesthood of the ministry or the hierarchy, and not just a difference of degree. Nevertheless, there is an ordered relation between them: one and the other has its special way of sharing the single priesthood of Christ."[10] — RF.

We are men who are called. We are called by Christ, called by God. That means that we are loved by Christ, loved by God. Do we think about this? "I know," says the Lord, "the ones I have chosen" (Jn 13:18). A divine plan conceived beforehand rests firmly on each one of us, so that of us it can be said what the prophet Jeremiah says to Israel in the name of God: "I have loved you with an everlasting love, so I am constant in my affection for you" (31:3). An identity entered in heaven, "in the book of life..." (cf. Rev 3:5).

Our gospel begins with our vocation. It seems to us justifiable to see in the history of the apostles the history of us priests. As for the first men that Jesus chose to be His own, the gospel story is very clear and very beautiful. The Lord's intention is obvious, and it is very interesting in the messianic setting and, later, in the context of the economy of Christianity. It is Jesus who takes the initiative; He Himself points this out: "You did not choose me, no, I chose you" (Jn 15:16; 15:19; cf. Jn 6:70) and the simple and delightful scenes which portray for us the calling of each disciple show fixed choices being carried out with precision (cf. Lk 6:13). It will be a pleasure for us to meditate on them. Whom does He call? He does not seem to take account of the social standing of those He chooses (cf. 1 Cor 1:27); nor does He seem to want to make use of those who offer themselves with superficial enthusiasm (cf. Mt 8:19-22).

This design in the gospels concerns us personally. I repeat: we are men who have been called. The familiar question of vocation concerns the personality and destiny of each one of us. How our vocations developed and were formed is the most interesting factor in the personal history of our lives. It would be foolish to try to reduce a vocation to a complex of trivial external circumstances. On the contrary, we should note the ever more assiduous and careful attention with which the Church nurtures, selects and assists priestly vocations.

This is a factor providing certainty in the confirmation of our identity—an identity that is often today subjected to specious analysis with the aim of declaring it unauthentic. In fact today it is an extremely difficult thing for a vocation to the Church to be based upon internal and external motives that could be honestly questioned. The saying of Paschal: "The most important thing in life is the choice of a profession: chance decides it"[11] does not hold good for us. It was not chance that decided for us. — Pope Paul VI, to Lenten preachers, 2-17-72.

What an invitation to great-hearted faithfulness springs forth for our priesthood, for us and for all our brothers who are devoted to the following and the service of Christ through sacramental ordination to the ministerial priesthood! How clearly has the "identity" of the Catholic priesthood been defined! What a benefit has been assured, today also, for the ministration of the word of God, the dispensation of grace and the pastoral direction of the People of God! What a full awareness of generous and joyful adhesion to the concept, which is paradoxical because it is evangelical, holy (that is, mystical and ascetical), simple and human in its practical and prophetic reality of our following of Christ, qualified as it is by the double and total gift of love to Christ Himself and, in Him and through Him, to our brothers and sisters and to the world. — Pope Paul VI, to College of Cardinals, 1-6-72.

We address you as "your fellow-presbyter and witness of the sufferings of Christ" (1 Pt 5:1), as the Representative on earth of Jesus, the Son of God born of the Blessed Virgin Mary, who has wished, by an unfathomable plan of love, to choose you individually as His close friends (cf. Jn 15:15), making you participants in the ministerial priesthood, which gives you a position of particular dignity and responsibility within the People of God.

3. *Dimensions*

An immense gift is the priesthood, entrusted to our frail men's hands so that we may cherish it with ever growing love. Priests were continually reminded of this, in several documents, by Vatican II, which, synthesizing the faith and life of the Church in the task of listening to the word of God with reverence and proclaiming it confidently,[12] stressed the sublime dignity of the priesthood, but also the duty of holiness that it entails.

So let the delicate and never-to-be-repeated memory of your priestly ordination always be present in your heart, to animate every apostolic action, to overcome every inevitable difficulty. — Pope Paul VI, to newly-ordained priests, 4-3-69.

By Christ you have been loved and you have been called, through a spiritual history and experience which has marked your life and your vocation, which is a sign of predilection on His part. He looked upon you and loved you (cf. Mk 10:21) and He chose you (cf. Jn 15:16); for your part, you responded and said yes to His love; you chose the better part (cf. Lk 10:42); you have given and consecrated yourselves to Him, without reserve and without repentance. You have understood to their very depths the demands of the kingdom of heaven; you have given everything, you have given your all for All, that is, for Him who is Life. — Pope Paul VI, Farewell to African Clergy, 8-14-69.

If the priest is the man of God, "another Christ," this is a sign that a stream of grace has followed through the history of his life: he is one called, chosen, preferred by the Lord's mercy. The Lord has loved him particularly; He has marked him with a special character, and thus qualified him to exercise divine authority.[13] He has made him fall in love with Himself, to the extent of maturing in him the fullest and greatest act of love of which the human heart is capable: complete, perpetual and happy donation of himself.... He has had the courage to make his life an offering, just like Jesus, for others, for all, for us. — Pope Paul VI, to a general audience, 10-13-71.

Today more than ever before there is need in the Church of priests who have a clear idea of their responsibility to Christ and to their fellowmen. The needs of the People of God are great and the urgency of preaching the redeeming gospel of the Lord to the ends of the earth is pressing. You have been called and chosen and sent forth to fulfill this role. We exhort each of you in the words Paul spoke to Timothy: "Always be steady, endure suffering, do the work of an evangelist, fulfill your ministry" (2 Tm 4:5). This is your vocation, this is your happiness: "Guard what has been entrusted to you" (1 Tm 6:20).

At the same time that We encourage you to realize the great responsibility that is yours and to accept courageously its challenge, We exhort you to do this in the name of Christ and relying on His grace. You must be convinced that the Lord is with you. As priests of this generation, the collective expression of your supernatural confidence must be that enjoined on one of the early Christian communities: "Let us hold fast the confession of our hope without wavering, for he who promised is faithful" (Heb 10:23). By the witness of your lives you must show the world the reason for your priestly dedication: "...because we have set our hope on the living God" (1 Tm 4:10). — Pope Paul VI, to newly-ordained priests, 3-3-71.

Undoubtedly, priests have no special shelter from the repercussions of the crisis of transformation which is upsetting the world today. Like all their brothers in the faith, they, too, experience hours of darkness in their journey toward God. Moreover, they suffer because of the frequently biased way in which certain facts of priestly life are interpreted and unjustly generalized. Therefore, We ask priests to remember that the situation of every Christian, and particularly of every priest, will always be a paradoxical and incomprehensible situation to those who have no faith. Hence, the present state of things urges the priest to deepen his faith, to realize ever more clearly to whom he belongs, with what powers he is invested, with what mission he is charged.

...To all priests, then, We say: Never doubt the nature of your ministerial priesthood, for it is not a commonplace office or service to be exercised for the ecclesial community, but a service which participates in a very special manner, through the sacrament of Orders and with an indelible character, in the power of the priesthood of Christ.[14] — Pope Paul VI, message to priests, 6-30-68.

1. Council of Trent, 23rd session, chapter 1, canon 1: Denzinger 957 and 961 (1764 and 1771).

2. Cf. Jn 20:21; LG 22.

3. LG 22.

4. Cf. *ibid.*

5. Cf. Roman Pontifical "Ordination of a Priest," preface. These words are already found in the Verona Sacramentary (L.C. Moehlberg, Rome, 1956, p. 122); also in Frankish Missal (L.C. Moehlberg, Rome, 1957, p. 9) and in the Book of Sacramentaries of the Roman Church (L.C. Moehlberg, Rome, 1960, p. 25) and Roman German Pontificals (Vogel-Elze, Vatican City, 1963, vol. I, p. 34).

6. Pontif. Rom., *De ordinatione presbyteri, in manuum unctione.*

7. LG 10.

8. *Ibid.,* 28.

9. PO 1.

10. LG 10.

11. *Pensèes* 97.

12. Cf. DV 1.

13. Cf. *Summa Theol.* III, 3, 5, 2.

14. LG 10, 28.

TRANSMISSION OF CHARISM

The office of priests, since it is connected with the episcopal order, also, in its own degree, shares the authority by which Christ builds up, sanctifies and rules His Body. Wherefore the priesthood, while indeed it presupposes the sacraments of Christian initiation, is conferred by that special sacrament; through it priests, by the anointing of the Holy Spirit, are signed with a special character and are conformed to Christ the Priest in such a way that they can act in the person of Christ the Head.[1] — PO 2.

We can place in relief certain dimensions which are proper to the Catholic priesthood, and, first of all, its character of sacredness. The priest is the man of God, the minister of the Lord. He can perform acts which transcend natural powers, because he acts *"in persona Christi"*; through him there passes a superior power, for at given moments he is, in his humility and his glory, its valid instrument, the channel of the Holy Spirit. Between him and the divine sphere there is a unique relationship, a divine delegation and trust.

This gift, however, is not possessed by the priest for himself, but for others, the sacred dimension is entirely oriented toward the apostolic dimension, that is, to the priestly mission and ministry. — Pope Paul VI, message to priests, 6-30-68.

When the time came for Him to leave this world and return to the Father, Jesus decided to choose and beckon other pastors after His heart. He called to Him those whom He desired (Mk 3:13), to make disciples of all nations, to the close of the age (Mt 28:18ff.). They will be His envoys, His messengers, His apostles.

They can be pastors only in His name, for the good of the flock and by the grace of His Spirit, to whom they must be faithful. The first of these was Peter, who, after his threefold confession of love of Jesus, was named pastor of His sheep and of His lambs (Jn 21:15-17). Then all the apostles. And after them, others still, but all in the same Spirit. And each one, in every age, must tend the Lord's flock entrusted to him, not domineering them, but by setting an example, with total altruism and generosity of heart (1 Pt 5:2ff.). Only thus when the chief Shepherd is manifested will they obtain the unfading crown of glory (1 Pt 5:4). — Pope Paul VI, vocation day message, 3-12-69.

We will try to sum up in a single word everything which can be thought and said concerning the event which is about to occur for you [ordination]. That word is transmission. Transmission of a divine power, a miraculous power of action, which *per se* belongs only to Christ.

Transmission of the power: Through the laying on of Our hands and the meaningful words which confer on the action a sacramental power, Christ sends down His Spirit from on high and pours into you that Spirit, the Holy Spirit, the vivifying and powerful Spirit. He comes to you not only to dwell in you, as in the other sacraments, but also to enable you to perform certain definite actions which are proper to Christ's priesthood, and to make you His efficacious ministers, vehicles of the Word and of grace. In this way He modifies your persons, in such a fashion that they not only represent Christ, but also act in a certain way as He, through a delegation which stamps an indelible "character" on your souls and likens you to Him, each of you as an *"alter Christus,"* another Christ.

Never forget that this marvel happens in you but not for you. It is for others, for the Church, which is to say, for the world to be saved. Your power is one of function, like the power of a special organ which works for the benefit of the whole body. Become instruments, become servants at the service of the brethren.

You can see the relationships which arise from this choice which has been made of you: relationships with God, with Christ, with the Church, with mankind. You understand what duties of prayer, charity and holiness, flow from your priestly ordination. You perceive what kind of a conscience you will always need to form in order to be equal to the office with which you are invested. You understand with what spiritual and human mindfulness you will need to look at the world, with what sentiments and what virtues you will need to exercise your ministry, with what dedication and courage you will have to live your lives, in what a spirit of sacrifice united with that of Christ.
— Pope Paul VI, pre-ordination message, 5-28-70.

By the laying on of hands there is communicated a gift of the Holy Spirit which cannot be lost (cf. 2 Tm 1:6). This reality configures the ordained minister to Christ the Priest, consecrates him[2] and makes him a sharer in Christ's mission under its two aspects of authority and service.

That authority does not belong to the minister as his own: it is a manifestation of the *exousia* (i.e. the power) of the Lord, by which the priest is an ambassador of Christ in the eschatological work of reconciliation (cf. 2 Cor 5:18-20). He also assists the conversion of human freedom to God for the building up of the Christian community.

The lifelong permanence of this reality, which is a sign, and which is a teaching of the faith and is referred to in the Church's tradition as the priestly character, expresses the fact that Christ associated the Church with Himself in an irrevocable way for the salvation of the

world, and that the Church dedicates herself to Christ in a definitive way for the carrying out of His work. The minister whose life bears the seal of the gift received through the sacrament of Orders reminds the Church that the gift of God is irrevocable. In the midst of the Christian community which, in spite of its defects, lives by the Spirit, he is a pledge of the salvific presence of Christ.

This special participation in Christ's priesthood does not disappear even if a priest for ecclesial or personal reasons is dispensed or removed from the exercise of his ministry. — Ministerial Priesthood, Nov. 1971, Synod Document.

1. LG 10.   2. Cf. PO 2.

WHO IS THE PRIEST?

Who is the priest? Is there really a priest in the Christian religion? And if there is a minister of the gospel, what is the role that he should assume? All the temptations of the early Protestant polemic have been revived. Perhaps even deeper temptations springing from a preternatural source have come to life — this is a mystery, not fantasy — temptations of doubt, not as a method of research, but as a disheartened response proceeding from ungrasped truth and from uncertainty to the point of blindness—a response which is assumed as a dramatic and condescending attitude by a person deprived of interior light.

These temptations have been felt even at the very center of the intimate self-awareness of the priest and have disturbed that blessed interior certitude about his role in the Church: *Tu es sacerdos in aeternum,* "you are a priest forever"; in its place there has been substituted a nagging question: Who am I? Does not the answer of the Church suffice—the answer that has always been given and that was taught to us from our years in the seminary, the answer that has burned as an everlasting flame in the center of our heart and has become part of our personal outlook?

Indeed it is a question that at first sight seems as superfluous as it is dangerous; but the fact is that it has been shot as an arrow into the heart of many priests, especially of some young men on the threshold of ordination, and of other brothers when they had arrived at the fullness of maturity. The tendency of our brothers, when they have found themselves in this difficult situation of doubt concerning themselves and the authority of the Church, a tendency *per se* hypothetically legitimate, but soon transformed into temptation and deviation because of the impossibility of finding a satisfying answer—the tendency has been to seek the definition of the priest's identity in the wrong place, or outside the household of the faith, in the writings of sociology especially, or of psychology, or in the comparison with Christian Churches separated from Catholic roots, or finally in a humanism which has the axiom: the priest is above all a man, a whole man, like all others....

We must search for the definition of the priest's identity in the thought of Christ. Only faith can tell us who we are and what we should be. The rest—what history, experience, society, the needs of the times, etc., can tell us—we will look for afterwards, with the responsible and wise assistance of the Church, as a logical derivation from an encounter in faith and from a commentary and application of it. Let then, the Lord speak to us. This is the theme... which each one of you can later develop on his own, in the inner sanctuary of the meeting with God.

And so let us humbly ask Jesus, our Master: what are we? Should we not perhaps consider what He thinks of us and what He wishes us to be and what our identity is, in His eyes? — Pope Paul VI, to Lenten preachers, 2-17-72.

...**What is** a priest? The question, at first naive and elementary, becomes heavy with deep and worrying doubts. Is the existence of a priesthood really justified in the economy of the New Testament, in view of the fact that the Levitical priesthood is finished, and only that of Christ fulfills the function of mediator between God and men; and men, raised to the level of "a chosen race" (1 Pt 2:9) have been reclothed with their own priesthood which authorizes them to adore the Father "in spirit and truth"? (Jn 4:24)

And then, what place and reason for existence is left for the priest in a society all tuned towards temporal and immanent goals, for the priest whose aims are transcendent and eschatological, and who is thus a stranger to the experience which is proper to the worldly man, in this overwhelming process of desacrilization, of secularization, which invades and transforms the modern world?

The doubt continues. Is the existence of a priesthood justified in the original intention of Christianity? Of a priesthood such as it is determined in its canonical definition? The doubt becomes critical under other aspects — psychological and sociological: is it possible? Does it serve any useful purpose? Can it still galvanize a lyrical and heroic vocation? Can it still constitute a way of life that is not alienated or frustrated?

The young intuitively guess this aggressive uncertainty, and many are discouraged. Now many vocations are extinguished by this adverse wind! And even some who are already priests sometimes feel this overpowering, interior torment; and for some it becomes fear, which alas in others is transformed into courage but only to flee, to defect: "Then the disciples...forsook him and fled"; the hour of Gethsemane! (Mt 26:56)

One hears of the crisis of the priesthood....

You are aware of the dangers, feel the pressures, desire defense....

Nothing is more necessary now than for our clergy to take up a firm stand of awareness and confidence in their own vocations. One could adapt the words of St. Paul to the present situation: "Consider your call, brethren" (1 Cor 1:26).

You know that there already exists a vast amount of literature on this subject. To books which undermine the security which reassures the Catholic priesthood, there are now books which answer not only by strengthening such security but which enhance it with new arguments, especially the most valid of all, that of an always more enlightened and convinced faith whence the life of a priest draws its inexhaustible source of light, courage, enthusiasm, and hope.

...Do not fear uncertainty over the priesthood. It could be providential, if we really know how to draw from it the stimulation to renew the genuine concept and updated exercise of our priesthood. But also, unfortunately, it could become destructive if one attributes more importance than is deserved to commonplace platitudes—circulated today with such facility—concerning this crisis of the priesthood, which some wish to make appear fatal, either by novelties of tendentious biblical studies, or by the authority of sociological phenomena, studied by means of statistical inquiries; or by surveys of psychological and moral phenomena.

These are interesting facts, if you wish, worthy of serious consideration by competent and responsible people, but they are never enough to shake our conception of the identity of the priesthood, provided this coincides with its authenticity, which the word of Christ and the derived and proven tradition of the Church delivers intact to our generation and, moreover, after the Council, in a way which has been deepened.

As you well know, such authenticity is maintained even in the face of the irreligious modern world, which precisely because it is so and because it has reached enormous progress in exploration and the conquest of things accessible to our experience, is conscious of, and will be still more conscious of the mystery of the universe that surrounds it and the illusion of one's own self-sufficiency, exposed by one's very own development to the danger of aridity and being no longer of use, and stimulated by the exasperating attempt to reach the ultimate truth and the life which never dies.

In a world such as ours, the need for someone to carry out a mission of transcendent truth, or supermotivated goodness, of eschatological salvation — the need for Christ — is increased, not cancelled....

We are sure that from the ever true knowledge of the Catholic Faith you will know how to draw living strength and new forms to continue the dialogue with the modern world. The Council offers you its richness which you will study with profit. And all of you, sons and brothers, have faith in your bishop! He has nothing of the attraction of life to promise to those who love this life. But to him who loves Christ, and loves the Church, and his brothers, he can offer that which strengthens such great love — faith, sacrifice, service, in fact the cross, and with this, strength, joy and peace, and also the extreme horizons of eternal hope. — Pope Paul VI, to Lenten preachers, 2-20-71.

We earnestly hope that in spite of the discussions which today surround the person and office of the priest, you will remain ever firm in the joy of your vocation. This joy does not have its source in material comforts or in human prestige — if such still exists; it comes rather from having a share in the special friendship of Jesus Christ (cf. Jn 15:16).

Dear brothers, be men of God, proclaiming by your whole conduct the primacy of the supernatural, the uprightness of your faith, the wholeheartedness of your self-giving to the Lord. It is freely that you have offered your whole being to Christ so as to bring to the world the message of salvation. You are aware that this service of the gospel can only be understood and lived in faith, prayer, penance and love; you know that it involves struggles and mortification and at times even misunderstanding. We urge you to hold fast with faith and generosity to all these commitments which conform you to the image of Christ the Priest.[1]

Be also servants of all your fellowmen, without distinction of origin or rank, servants of those who are near as of those who are far, of those who search and of those who suffer; and as shining witnesses to the liberation brought by Christ accept and satisfy their longings. — Pope Paul VI, to the clergy (Australia), 12-10-70.

The priest is no longer for himself; he is for the ministry of Christ's Mystical Body. He is a servant, an instrument of the Word and of grace. The proclamation of the gospel, the celebration of the Eucharist, the remission of sins, the exercise of pastoral activity, the life of faith and worship, and the radiation of charity and holiness are his duty, a duty that reaches the point of self-sacrifice, of the cross, as for Jesus. It is a very heavy burden. But Jesus bears it with His chosen one and makes him feel the truth of His words: "My yoke is easy and my burden light" (Mt 11:30). For, as Saint Augustine

teaches us, "my weight is my love." [2] When love of Christ
becomes the single supreme principle of the life of a priest,
it makes all easy, all possible, all happy. — Pope Paul VI,
to newly-ordained priests in the Philippines, 11-28-70.

We will do no more than
recommend you to meditate on your ordination for the rest
of your lives. Today sees the beginning for you of a subject
for thought, prayer and action, which you must always recall, examine, explore and seek to understand. It must be
stamped on your consciousness, just as the sacramental
character is already stamped on your souls, on your being
as men, on your being as Christians. Think of it! Today
you have become priests! Try to give a definition of yourselves and the words come with effort and difficulty;
the reality which they try to express is still more difficult,
mysterious and inexpressible.

What has taken place in you makes one truly marvel!
"How can I repay the Lord for his goodness to me?"
(Ps 115:12) each of you can say, on feeling himself invested
by the transforming action of the Holy Spirit. You become
for yourselves something to wonder at and revere. Never
forget it. Though the world does not know of it, and though
many seek to strip the priest's personality of it, your
"sacrality" must be kept ever present in your minds
and in your conduct. It derives from a new qualifying
presence of the Holy Spirit in your souls; if you are watchful in love, you will also experience it within you (cf. Jn
14:17, 14:22-23). Never doubt your priestly identity;
seek rather to understand it. — Pope Paul VI, to newly-
ordained priests in the Philippines, 11-28-70.

1. Cf. Letter to the Cardinal Secretary of State, Feb. 2, 1970; AAS
(1970) II; 2-29-70.
2. *Confessions*, 13:9.

Priests, while engaging in prayer and adoration, or preaching the word, or offering the Eucharistic Sacrifice and administering the other sacraments, or performing other works of the ministry for men, devote all this energy to the increase of the glory of God and to man's progress in the divine life. — PO 2.

The Priesthood Is Commitment

**TO SERVE THE LORD
TO SERVE OUR BROTHERS**

TO SERVE THE LORD

We ought to think about certain aspects of this vocation which came to us. It marked the highest moment for the exercise of our freedom: we freely thought, reflected, willed and decided. It brought about the great choice of our life; like the words "I do" spoken by the person contracting marriage, our response to it, in contrast to the wordiness of the man lacking ideals greater than himself, was a commitment of our life: a commitment of the form, the extent, and the duration of our self-offering. It is therefore the most beautiful and the most ideal historical page of our human existence. It would be tragic to underestimate it.

Our response at once qualified our entire life with its awesome "yes," making our life that of one who is set aside from the ordinary manner in which others lead their lives. St. Paul says it of himself: "Set apart for the gospel of God." It is a "yes" which in a moment tore us from everything that we had: "they left everything and followed him" (Lk 5:11); it is a "yes" which placed us in the ranks of the idealists, dreamers, madmen, even of those who seemed like fools, but also, thank God, in the ranks of the strong, of those who know why they are living and for whom they are living — "I know who it is that I have put my trust in" (1 Tm 1:12)—of those who have set themselves to the task of serving and giving their lives, their whole lives, for others. This is what we are called to. We are indeed set apart from the world, but we are not separated from that world for which we must be, with Christ and like Christ, ministers of salvation.[1]—Pope Paul VI, to Lenten preachers, 2-17-72.

You will allow Us to recall here with emotion the last discourse which death prevented Pius XII from pronouncing, and which remains like the extreme and solemn appeal of that great Pontiff for priestly sanctity:

"The sacramental nature of the Order," it says, "seals on behalf of God an eternal pact of His love, of predilection, demanding in exchange sanctification of the chosen human being.... The cleric will be a chosen person among the people, he will be privileged with divine favor, a custodian of divine power, in one word, an *alter Christus*.... He does not belong to himself in the same way as he does not belong to relatives, friends, nor does he belong to a specific country—universal charity will be his life. His very thoughts, will and feelings are not his own but belong to Christ, his life."—SNP.

Help us, [Lord], to understand how we, yes, we, miserable human clay taken into Your miraculous hands, how we have been made ministers of Your unique efficacious mediation.[2] It is left up to us, Your representatives and the dispensers of Your divine mysteries (1 Cor 4:1; 1 Pt 4:10) to diffuse the treasures of Your word, of Your grace, of Your example among men to whom our life is from today on completely and forever dedicated (cf. 2 Cor 4:5).

This ministerial mediation puts us, fragile and humble though we still be, in a position indeed of dignity and honor (2 Cor 3:7), of power[3] and of exemplariness.[4] This same mediation so qualifies our life morally and socially and tends to assimilate the sentiment of our personal consciousness to that which filled Your divine heart, O Christ (Phil 2:5; Eph 5:1), for we too, as though living with You and in You, have become both priests and victims (Gal 2:19-20), ready with all our being to fulfill, like You, Lord, the will of the Father (cf. Ps 102:21; Heb 13:21), obedient unto death, as You were, unto death on the cross (Phil 2:8), for the salvation of the world (1 Cor 11:26). —Pope Paul VI, to newly-ordained priests and deacons, 9-5-68.

1. Cf. Ench. Cler., 104, 360, 1387.
2. Cf. S. Th. III, 26, 1 ad 1.
3. Cf. 1 Cor 11:24-25; Jn 20:33; Acts 1:22; 1 Pt 5:2 etc.
4. Cf. 1 Cor 4:16; 11:1; Phil 3:17; 1 Pt 5:3.

TO SERVE OUR BROTHERS

The work of redemption is not accomplished in the world and in time without the ministry of dedicated men — men who, through an oblation of total human charity, implement the plan of salvation and of infinite divine charity.

Had God willed it, this divine charity could have spread itself and performed salvation directly. But the design is a different one. God will save men in Christ through a service rendered by men. God did not give the world only a revelation and a religion. He gave a Church, an organized society, a flexible community, in which brothers work for the salvation of other brothers.

He set up a hierarchy; He instituted a priesthood. Where the priesthood of Christ reaches, there reaches the message and the virtue of Christ's salvation. The Lord willed that the spreading of the gospel should depend on the number and the zeal of the workers of the gospel. — Pope Paul VI, address on seminaries and vocations, 11-4-63.

The purpose which priests pursue in their ministry and by their life is to procure the glory of God the Father in Christ. That glory consists in this — that men working freely and with a grateful spirit receive the work of God made perfect in Christ and then manifest it in their whole lives. Hence, priests, while engaging in prayer and adoration, or preaching the word, or offering the Eucharistic Sacrifice and administering the other sacraments, or performing other works of the ministry for men, devote all this energy to the increase of the glory of God and to man's progress in the divine life. — PO 2.

The Priesthood...was instituted by Christ for the salvation of His Church and of mankind. Our joy in the priesthood is all the greater even though today We find — to Our immense sorrow and to the regret of the faithful Church — this mysterious and admirable ministerial priesthood being contested, called in question, depreciated, betrayed and denied. It is a divine institution, which flowed from the heart of Christ at the very hour in which Christ turned Himself into sacrificial food to be communicated to each of His followers and to make Himself, the Redeemer, the principle of charity and unity for the whole of the mystical Body, the Church, by overcoming the narrow bounds of time and space.

Indeed, Christ's intention was that the Eucharist should be a means of overcoming that solitude in which every man with a personal life finds himself, whether he be a child or an old man. It is a means of overcoming that distance which history and geography put between the generations and among the various situations in which man is scattered over the earth.

A human instrument was needed for accomplishing that unheard of and wonderful plan; there was need of a delegated power which might renew the sacramental miracle, a ministry to announce and distribute the Word made the bread of life, flesh and blood of the paschal Lamb, the Savior and Liberator (as was done in the prophetic and symbolic episode of the multiplication of the loaves). There was need of a qualified minister, there was need of a qualified ministry, of the Priesthood of Christ Himself, transfused into men, who would be raised up from being disciples to become apostles and priests.

It will be a great good fortune, and there will be great exultation in the Church and in the world when theology, liturgy, spirituality and, We may add, sociology, bring out afresh those secret and light-filled truths into our day, in the way proper to the divine realities which they contain and the cognoscitive capacities of modern man. The divine Priesthood of Christ, as communicated in the ministerial priesthood, will then be vindicated, in its dignity and in its mission. For this reason, dearest brethren and sons, We have welcomed the simple but sincere honors which have been given to Our priestly jubilee — not so much to Us, who are frail clay, but to the Priesthood of Christ, to the divine treasure which has been entrusted to Us as to every other priest (cf. 2 Cor 4:7). — Pope Paul VI, to a general audience, 6-18-71.

Dear sons and dear brothers, if you only knew how deeply We are moved by your presence and by the title you and We bear..., yes! the title of priests. We are always moved whenever We meet Our brethren in the priesthood and speak of our common election to this holy state, of the grandeur of our vocation and of the mystery of God's calling. Why has the Lord chosen us? What is this mission to which we have been destined? What is it that passes through us as we dispense graces, charisms and power? And for what purpose? It is for the people of God. In the Church, we priests are the instruments and the channels of the Word, of grace, of spiritual direction and of government. We are those who must make an organic body of the great human family. It is for us to weld it together in all its parts. We must hold the faithful together, watch over them, calm them when necessary and also awaken them. — Pope Paul VI, to priests and seminarians, 12-26-68.

A priest no longer belongs to himself. His very spiritual life is conditioned by the communion of the brethren to whom our ministry is directed. He is at their disposal, at their service. Whatever helps to edify them is a matter of obligation for a priest. — Pope Paul VI, to a general audience, 6-10-70.

...**Whatever be the** ministry for which you [new priests] are intended, you will be loyal continuers of Christ among men, for the glory of God. Through you, Christ will continue to pray to the Father, to sacrifice Himself in the Blessed Sacrament, to sanctify souls with the contact of His grace, which you have received through the apostolic imposition of hands. Through you, Christ will continue to preach, to announce the plan of Messianic salvation, to choose especially the children, the young and the suffering. You will always be faithful to these tasks, if you wish to give your life a triple stamp: love for the Word of God, for the Holy Eucharist, and for the Church.

   — for the Word of God, in the first place, in order to study it as deeply as our littleness permits, because the priest is the specialist of God, and must become more familiar every day with the Spirit of God, speaking through the Scriptures. Hence meditation, desired and awaited and prepared as the bracing daily meeting with God who speaks in the silence of the heart; hence preaching, which will not lose its bite, its flavor and its content to the extent that it is fed at the real sources of the Bible; hence "our citizenship is in heaven" (Phil 3:20), which makes the ministry fruitful and safeguards priestly life.

— love for the Holy Eucharist, the center of your life, because that is what you have been expressly delegated for. As We said years ago to confrères of yours, "the priest is the generating minister of so great a Sacrament, and then the first worshiper and wise revealer and tireless distributor." [1]

It is essentially on your personal eucharistic life, on your way of celebrating Mass and encouraging attendance at it, that the degree of intensity of faith depends in the communities entrusted to you. This subject would call for a long treatment, but We have dealt with it on other occasions, nor do you lack the classic texts of patristics and theology to help you to live your vocation deeply. This vocation, which is eucharistic first of all, really makes us the *"alter Christus"* for which the souls of those who lack God are athirst.

— love for the Church, finally, which has trusted and trusts you, has transmitted to you the ineffable powers Christ entrusted to her, and makes you the messengers of truth, justice and peace. She sends you to be brothers among brothers, opens to you the boundless fields of the ripening harvest, Christ's innumerable flocks of sheep, which are languishing in so many parts of the world not only because of the lack of assistance, bread, aid, but also and above all because of the lack of priests to satisfy their expectations, allay their anxieties and transmit to them the love that comes from Christ's own heart: "When he saw the crowds, he had compassion for them, because they were harassed and helpless, like sheep without a shepherd" (Mt 9:36).

This is what We wanted to tell you, beloved brothers in the one priesthood of the Savior. Our souls have met and understood one another, in the outpouring of Christian love which makes us feel God's presence: "Where there is charity and love, there is God." We will follow you with Our prayer, each in the way that the Lord has marked out for you, and which as life will show you is one plan of incommensurable and perpetual love; We will be near you spiritually with Our affection in the joyful and sad moments of your lives as priests, dedicated to God; you will always be in Our heart. — Pope Paul VI, to young priests, 6-12-71.

You, [Lord], have deigned to impress a new interior indelible mark on the personal being of these Your chosen ones, a mark which likens them to You and because of which each one of them is and will be called another Christ. You have impressed on them Your human and divine countenance, conferring not only Your inexpressible likeness, but also Your power, Your virtue, a capacity to perform actions which only the divine efficacy of Your word attests and that of Your will realizes.

They are Yours, O Lord, these Your sons, who by a new title have become Your brothers, Your ministers. By means of their priestly service Your presence and Your sacramental sacrifice, Your gospel, Your grace, Your Spirit, in one word, the work of Your salvation will be communicated to men who are disposed to receive it; an immeasurable radiation of Your charity will diffuse itself through the present and future generation....

They are Yours, Lord, these servants of Your designs of supernatural love; and they are Ours, because they are joined with Us in the great work of evangelization as the most qualified collaborators of Our ministry, as Our beloved sons, indeed, as brothers of Our dignity and Our function, as valiant co-workers in the building of Your Church, as servants and guides, as consolers and friends of the People of God, dispensers, like Us, of Your mysteries. — Pope Paul VI, to newly-ordained priests and deacons of Colombia, 9-5-68.

1. To participants at the Thirteenth National Week of Pastoral Orientation, 9-6-63; *Insegnamenti*, I, p. 121.

CHRISTOLOGICAL DIMENSION

Since every priest in his own fashion acts in place of Christ Himself, he is enriched by a special grace, so that, as he serves the flock committed to him and the entire People of God, he may the better grow in the grace of Him whose tasks he performs. — PO 12.

Made in the Likeness of Christ

IN THE PRIESTHOOD OF CHRIST

OTHER CHRISTS

DISCIPLESHIP

HOLINESS: THE FORCE
        BEHIND THE MINISTRY

PERFECT MANHOOD IN CHRIST

WITNESS VALUE

IN THE PRIESTHOOD OF CHRIST

Jesus Christ, the Son of God and the Word, "whom the Father sanctified and sent into the world" (Jn 10:36), and who was marked with the seal of the fullness of the Holy Spirit (cf. Lk 4:1, 18-21; Acts 10:38), proclaimed to the world the Good News of reconciliation between God and men. His preaching as a prophet, confirmed by signs, reaches its summit in the Paschal Mystery, the supreme word of the divine love with which the Father addressed us. On the cross Jesus showed Himself to the greatest possible extent to be the Good Shepherd who laid down His life for His sheep in order to gather them into that unity which depends on Himself (cf. Jn 10:1ff.; 11:52). Exercising a supreme and unique priesthood by the offering of Himself, He surpassed, by fulfilling them, all the ritual priesthoods and holocausts of the Old Testament and indeed of the pagans. In His sacrifice He took on Himself the miseries and sacrifices of men of every age and also the efforts of those who suffer for the cause of justice or who are daily oppressed by misfortune. He took on Himself the endeavors of those who abandon the world and attempt to reach God by asceticism and contemplation as well as the labors of those who sincerely devote their lives to a better present and future society. He bore the sins of us all on the cross; rising from the dead and being made Lord (cf. Phil 2:9-11), He reconciled us to God; and He laid the foundation of the people of the New Covenant, which is the Church.

He is the "one mediator between God and men, the man Christ Jesus" (1 Tm 2:5), "for in him were created all things" (Col 1:16; cf. Jn 1:3ff.) and everything is brought together under Him, as head (cf. Eph 1:10). Since He is the image of the Father and manifestation of the unseen God (cf. Col 1:15), by emptying Himself and by being raised up He brought us into the fellowship of the Holy Spirit which He lives with the Father.

When therefore we speak of the priesthood of Christ, we should have before our eyes a unique, incomparable reality, which includes the prophetic and royal office of the Incarnate Word of God.

So Jesus Christ signifies and manifests in many ways the presence and effectiveness of the anticipatory love of God. The Lord Himself, constantly influencing the Church by His Spirit, stirs up and fosters the response of all those who offer themselves to this freely given love. —Ministerial Priesthood, Nov. 1971, Synod Document.

The Christian priesthood, being of a new order, can be understood only in the light of the newness of Christ, the Supreme Pontiff and eternal Priest, who instituted the priesthood of the ministry as a real participation in His own unique priesthood.[1] The minister of Christ and dispenser of the mysteries of God (1 Cor 4:1), therefore, looks up to Him directly as his model and supreme ideal (cf. 1 Cor 11:1). The Lord Jesus, the only Son of God, was sent by the Father into the world and He became man, in order that humanity which was subject to sin and death might be reborn, and through this new birth (Jn 3:5; Ti 3:5) might enter the kingdom of heaven. Being entirely consecrated to the will of the

Father (Jn 4:34; 17:4), Jesus brought forth this new creation by means of His paschal mystery (2 Cor 5:17; Gal 6:15); thus, He introduced into time and into the world a new form of life which is sublime and divine and which transforms the very earthly condition of human nature (cf. Gal 3:28). —SCl 19.

We should like to remind you today that [ordination] is not a goal where you may rest once you have reached it. It is indeed the end of a long and laborious climb, but it is also the beginning of a journey with ever widening horizons. Jesus said: "Go, therefore, and make disciples of all nations" (Mt 28:19), and with that He pointed out a road upon which there is no rest and no turning back.

When He makes you sharers in His priesthood He will send you out as dispensers of His grace, and He will entrust the fullness of the gospel message to you, which message proclaims that the poor in spirit, the meek, those that mourn, those that hunger and thirst for justice, the merciful of heart, the peacemakers, the persecuted, are blessed (Mt 5:3, 10).

Our exhortation to you is therefore this: Love your priesthood, live it thoroughly, and by so doing respond to the pressing call made by Vatican Council II: "...Priests should grow in love for God and neighbor through the daily exercise of their duty. They should preserve the bond of priestly fraternity, abound in every spiritual good, and give living evidence of God to all men."[2] —Pope Paul VI, to deacons from Bohemia and Moravia, 4-24-69.

1. LG 28.
2. LG 41.

OTHER CHRISTS

Through the sacred sign of Holy Orders you have become more like unto Christ. You have become His own — His brothers. He has imprinted His divine countenance. With the apostle you can now say: "It is now no longer I who live, but Christ lives in me" (Gal 2:20).

Through your priestly service will be revealed in greater measure: His presence, His divine sacrifice, His salvific message, His grace, the spirit of His love and peace and the Redemption of men, who are entrusted to your loving care. —Pope Paul VI, to newly-ordained priests, 10-12-68.

You will be able to understand something of your priesthood by trying to comprehend two orders of relationships set up by it. The first order concerns the relationships with Christ which you have taken on by your priestly ordination. You know that in the religious dispensation of the New Testament there is only one true priesthood, that of Jesus Christ, the one mediator between God and mankind (1 Tm 2:5). But by virtue of the sacrament of Orders you have become sharers in Christ's priesthood so that not only do you represent Christ, not only do you exercise His ministry, but you live Christ. Christ lives in you.

Inasmuch as you are associates with Him in a degree that is so high and so filled with a sharing in His mission of salvation, you can say, as Saint Paul said of himself: "I live now not with my own life but with the life of Christ who lives in me" (Gal 2:20). This is something that opens to the priest the way of ascent for his spirituality, the highest way open to man, one that reaches the summits of ascetical and mystical life. If ever some day you feel lonely, if ever some day you feel that you are weak secular men, if ever some day you are tempted to abandon the sacred commitment of your priesthood, remember that you are "through Him, with Him and in Him"; each one of you is "another Christ." — Pope Paul VI, to newly-ordained priests in the Philippines, 11-28-70.

Christ is with us. We must have confidence in Him, since "we can do all things in him who strengthens us" (Phil 4:13). Christ chose us in spite of our weakness, and He will by no means permit us to lack suitable aid for the right fulfillment of our office as pastors. He has made us His own as He made Paul (cf. Phil 3:12). Let us model our lives on Him, that our whole way of acting may be impregnated with His grace. He is the eternal Priest, the example and model of the apostolic way of life. To use the words of St. Ambrose, an admirable shepherd of souls: "Let His image shine in our profession of faith, in our love, in our works and deeds. Thus, if possible, His whole beauty will find expression in us.

"Let Him be our head, since 'Christ is the head of every man' (1 Cor 11:3); let Him be our eye, that through Him we may see the Father; let Him be our voice, that through Him we may speak to the Father; let Him be our right hand, that through Him we may offer our sacrifice to God the Father." [1]

To bring this into effect, we receive help from the Virgin Mother of God, the Mother of the Church, who more than anyone else gave expression in herself to the image of her Son. Let us therefore place our confidence surely and immovably in her who joins us in continuous prayer, as once she joined with Peter and the disciples (cf. Acts 1:14), that a new day of Pentecost may dawn for the holy Church. — Pope Paul VI, at closing of Synod, 11-18-71.

1. *De Isaac et anima*, 8:7.

DISCIPLESHIP

We are called. But for what purpose? Our identity is enriched by another essential characteristic: we are *disciples*. We are, so to speak, *the* disciples. The term "disciple" necessarily involves another term: "master." Who is our Master? It is absolutely essential to remember this: "You have only one Master, and you are all brothers, you have only one Teacher, Christ" (Mt 23:8-10). Jesus wanted to be known by this title Master (cf. Jn 13:13). After speaking to the crowd, after instructing everyone, Jesus taught the group of His special followers, the disciples, recognizing that they had a prerogative of supreme importance: "the mysteries of the kingdom of heaven are revealed to you, but they are not revealed to them" (Mt 13:11). Because those whom He called were disciples, they were raised to the position of teachers, not of their own doctrine, clearly, but of the doctrine revealed to them by Christ. In spite of the infinite difference, this is analogous to what Christ said of Himself: "My teaching is not from myself; it comes from the one who sent me" (Jn 7:16). Therefore, inasmuch as we are disciples, we can also say that our priestly identity carries with it a connotation of magisterium: we are disciples and we are teachers; we listen to the word of Christ and we proclaim that same Word. —Pope Paul VI, to Lenten preachers, 2-17-72.

The characteristic of disciples, upon which we are now concentrating our attention, is a very important one. As you know, dear brothers, this characteristic involves a twofold duty for the life of the priest in search of authenticity. The first duty is that of studying Christ's teaching. This study branches out in various directions, all of which are concerned with essential aims for our definition as priests. We hasten to say that this duty is that of *listening*, listening to the voice of Christ's Spirit, that is, to the inspirations that have the mark of true supernatural origin (cf. Rev 2:6ff.; Mt 10:19; Jn 14:26). We must listen, therefore, to the voice of the Church when she speaks in the exercise of her magisterium, whether ordinary or extraordinary (cf. Lk 10:16). We must listen to the echo of Christ's voice in the words of those who speak to us in the name of the Lord, as do the bishop, the spiritual director or some good and wise friend. We must listen also to the voice of the People of God, when it recalls us to our duties or occasionally asks from us some service which is in accordance with our ministry. But we must act with due prudence, which is so necessary in such circumstances, for here it is easy to suffer from excess, from the pressure of publicity or the presence of outside interests or methods. We must listen through the study of the sacred sciences; often lay experts are better informed about their own subjects than we are about religious teachings (cf. Lk 16:8). Finally we must listen through mental prayer and meditation. We are all well aware that this is meant for the nourishment of our personal spiritual life (cf. Jn 8:31). We can truly say with Jesus: "Blessed are those who hear the word of God and keep it" (Lk 11:28; cf. 8:21).

The second duty if we are to be true disciples, is to imitate. How much there is to say about this second consequence of the fact that we are members of Christ's school, precisely at this time when we are assailed by secularization and the attempt to cause the clergy to lose its external marks, and, unfortunately, its interior ones too. So-called "human respect," which caused even Peter to fall, could tempt us also to hide what we are and make us forget Saint Paul's exhortation: "Do not model yourselves on the behavior of the world around you" (Rom 12:2). In fact the "imitation of Christ" must be the practical study for our conduct. We will not say anything further on a subject which is so well known and so closely connected with the intrinsic demands of priestly identity. In the thought of Jesus there is still another essential characteristic needed for our identity. It is the fact that He has promoted us from disciples to apostles. As a synthesis of what We are saying, listen to the words of the Evangelist Saint Luke: Christ "summoned his disciples and picked out twelve of them; he called them apostles" (Lk 6:13). *Servatis servandis,* it does not seem exaggerated to us that this supreme title of apostle should be applied to priests, and indeed that certain powers and functions proper to the priest of Christ should be looked for in this very title.

Each one of us can say: "I am an apostle." What does *apostle* mean? It means "sent." Sent by whom? And sent to whom? Jesus Himself gives us the answer to both these questions on the evening of His Resurrection: "As the Father sent me, so am I sending you" (Jn 20:21). Think of it. Here is something that leaves us really amazed. Where does my priesthood come from and where does it lead? What else is it but the channel of the divine life, serving, by an extension of the saving mission of Christ, God and Man, to communicate the divine mysteries to mankind? Let people consider us, Saint Paul says, as "stewards entrusted with the mysteries of God" (1 Cor 4:1). We are ministers of God (2 Cor 6:4). We are friends of Christ. Ours is a mission which sets up a personal relationship with Christ, a relationship which is singular and different from that which He has with all others: "I call you friends, because I have made known to you everything I have learned from my Father. You did not choose me; no, I chose you" (Jn 15:15-16). This is a friendship which has its roots in the uncreated love of the Trinity itself: "As the Father has loved me, so I have loved you. Remain in my love" (Jn 15:9). We are servants of the brethren; we will never succeed in giving this term enough fullness of meaning with regard both to ourselves and even more to our mission. Christ wished thus to define His mission (cf. Mt 20:28) and He wished ours to be similar, in deep humility and in perfect charity: "...and you should wash each other's feet!" (Jn 13:14). But at the same time what dignity and what powers such service involves! It is the service of an ambassador! "We are ambassadors for Christ; it is as though God were appealing through us" (2 Cor 5:20). In addition we have the sacramental powers that make us instruments of the very action of God in men's hearts. It is no longer just our human activity that marks us, but the conferral of the divine power working through our ministry. — Pope Paul VI, to Lenten preachers.

HOLINESS:
THE FORCE BEHIND THE MINISTRY

They [priests] have received in the sacrament of Baptism the symbol and gift of such a calling and such grace that even in human weakness (cf. 2 Cor 12:19). They can and must seek for perfection, according to the exhortation of Christ: "Be you therefore perfect, as your heavenly Father is perfect" (Mt 5:48). Priests are bound, however, to acquire that perfection in a special fashion. They have been consecrated by God in a new manner at their ordination and made living instruments of Christ the Eternal Priest that they may be able to carry on in time His marvelous work whereby the entire family of man is again made whole by power from above.[1] Since, therefore, every priest in his own fashion acts in place of Christ Himself, he is enriched by a special grace, so that, as he serves the flock committed to him and the entire People of God, he may the better grow in the grace of Him whose tasks he performs, because to the weakness of our flesh there is brought the holiness of Him who for us was made a High Priest "holy, guiltless, undefiled, not reckoned among us sinners" (Heb 7:26). — PO 12.

In the world of today, when people are so burdened with duties and their problems, which oftentimes have to be solved with great haste, and range through so many fields, there is considerable danger of dissipating their energy. Priests, too, involved and constrained by so many obligations of their office, certainly have reason to wonder how they can coordinate and balance their interior life with feverish outward activity. Neither the mere external performance of the works of the ministry, nor the exclusive engagement in pious devotion, although very helpful, can bring about this necessary coordination. Priests can arrive at this only by following the example of Christ our Lord in their ministry. His food was to follow the will of Him who had sent Him to accomplish His work (cf. Jn 4:34).

In order to continue doing the will of His Father in the world, Christ works unceasingly through the Church. He operates through His ministers, and hence He remains always the source and wellspring of the unity of their lives. Priests, then, can achieve this coordination and unity of life by joining themselves with Christ to acknowledge the will of the Father. For them this means a complete gift of themselves to the flock committed to them (cf. 1 Jn 3:16). Hence, as they fulfill the role of the Good Shepherd, in the very exercise of their pastoral charity they will discover a bond of priestly perfection which draws their life and activity to unity and coordination. This pastoral charity[2] flows out in a very special way from the Eucharistic Sacrifice. This stands as the root and center of the whole life of a priest. What takes place on the altar of sacrifice, the priestly heart must make his own. This cannot be done unless priests through prayer continue to penetrate more deeply into the mystery of Christ. — PO 14.

Well do you know how much the Church and the souls of the faithful expect from you: a fidelity true to the demands of the sacramental character, an attitude of service consecrated to others, a daily dedication to your sanctification, in order not to obscure the authentic character of your mission, not to deny your mysterious and stupendous reality.

You are heirs and instruments of Christ; mediators of His gifts. Therefore you are expected — and of this you are gloriously aware — to be transparent and convincing witnesses to Christ; Christ strong and humble, sincere and obedient, meditative and active, who extends and realizes the mystery of His redemption, and through your words and your priestly actions continues His work for the salvation of the world. Live up to what you are, what you represent, what you deal with. — Pope Paul VI, to young Spanish priests, 4-4-68.

The apostolate would lose its interior roots and its best and original forms, together with its highest ends, if the apostle were not a man of prayer and meditation. The texture of the people educated in participation in the liturgy would lack true spiritual cohesion and true fruits from communion with the divine mysteries being celebrated, if the minister and the individual faithful themselves did not acquire a religious fervor of their own from the rite and put some of their own into it. The Church would no longer be the Church, if divine charity were not put before the practice of fraternal charity and also infused into it.

This requires the soul to have a silent colloquy, listening and contemplating within itself, speaking its childlike, superlative words, stammering, mournful, imploring, exultant and singing words, perhaps comprehensible only by God, words uttered in an indescribable manner alone with the Spirit and perhaps by the Spirit Himself in us: "with unutterable groanings" (Rom 8:26). There are no substitutes for the spiritual life. For us especially who are the Lord's ministers, it cannot, it must not be lacking. —Pope Paul VI, to Lenten preachers, 2-9-70.

In us God has His living instrument, His minister, and so His spokesman, the echo of His voice, His tabernacle, the historical and social sign of His presence with mankind, the burning hearth radiating His love for man. This prodigious fact—Lord, help us never to forget it!—carries with it a duty, the first and most pleasant of our priestly life: that of intimacy with Christ, in the Holy Spirit, and so with You, Father (cf. Jn 16:27); in other words, the obligation of an authentic and personal interior life, one that is not only jealously preserved in the fullness of grace, but that is also expressed in a continuous reflexive act of awareness, of dialogue, of loving contemplative suspense.[3]

The oft-repeated words of Christ at the Last Supper: "abide in my love" (Jn 15:9; 15:4; etc.) are meant for us, dear sons and brothers. This yearning for union with Christ and His revelation about the divine and human world is the first attitude characteristic of the minister who has been made Christ's representative and has been invited through the charism of Sacred Orders to personify Him existentially in himself. This is most important for us: it is indispensable. And do not think that this absorption of our conscious spirituality into intimate dialogue with Christ arrests or slows up the dynamism of our ministry, that it delays, in other words, the carrying out of our external apostolate and serves perhaps also as an escape from the harassing and burdensome effort of our dedication to the service of others, to the mission entrusted to us; no, this assimilation is the stimulus to ministerial action, the fount of apostolic energy; it renders effective the mysterious relationship existing between love for Christ and pastoral dedication (cf. Jn 21:15ff.).

So it is, indeed, that the spirituality of a priest as a representative of God with the people turns itself to that other pole, namely, the priest as a representative of the people with God. And this it does not only to lavish our entire activity and our whole heart on men who are loved for the sake of Christ, but likewise, in a previous psychological moment, to assume in ourselves their representation: we gather in ourselves, in our love and in our responsibility, the People of God. We are not only ministers of God, but we are also ministers of the Church[4]; in fact, we should always remember that the priest celebrating holy Mass is acting in the name of the people,[5] and so, as far as the sacramental validity of the sacrifice is concerned, the priest acts "in the person of Christ," but as regards its application, he acts as a minister of the Church.[6]

We beg the Lord then to infuse in us a sense of the People we represent, the People we gather together in our priestly office and in our hearts consecrated to their salvation; the People we assemble together in an ecclesial community and gather around the altar, for whom we are interpreters in their needs and prayers, in their sufferings and hopes, in their weakness and in their strength. In the exercise of our ministry of worship, we are the People of God. In our representative and ministerial capacities, we bring together the various elements that make up the Christian community: children, young people, families, workers, the poor, the sick, and also those who are far away and even our adversaries. We are the love which unites the people of this world. We are the heart of that people; we are their voice adoring and praying, exulting and weeping. We are their expiation (cf. 2 Cor 5:21), we are the messengers of their hope! —Pope Paul VI to newly-ordained priests, 9-5-68.

Those who exercise the ministry of the spirit and of justice (cf. 2 Cor 3:8-9) will be confirmed in the life of the spirit, so long as they are open to the Spirit of Christ, who gives them life and direction. By the sacred actions which are theirs daily as well as by their entire ministry which they share with the bishop and their fellow priests, they are directed to perfection in their lives. Holiness does much for priests in carrying on a fruitful ministry. Although divine grace could use unworthy ministers to effect the work of salvation, yet for the most part God chooses, to show forth His wonders, those who are more open to the power and direction of the Holy Spirit, and who can by reason of their close union with Christ and their holiness of life say with St. Paul: "And yet I am alive; or rather, not I; it is Christ that lives in me" (Gal 2:20). —PO 12.

The activities of the apostolate...furnish an indispensable nourishment for fostering the spiritual life of the priest: "By assuming the role of the Good Shepherd, they will find precisely in the pastoral exercise of love the bond of priestly perfection which will unify their lives and activities."[7] In the exercise of his ministry the priest is enlightened and strengthened by the action of the Church and the example of the faithful. The renunciations imposed by the pastoral life itself help him to acquire an ever greater sharing in Christ's cross and hence a purer pastoral charity.

This same charity of priests will also cause them to adapt their spiritual lives to the modes and forms of sanctification which are more suitable and fitting for the men of their own times and culture. Desiring to be all things to all men, to save all (cf. 1 Cor 9:22), the priest should be attentive to the inspiration of the Holy Spirit in these days. Thus he will announce the Word of God not only by human means but he will be taken as a valid instrument by the Word Himself, whose message is "living and active and sharper than any two-edged sword" (Heb 4:12). — Ministerial Priesthood, Nov. 1971, Synod Document.

Priests who perform their duties sincerely and indefatigably in the Spirit of Christ arrive at holiness by this very fact.

Since they are ministers of God's word, each day they read and hear the word of God, which it is their task to teach others. If at the same time they are ready to receive the word themselves they will grow daily into more perfect followers of the Lord. — PO 13.

1. Cf. Pius XI, encyclical letter, *Ad Catholici Sacerdotii*, 12-20-35: AAS 28 (1936), p. 10.
2. "May it be a duty of love to feed the Lord's flock" (St. Augustine, "Tract on John," 1967), 123, 5: P. 35.
3. Cf. St. Gregory, Regula Past. I: "contemplatione suspendus."
4. Cf. MD, AAS (1947), p. 539.
5. AAS (1954), p. 668.
6. Cf. Journet, 1, p. 110, n. 1, I ed.; cf. S. Th. III, 22, 1; cf. also 2 Cor 5:11.   7. PO 14.

PERFECT MANHOOD IN CHRIST

Christ, whom the Father sanctified, consecrated and sent into the world (cf. Jn 10:36) "gave himself for us that he might redeem us from all iniquity and cleanse for himself an acceptable people, pursuing good works" (Ti 2:14), and thus through suffering entered into His glory (Lk 24:26). In like fashion, priests consecrated by the anointing of the Holy Spirit and sent by Christ must mortify the works of the flesh in themselves and give themselves entirely to the service of men. It is in this way that they can go forward in that holiness with which Christ endows them to perfect manhood (cf. Eph 4:13). — PO 12.

Holiness begins from Christ; and Christ is its cause. For no act conducive to salvation can be performed unless it proceeds from Him as from its supernatural source. "Without me," He says, "you can do nothing" (cf. Jn 15:5). If we grieve and do penance for our sins, if, with filial fear and hope, we turn again to God, it is because He is leading us. Grace and glory flow from His inexhaustible fullness. Our Savior is continually pouring out His gifts of counsel, fortitude, fear and piety, especially on the leading members of His Body, so that the whole Body may grow ever more and more in holiness and in integrity of life. — MC 51.

Christ proved His love for His spotless bride not only at the cost of immense labor and constant prayer, but by His sorrows and His sufferings which He willingly and lovingly endured for her sake. "Having loved his own...he loved them unto the end" (Jn 13:1). Indeed it was only at the price of His blood that He purchased the Church (cf. Acts 20:28). Let us then follow gladly in the bloodstained footsteps of our King, for this is necessary to ensure our salvation: "For if we have been planted together in the likeness of his death, we shall be also in the likeness of his resurrection" (Rom 6:5), and "if we be dead with him, we shall also live with him" (2 Tm 2:11). Also our zealous love for the Church demands it, and our brotherly love for the souls she brings forth to Christ. — MC 106.

The precept of penitence must be satisfied in a more perfect way by priests, who are more closely linked to Christ through sacred character, as well as by those who in order to follow more closely the abnegation of the Lord and to find an easier and more efficacious path to the perfection of charity practice the evangelical counsels.[1] — POE.

The whole personal sanctification of the priest must be modeled on the Sacrifice he celebrates, in conformity with the invitation of the Roman Pontifical: "Know what you do. Imitate that which you handle." But here let Us leave the words to Our immediate predecessor, who wrote in his exhortation *Menti Nostrae:* "As the whole life of the Savior was ordained to the sacrifice of Himself, so the life of the priest which should reproduce in itself the image of Christ, ought also to be with Him and through Him and in Him, a pleasing sacrifice.... Consequently he will not merely celebrate Holy Mass, but will live it out intimately in his daily life. In no other way can he obtain that supernatural vigor which will transform him and make him a sharer in the life of sacrifice of the Redeemer."

And the same Pontiff concluded: "The priest should, therefore, study to reproduce in his own soul the things that are effected upon the altar. As Jesus Christ immolates Himself, so His minister should be immolated with Him. As Jesus expiates the sins of men, so he, by following the hard road of Christian asceticism, should labor at the purification of himself and of others." — SNP

Priests act especially in the person of Christ as ministers of holy things, particularly in the Sacrifice of the Mass, the sacrifice of Christ who gave Himself for the sanctification of men. Hence, they are asked to take example from that with which they deal, and inasmuch as they celebrate the mystery of the Lord's death they should keep their bodies free of wantonness and lusts.[2] — PO 13.

Among the virtues that priests must possess for their sacred ministry none is so important as a frame of mind and soul whereby they are always ready to know and do the will of Him who sent them and not their own will (cf. Jn 4:34; 5:30; 6:38). The divine task that they are called by the Holy Spirit to fulfill (cf. Acts 13:2) surpasses all human wisdom and human ability. "God chooses the weak things of the world to confound the strong" (1 Cor 1:27). Aware of his own weakness, the true minister of Christ works in humility trying to do what is pleasing to God (cf. Eph 5:10). Filled with the Holy Spirit (cf. Acts 20:22), he is guided by Him who desires the salvation of all men. He understands this desire of God and follows it in the ordinary circumstances of his everyday life. With humble disposition he waits upon all whom God has sent him to serve in the work assigned to him and in the multiple experiences of his life. — PO 15.

One's thoughts go spontaneously to the gospel story enshrined in the humble scene of Nazareth, where God's Son lived in obedience, growing in wisdom, in years and in favor (Lk 2:51). One's thoughts go to the social condition in which Christ chose to be a citizen of the earth and our brother, in open contrast with current mentality, with our unsatisfied claims, with the human will for power; so much so, that as the gospel text emphasized, His fellow-townsmen "were astonished and said, 'Where did this man get this wisdom and these mighty works? Is not this the carpenter's son? Is not his mother called Mary?... Where then did this man get all this?' And they took offense at him" (Mt 13:54-56).

Here then is a first lesson flowing from these reflections: continual recourse to the gospel. It is our duty. It is our strength. Today, especially we must take particular interest in the mystery of Christ's poverty. The Council spoke of it when it said, "Prompted by the Holy Spirit, the Church must walk the same road which Christ walked: a road of poverty and obedience, of service and self-sacrifice,"[3] and also when it said that the spirit of poverty and of love are "the glory and authentication of the Church of Christ."[4] — Pope Paul VI, to new cardinals, 5-8-69.

Try to give your conduct a strong, austere and upright character, give your existence, when necessary, a capacity of stout resistance, not "bourgeois," not slack, not absent-minded, not dissipated. Be really energetic, even if you must sometimes undergo some discipline of our environment, some obedience, some mortification, some Christian penance. The priest must have a character tempered in this spiritual and moral energy, which he must first exert on himself in order to be able later to indicate to others, in human words, also sweet and convincing, the difficult ways to the kingdom of God. "My way is narrow," the Lord said. One cannot travel along it comfortably, walking in a free and easy way, with as little effort as possible, lazily and sadly. One must walk heroically in Christ's footsteps. — Pope Paul VI, to students of the major Roman Seminary, 2-22-71.

1. Cf. PO 12, 13, 16 and 17; LG 41; AG 24; LG 42; PC 7, 12, 13, 14 and 25; OT 2, 8 and 9.
2. Cf. Roman Pontifical on the ordination of priests.
3. AG 5.
4. GS 88.

WITNESS VALUE

We should not dedicate ourselves to the apostolate, unless we know how to back it up with the example of Christian and priestly virtues. We are very much under observation: "we have been made a spectacle to the world" (1 Cor 4:9): the world watches us today in a particular way with regard to poverty, to simplicity of life, to the degree of fidelity we practice in our use of temporal goods; the angels watch us in the transparent purity of our only love of Christ, which is so clearly shown in the strong and joyful observance of our priestly celibacy; and the Church watches us with regard to the communion which makes us a unity, and to the laws, which we must always recall, of its visible and organic structure. Blessed be this our tormented and paradoxical time, which almost obliges us to the sanctity corresponding to our office, so representative and so responsible, and which obliges us to recover, in the contemplation and the ascetics of the ministers of the Holy Spirit, that interior personal treasure, from which the extremely compelling dedication to our office almost turns us aside! — Pope Paul VI to Latin American bishops, 9-5-68.

How in fact shall we be able to proclaim fruitfully the word of God, if it is not familiar to us through being the subject of our daily meditation and prayer? And how can it be received unless it is supported by a life of deep faith, active charity, total obedience, fervent prayer and humble penance? Having insisted, as is Our duty, on teaching the doctine of the faith, We must add that what is often most needed is not so much an abundance of words as speech in harmony with a more evangelical life. Yes, it is the witness of saints that the world needs, for, as the council reminds us, God "speaks to us in them, and gives us a sign of His kingdom, to which we are powerfully drawn."[1] — Pope Paul VI, Apostolic Exhortation to all Bishops, 12-8-72.

Let [priests], as fathers in Christ, take care of the faithful whom they have begotten by baptism and their teaching (cf. 1 Cor 4:15; 1 Pt 1:23). Becoming from the heart a pattern to the flock (1 Pt 5:3), let them so lead and serve their local community that it may worthily be called by that name, by which the one and entire people of God is signed, namely, the Church of God (cf. 1 Cor 1:2; 2 Cor 1:1). Let them remember that by their daily life and interests they are showing the face of a truly sacerdotal and pastoral ministry to the faithful and the infidels, to Catholics and non-Catholics, and that to all they bear witness to the truth and life. — LG 28.

The priestly life certainly requires an authentic spiritual intensity in order to live by the Spirit and to conform to the Spirit (Gal 5:25); it requires a truly virile asceticism both interior and exterior in one who, belonging in a special way to Christ, has in Him and through Him crucified the flesh with its passions and desires (Gal 5:24), not hesitating to face arduous and lengthy trials in order to do so (cf. 1 Cor 9:26-27). In this way Christ's minister will be the better able to show to the world the fruits of the Spirit which are "love, joy, peace, patience, kindness, goodness, long-suffering, mildness, faithfulness, gentleness, self-control, chastity" (Gal 5:22-23). — SCl 78.

We know your enthusiasm, your holy resolutions, your love for Christ and the Church. Be therefore always the faithful friends and worthy ministers of that Jesus whom you have chosen as the great aim of your lives. Bear witness of Him to the brethren, by word and example, in a priesthood lived in accordance with the demanding commitments of these times and the wise directives of the Second Council of the Vatican, which are the very directives of the gospel. — Pope Paul VI, to newly-ordained priests from Bratislava, 7-17-69.

1. LG 50; AAS 57, (1965), p. 56.

> Those who commune with Christ share in God's love, the mystery of which, kept hidden from the beginning of time (cf. Eph 3:9), is revealed in Christ. —PO 13.

Vertical Thrust

POINT OF CONTACT

STRENGTHENING THE SPIRIT

CANTICLE OF DIVINE PRAISE

POINT OF CONTACT

From a lively consciousness of his vocation and his consecration as the instrument of Christ for the service of men, the priest derives the consciousness of another dimension of his personality, that of mysticism and asceticism. If every Christian is the temple of the Holy Spirit, what must be the interior conversation of the priestly soul with the inhabiting presence, which transfigures, torments and inebriates him? These words of the Apostle are addressed to us priests: "But we carry this treasure in vessels of clay, to show that the abundance of the power is God's and not ours" (2 Cor 4:7).

Priestly sons and brothers, how do we affirm and nourish this awareness? How do we tend the lamp of contemplation? How seriously do we attend to this inmost focal point of our personality, retreating briefly for interior conversation from the constant onslaught of external duties? Have we kept our taste for personal prayer and meditation, for the breviary? And how can we hope to give our activity full efficacy if we do not draw from the interior fount of conversation with God those choicest energies which He alone can give? —Pope Paul VI, message to priests, 6-30-68.

Faithfulness to prayer is for the priest a duty of personal piety, of which the wisdom of the Church has defined precisely several important points, like the daily mental prayer, the visit to the most Blessed Sacrament, the rosary and the examination of one's conscience. And it is also a strict obligation contracted with the Church when it is a question of the daily recitation of the Divine Office. Probably because they have neglected some of these regulations some members of the clergy have found themselves the victims of an outward instability, of interior impoverishment, and exposed one day without defense to the temptations of life....

Together with St. Pius X, "We consider it certain that if the priest is to hold worthily the height of his rank and office, he must be particularly dedicated to the practice of prayer.... The priest must obey the commandment of Christ more intensely than others. One must always pray; a precept so much recommended by St. Paul—insist on prayer, watchfully giving thanks—pray without interruption."

And in concluding this point, We Ourselves gladly repeat the password given to priests by Our immediate predecessor, Pius XII, from the very beginning of his pontificate: "Pray, pray always more and more with greater insistence." —SNP.

Try to have an inner life, to be, as we used to say, living "duplicates," in contact with exterior life and then with personal conscience, which has, for one who listens to them, its multiple voices: psychological, moral, spiritual.... The latter especially we call inner life, which would be better termed a voice listened to, an echo of the Spirit "who speaks in you," vocation, the secret, delicate and powerful conversation of the Lord with our heart, and which is expressed on the part of the soul in a language of faith and religious prayer. Oh, yes! Try to pray to the Lord. Do not pray mechanically. Do not leave the usual, prescribed meeting with God without drawing out of yourself a personal cry of sincerity and an affectionate moment of conversation with Him. Remember, then: first, inner life. — Pope Paul VI to students of the major Roman seminary, 2-22-71.

STRENGTHENING THE SPIRIT

The following must be features of the priest's life: a) he must learn "to live in familiar and constant company with the Father through His Son, Jesus Christ, in the Holy Spirit."[1]

b) he ought to be able to find Christ habitually in the intimate communion of prayer;

c) he should have learned to keep by his side the word of God in Sacred Scripture, with an affection rooted in faith, and to give it to others;

d) he should be willing and happy to visit and adore Christ sacramentally present in the Eucharist;

e) he ought to have, as the Church desires, a fervent love for the Virgin Mary, Mother of Christ, who was in a special way associated with the work of the redemption;

f) he should readily consult the documents of sacred tradition, the works of the Fathers, and the examples of the saints;

g) he must know how to examine and judge himself, his conscience and his motives, with honesty and sincerity. — RF.

The priest's individual efforts at his own sanctification find new incentives in the ministry of grace and in the ministry of the Eucharist, in which all the riches of the Church are contained.[2] Acting in the person of Christ, the priest unites himself most intimately with the offering, and places on the altar his entire life, which bears the marks of the holocaust. —SCl 29.

The Church has this lofty doctrine in mind when she invites her ministers to a life of asceticism and recommends them to celebrate the Eucharistic Sacrifice with profound piety. Is it not perhaps because they did not fully understand the close link, and almost reciprocity, uniting the daily gift of oneself with the offering of the Mass, that certain priests little by little lost the first love of their ordination? This was the experience of the Curé of Ars: "The cause," he said, "of the slackness of the priest is that he does not pay attention to the Mass."...

...With paternal affection, We ask Our beloved priests to examine themselves periodically on the manner in which they celebrate the holy mysteries and their spiritual state of mind when they go up to the altar and the fruits they strive to derive from it. The centenary of this admirable priest (St. John Vianney) who derived from the comfort and fortune of celebrating the holy Mass the courage of his own sacrifice invites them to it. We are firmly confident that his intercession will obtain for them abundant graces of light and of strength. —SNP

...**In the life** of a priest nothing could replace the silent and prolonged prayer before the altar. The adoration of Jesus, our God, thanksgiving, reparation for our sins and for those of men, the prayer for so many intentions entrusted to him, combine to raise the priest to a greater love for the Divine Master, to whom he has promised faithfulness and for men who depend on his priestly ministry. With the practice of this enlightened and fervent worship of the Eucharist, the spiritual life of the priest increases and there are prepared the missionary energies of the most valuable apostles. — SNP

In the fulfillment of [priests'] ministry with fidelity to the daily colloquy with Christ, a visit to and veneration of the most holy Eucharist, spiritual retreats and spiritual direction are of great worth. In many ways, but especially through mental prayer and the vocal prayers which they freely choose, priests seek and fervently pray that God will grant them the spirit of true adoration whereby they themselves, along with the people committed to them, may intimately unite themselves with Christ the Mediator of the New Testament, and so as adopted children of God may be able to call out "Abba, Father" (Rom 8:15). — PO 18.

...**In order that,** in all conditions of life, they may be able to grow in union with Christ, priests, besides the exercise of their conscious ministry, enjoy the common and particular means, old and new, which the Spirit never ceases to arouse in the People of God and which the Church commends, and sometimes commands,[3] for the sanctification of her members. Outstanding among all these spiritual aids are those acts by which the faithful are nourished in the Word of God at the double table of the Sacred Scripture and the Eucharist.[4] The importance of frequent use of these for the sanctification of priests is obvious to all. The ministers of sacramental grace are intimately united to Christ our Savior and Pastor through the fruitful reception of the sacraments, especially sacramental Penance, in which, prepared by the daily examination of conscience, the necessary conversion of heart and love for the Father of mercy is greatly deepened. Nourished by spiritual reading, under the light of faith, they can more diligently seek signs of God's will and impulses of His grace in the various events of life, and so from day to day become more docile to the mission they have assumed in the Holy Spirit. — PO 18.

We wish to trust that the ministers of the Lord will themselves be the first, according to the precepts of canon law, to practice regularly and fervently the sacrament of Penance, so necessary for their sanctification, and that they will give the greatest importance to the pressing insistence that Pius XII on several occasions and with sadness addressed to them in this respect. — SNP.

1. OT 8.   2. PO 5.   3. Cf. Code of Canon Law, 125ff.
4. Cf. PC 6; DV 21.

CANTICLE OF DIVINE PRAISE

Christ Jesus, high priest of the new and eternal covenant, taking human nature, introduced into this earthly exile that hymn which is sung throughout all ages in the halls of heaven. He joins the entire community of mankind to Himself, associating it with His own singing of this canticle of divine praise.

For He continues His priestly work through the agency of His Church, which is ceaselessly engaged in praising the Lord and interceding for the salvation of the whole world. She does this, not only by celebrating the Eucharist, but also in other ways, especially by praying the Divine Office. — SC 83.

The hymn of praise, which resounds eternally in the heavenly halls, and which Jesus Christ the High Priest introduced into this land of exile, has always been continued by the Church in the course of so many centuries, with constancy and faithfulness, in the marvelous variety of its forms.

...In celebrating the Divine Office, those who as a result of having received sacred Orders are destined in a particular way to be the sign of Christ the Priest, and those who with the vows of religious profession have dedicated themselves to the service of God and the Church in a special way, should not feel impelled solely by a law they must observe but rather by recognition of the intrinsic importance of prayer and by its pastoral and ascetic usefulness. It is highly desirable that the public prayer of the Church should spring from a general spiritual renewal and from awareness of the intrinsic necessity of the whole body of the Church. The latter, like her Head, cannot be presented except as a praying Church. — Apostolic Constitution on the Breviary.

Like Christ Himself, His minister is wholly and solely intent on the things of God and the Church (cf. Lk 2:49; 1 Cor 7:32-33), and he imitates the great High Priest who stands in the presence of God ever living to intercede in our favor (Heb 9:24; 7:25). So, he receives joy and encouragement unceasingly from the attentive and devout recitation of the Divine Office, by which he dedicates his voice to the Church who prays together with her Spouse,[1] and he recognizes the necessity of continuing his diligence at prayer, which is the profoundly priestly occupation (Acts 6:4). — SCl 28.

In the recitation of the Divine Office, [priests] offer the voice of the Church which perseveres in prayer in the name of the whole human race, together with Christ who lives on still to make intercession on our behalf. — PO 13.

1. Cf. PO 13.

> Through virginity, or celibacy observed for the kingdom of heaven (cf. Mt 19:12), priests are consecrated to Christ by a new and exceptional reason. They adhere to Him more easily with an undivided heart (1 Cor 7:32-34); they dedicate themselves more freely in Him and through Him to the service of God and men. — PO 16.

A Total Giving

FULLNESS OF LOVE

PASTORAL STIMULUS

CELIBACY AND PERSONALITY

ON-GOING FIDELITY

CELIBACY AND LONELINESS

A SIGN TO ALL MEN

FULLNESS OF LOVE

Jesus, who selected the first ministers of salvation, wished them to be introduced to the understanding of the mysteries of the kingdom of heaven (Mt 13:11; Mk 4:11; Lk 8:10), to be co-workers with God under a very special title, and His ambassadors (2 Cor 5:20). He called them friends and brethren (Jn 15:15; 20:17), for whom He consecrated Himself so that they might be consecrated in truth (Jn 17:19); He promised a more than abundant recompense to anyone who should leave home, family, wife and children for the sake of the kingdom of God (Lk 18:29-30).

More than this, in words filled with mystery and hope, He also commended[1] an even more perfect consecration to the kingdom of heaven by means of celibacy, as a special gift (Mt 19:11-12). The motive of this answer to the divine call is the kingdom of heaven (*ibid.*, v. 12); similarly, the ideas—of this kingdom (Lk 18:30), of the gospel (Mk 10:29), and of the name of Christ (Mt 19:29), are what motivate those invited by Jesus to the difficult renunciations of the apostolate, by a very intimate participation in His lot (cf. Mk, *loc. cit.*). —SCl 22.

As for those men "who were not defiled with women, being virgins," the Apostle John asserts that, "they follow the Lamb wherever he goes" (Rev 14:4). Let us meditate then on the exhortation Augustine gives to all men of this class: "You follow the Lamb because the body of the Lamb is indeed virginal.... Rightly do you follow Him in virginity of heart and body wherever He goes. For what does following mean but imitation? Christ has suffered for us, leaving us an example, as the Apostle Peter says 'that we should follow in His footsteps.'"[2]

Hence all these disciples and spouses of Christ embraced the state of virginity, as St. Bonaventure says, "in order to become like unto Christ the Spouse, for that state makes virgins like unto Him."[3] It would hardly satisfy their burning love for Christ to be united with Him by the bonds of affection, but this love had perforce to express itself by the imitation of His virtues, and especially by conformity to His way of life, which was lived completely for the benefit and salvation of the human race. If priests, religious men and women, and others who in any way have vowed themselves to the divine service, cultivate perfect chastity, it is certainly for the reason that their Divine Master remained all His life a virgin. —SV.

Christ, the only Son of the Father, by the power of the Incarnation itself was made Mediator between heaven and earth, between the Father and the human race. Wholly in accord with this mission, Christ remained throughout His whole life in the state of celibacy, which signified His total dedication to the service of God and men. This deep connection between celibacy and the priesthood of Christ is reflected in those whose fortune it is to share in the dignity and in the mission of the Mediator and eternal Priest; this sharing will be more perfect the freer the sacred minister is from the bonds of flesh and blood.[4] —SCl 21.

The response to the divine call is an answer of love to the love which Christ has shown us so sublimely (Jn 15:13; 3:16). This response is included in the mystery of that special love for those souls who have accepted His most urgent appeals (cf. Mk 10:21). Grace with a divine force increases the longings of love. And love, when it is genuine, is total, exclusive, stable and lasting, an irresistible spur to all forms of heroism. And so, the free choice of sacred celibacy has always been considered by the Church "as something that signifies and stimulates charity"[5]: it signifies a love without reservations, it stimulates to a charity which is open to all. Who can see in such a life so completely dedicated and motivated as shown above, the sign of spiritual poverty, of self-seeking, and not rather see that celibacy is and ought to be a rare and very meaningful example of a life whose motivation is love, by which man expresses his own unique greatness? Who can doubt the moral and spiritual richness of such a consecrated life, consecrated not to any human ideal no matter how noble, but to Christ and to His work to bring about a new form of humanity in all places and for all generations? —SCl 24.

This biblical and theological vision associates our ministerial priesthood with the priesthood of Christ; it is modeled on the total and exclusive dedication of Christ to His mission of salvation, and makes it the cause of our assimilation to the form of charity and sacrifice proper to Christ our Savior. This vision seems to Us so profound and rich in truth, both speculative and practical, that We invite you, venerable brothers, and We invite you, eager students of Christian doctrine and masters of the spiritual life, and all priests who have gained a supernatural insight into your vocation—to persevere in the study of this vision, and to go deeply into the inner recesses and wealth of its reality. In this way, the bond between the priesthood and celibacy will be seen in an ever improving union, owing to its clear logic and to the heroism of a unique and limitless love for Christ the Lord and for His Church. — SCl 25.

"**Made captive** by Christ Jesus" (Phil 3:12) unto the complete abandonment of one's entire self to Him, the priest takes on the likeness of Christ most perfectly, even in the love with which the eternal Priest has loved the Church His Body and offered Himself entirely for her sake, in order to make her a glorious, holy and immaculate Spouse (cf. Eph 5:25-27).

The consecrated celibacy of the sacred ministers actually manifests the virginal love of Christ for the Church, and the virginal and supernatural fecundity of this marriage, by which the children of God are born but not of flesh and blood (Jn 1:13).[6] — SCl 26.

The spontaneous and complete dedication of sacred celibacy, traditional in the Latin Church, could not but have in the Synod the expression which we know, not only of convinced confirmation but also of present and historical renewal.

...We are certain that the present generation and even more the young and future generations of the clergy will willingly accept this discipline, and live it with humble splendor. That man esteems this discipline who loves with a heart open to the Holy Spirit and sacrificed for the better rendering of his personal service to the Church and to the People of God. Vocations will flourish if the cross is their powerful attraction. — Pope Paul VI, to College of Cardinals, 1-6-72.

1. PO 16.
2. 1 Pt 2:21; St. Augustine, *De sancta virginitate*, c. 27; P.L. XL, 411.
3. St. Bonaventure, *De perfectione evangelica*, Q. 3, a. 3.
4. PO 16.   5. LG 42.   6. Cf. LG 42; PO 16.

PASTORAL STIMULUS

Celibacy is to be embraced and esteemed as a gift. Perfect and perpetual continence for the sake of the kingdom of heaven, commended by Christ the Lord (cf. Mt 19:22) and through the course of time as well as in our own days freely accepted and observed in a praiseworthy manner by many of the faithful, is held by the Church to be of great value in a special manner for the priestly life. It is at the same time a sign and a stimulus for pastoral charity and a special source of spiritual fecundity in the world.[1] — PO 16.

...Indeed, celibacy has a many-faceted suitability for the priesthood, for the whole priestly mission is dedicated to the service of a new humanity which Christ, the victor over death, has aroused through His Spirit in the world and which has its origin "not of blood, nor of the will of the flesh, nor of the will of man but of God" (Jn 1:13). Through virginity, then, or celibacy observed for the kingdom of heaven (cf. Mt 19:12), priests are consecrated to Christ by a new and exceptional reason. They adhere to Him more easily with an undivided heart (cf. 1 Cor 7:32-34), they dedicate themselves more freely in Him and through Him to the service of God and men, and they more expeditiously minister to His kingdom and the work of heavenly regeneration, and thus they are apt to accept, in a broad sense, paternity in Christ. — PO 16.

The consecration to Christ, by virtue of a new and lofty title like celibacy, evidently gives to the priest, even in the practical field, the maximum efficiency and the best disposition of mind, psychologically and affectively, for the continuous exercise of a perfect charity. This charity will permit him to spend himself wholly for the welfare of all, in a fuller and more concrete way (2 Cor 12:15).[2] It also guarantees him obviously a greater freedom and flexibility in the pastoral ministry,[3] in his active and loving presence in the world, to which Christ has invited him (Jn 17:18), so that he may pay fully to all the children of God the debt due them (Rom 1:14). — SCl 32.

"**Unless a grain** of wheat falls into the earth and dies, it remains alone; but if it dies, it bears much fruit" (Jn 12:24). And the Apostle Paul did not hesitate to expose himself to a daily death, in order to obtain among his faithful glory in Christ Jesus (1 Cor 15:31). In a similar way, by a daily dying to himself, and by giving up the legitimate love of a family of his own for the love of Christ and of His kingdom, the priest will find the glory of an exceedingly rich and fruitful life in Christ, because like Him and in Him, he loves and dedicates himself to all the children of God. — SCl 30.

1. Cf. LG 42, AAS 57 (1965), pp. 47-49.
2. OT 10.   3. PO 16.

CELIBACY AND PERSONALITY

Celibacy, as a personal option for some more important good, even a merely natural one, can promote the full maturity and integration of the human personality. This is all the more true in regard to celibacy undertaken for the kingdom of heaven, as is evident in the lives of so many saints and of the faithful who, living the celibate life, dedicated themselves totally to promoting human and Christian progress for the sake of God and men. —Ministerial Priesthood, Nov. 1971, Synod Document.

The natural and lawful desire a man has to love a woman and to raise a family are renounced by celibacy, but marriage and the family are not said to be the only way for fully developing the human person. In the priest's heart love is by no means extinct. His charity is drawn from the purest source (cf. 1 Jn 4:8-16), practiced in the imitation of God and Christ, and no less than any other genuine love is demanding and real (cf. 1 Jn 3:16-18). It gives the priest a limitless horizon, deepens and gives breadth to his sense of responsibility—a sign of mature personality—and inculcates in him as a sign of a higher and greater fatherhood, a generosity and refinement of heart[1] which offer a superlative enrichment. —SCl 56.

The Church is not unaware that the choice of consecrated celibacy, since it involves a series of hard renunciations which affect the very depths of a man, presents also grave difficulties and problems to which the men of today are particularly sensitive. In fact, it might seem that celibacy conflicts with the solemn recognition of human values by the Church in the recent Council. And yet a more careful consideration reveals that the sacrifice of human love as experienced in a family and as offered by the priest for the love of Christ, is really a singular tribute paid to that superior love. Indeed, it is universally recognized that man has always offered to God what is worthy of both the giver and the receiver.

On the other hand, the Church cannot and should not set aside the fact that the choice of celibacy—provided that it is made with human and Christian prudence and responsibility — is governed by grace which, far from destroy-ing or doing voilence to nature, elevates it and imparts to it supernatural powers and vigor. God, who has cre-ated and redeemed man, knows what He can ask of him and gives him everything necessary to be able to do what his Creator and Redeemer asks of him. St. Augustine, who had fully and painfully experienced in himself the nature of man, exclaimed: "Grant what You command, and command what You will."[2] — SCl 50, 51.

A true knowledge of the real difficulties of celibacy is very useful, even necessary, for the priest, so that he may be fully aware of what his celi-bacy requires to be genuine and beneficial. But with equal fidelity to the truth, these difficulties must not be given greater value or weight than they actually have in the human or religious sphere, or declared impossible of solu-tion.

After what science has now ascertained,[3] it is not just to continue repeating that celibacy is against nature because it runs counter to lawful physical, psychological and affective needs or to claim that a completely mature human personality demands fulfillment of these needs. Man, created to God's image and likeness (Gen. 1:26-27) is not just flesh and blood; the sexual instinct is not all that he has; man is also, and pre-eminently, understanding, choice, freedom, and thanks to these powers, he is, and must remain, superior to the rest of creation; they give him mastery over his physical, psychological and affective appetites.

The true, deep reason for dedicated celibacy is, as We have said, the choice of a closer and more complete relationship with the mystery of Christ and the Church for the good of all mankind: in this choice there is no doubt, that those highest human values are able to find their fullest expression. — SCl 52, 53, 54.

It may not be asserted, as some do, that the "mutual help,"[4] which is sought in Christian marriage, is a more effective aid in striving for personal sanctity than the solitude of the heart, as they term it, of virgins and celibates. For although all those who have embraced a life of perfect chastity have deprived themselves of the expression of human love permitted in the married state, nonetheless it cannot thereby be affirmed that because of this privation they have diminished and despoiled the human personality. For they receive from the Giver of heavenly gifts something spiritual which far exceeds that "mutual help" which husband and wife confer on each other. They consecrate themselves to Him who is their source, and who shares with them His divine life, and thus personality suffers no loss, but gains immensely. For who, more than the virgin, can apply to himself that marvelous phrase of the Apostle Paul: "I live, now not I; but Christ lives in me" (Gal 2:20). —SV.

1. Cf. 1 Thes 2:11; 1 Cor 4:15; 2 Cor 6:13; Gal 4:19; 1 Tm 5:1-2.
2. *Confessions* X. 29. 40: P.L. 32. 796.
3. Cf. SCl 10.   4. Cf. C.I.C., Can. 1013, section 1.

ON-GOING FIDELITY

Perfect chastity demands, first, a free choice by Christians before they consecrate themselves to God and then, from God, supernatural help and grace (cf. 1 Cor 7:7). Our divine Redeemer Himself has taught us this in the following words: "All men take not his word, but they to whom it is given....

He that can take it, let him take it" (Mt 19:11, 12). Saint Jerome, intently pondering this sacred phrase of Jesus Christ, exhorts all "that each one study his own powers, whether he can fulfill the precepts of virginal modesty. For of itself chastity is charming and attractive to all. But one's forces must be considered, that he who can may take it. The Lord's word is as it were an exhortation, stirring on His soldiers to the prize of purity. He that can take it, let him take it: let him who can, fight, conquer and receive his reward."[1]

For virginity is a difficult virtue; that one be able to embrace it there is needed not only a strong and declared determination of completely and perpetually abstaining from those legitimate pleasures derived from marriage, but also a constant vigilance and struggle to contain and dominate rebellious movements of body and soul, a flight from the importunings of this world, a struggle to conquer the wiles of satan.... Hence a chastity dedicated to God demands strong and noble souls, souls ready to do battle and conquer "for the sake of the kingdom of heaven" (Mt 19:12). — SV.

Although chastity pledged to God is a difficult virtue, those who after serious consideration generously answer Christ's invitation and do all in their power to attain it, can perfectly and faithfully preserve it. For since they have eagerly embraced the state of virginity or celibacy, they will certainly receive from God that gift of grace through whose help they will be able to carry out their promise. Wherefore, if there are any "who do not feel they have the gift of chastity even though they have vowed it,"[2] let them not declare they cannot fulfill their obligations in this matter. "For," says the Council of Trent, quoting St. Augustine, "'God does not command the impossible, but in commanding serves notice that one do what he can, and pray for what he cannot,'[3] and He helps us to accomplish it."[4] — SV.

This sacred synod exhorts all priests who, in following the example of Christ, freely receive sacred celibacy as a grace of God, that they magnanimously and wholeheartedly adhere to it, and that persevering faithfully in it, they may acknowledge this outstanding gift of the Father which is so openly praised and extolled by the Lord (cf. Mt 19:1). Let them keep before their eyes the great mysteries signified by it and fulfilled in it. Insofar as perfect continence is thought by many men to be impossible in our times, to that extent priests should all the more humbly and steadfastly pray with the Church for that grace of fidelity, which is never denied those who seek it, and use all the supernatural and natural aids available. They should especially seek, lest they omit them, the ascetical norms which have been proved by the experience of the Church and which are scarcely less necessary in the contemporary world. This holy synod asks not only priests but all the faithful that they might receive this precious gift of priestly celibacy in their hearts and ask of God that He will always bestow this gift upon His Church. — PO 16.

The priest must not think that ordination makes everything easy for him and screens him once for all from every temptation or danger. Chastity is not acquired all at once but results from a laborious conquest and daily affirmation. Our world today stresses the positive values of love between the sexes but has also multiplied the difficulties and risks in this sphere. In order to safeguard his chastity with all care and affirm its sublime meaning, the priest must consider clearly and calmly his position as a man exposed to spiritual warfare against the seductions of the flesh in himself and in the world, continually renewing his resolution to give an ever increasing and ever better perfection to the irrevocable offering of himself which obliges him to a fidelity that is complete, loyal and real.

Christ's priest will receive new strength and joy daily as he deepens in his meditation and prayer the motives for his gift and the conviction that he has chosen the better part. He will ask humbly and perseveringly for the grace of fidelity, never denied to those who ask it sincerely.[5] — SCl 73.

We know well that in the world of today particular difficulties threaten celibacy from all sides; priests have indeed already repeatedly experienced them in the course of the centuries. But they can overcome these difficulties if suitable conditions are fostered, namely: growth of the interior life through prayer, renunciation and fervent love for God and one's neighbor and by other aids to spiritual life; human balance through well-ordered integration into the fabric of social relationships; fraternal association and companionship with other priests and with the bishop, through pastoral structures better suited to this purpose and with the assistance also of the community of the faithful. — Ministerial Priesthood, Nov. 1971, Synod Document.

Rightly jealous of his full self-giving to the Lord, the priest should know how to guard against sentimental tendencies which imperil an affectivity not sufficiently enlightened or guided by the Spirit. He should beware of looking for spiritual or apostolic pretexts for what are in fact dangerous inclinations of the heart. — SCl 77.

In order to acquire perfect mastery of the spirit over the senses, it is not enough to refrain from acts directly contrary to chastity, but it is necessary also generously to renounce anything that may offend this virtue nearly or remotely; at such a price will the soul be able to reign fully over the body and lead its spiritual life in peace and liberty. Who then does not see, in the light of Catholic principles, that perfect chastity and virginity, far from harming the normal unfolding of man or woman, on the contrary endow them with the highest moral nobility. — SV.

Modesty is nourished by the fear of God, that filial fear which is founded on the virtue of profound Christian humility, and which creates in us utter abhorrence for the slightest sin, as Our predecessor, St. Clement I, stated in these words, "He who is chaste in flesh should not be proud, for he should know that he owes the gift of continence to another."[6] How important Christian humility is for the protection of virginity, no one perhaps has taught more clearly than Augustine. "Because perpetual continence, and virginity above all, is a great good in the saints of God, extreme vigilance must be exercised lest it be corrupted by pride.... The more clearly I see the greatness of this gift, the more truly do I fear lest it be plundered by thieving pride. No one therefore protects virginity, but God Himself who bestowed it: and 'God is charity' (1 Jn 4:8). The guardian therefore of virginity is charity; the habitat of this guardian is humility."[7] — SV.

...**Never should** it be forgotten that perfect chastity is a great gift of God. For this reason Jerome wrote these succinct words, "It is given to those (cf. Mt 19:11), who have asked for it, who have desired it, who have worked to receive it. For it will be given to everyone who asks, the seeker will find, to the importunate it will be opened."[8] Ambrose adds that the constant fidelity of virgins to their Divine Spouse depends upon prayer.[9] With that fervent piety for which he was noted St. Alphonsus Liguori taught that there is no help more necessary and certain for conquering temptations against the beautiful virtue of chastity than instant recourse to God in prayer.[10] — SV.

The priest should apply himself above all else to developing, with all the love grace inspires in him, his close relationship with Christ, searching the inexhaustible and enriching mystery; he should also acquire an ever deeper sense of the mystery of the Church. There would be the risk of his state of life seeming unreasonable and unfounded if seen apart from this mystery.

Priestly piety, nourished at the table of God's Word and the Holy Eucharist, lived within the cycle of the liturgical year, inspired by a warm and enlightened devotion to the Virgin Mother of the supreme and eternal high Priest and Queen of the Apostles,[11] will bring him to the source of a true spiritual life which alone provides a solid foundation for the observance of celibacy. — SCl 75.

1. St. Jerome, *Comment. in Matt.*, 19, 12; P.L. 26, 136.
2. Cf. Conc. Trid. Session 24, canon 9.
3. Cf. St. Augustine, *De natura et gratis*, n. 50; P.L. XLIV, 271.
4. Conc. Trid., Session 6, c. 11.
5. PO 16, 18.
6. St. Clement of Rome, *Ad Corinthios*, 38, 2; (Funk-Diekamp). *Patres Apostolici*, Vol. 1, p. 148.
7. St. Augustine, *De sancta virginitate*, cc. 33, 51; P.L. XL, 415, 426; cf. cc. 31-32, 38; 412-415, 419.
8. Cf. *ibid.*, VII, 8: St. Jerome, *Comm. in Matt.* 19:11; P.L. XXVI, 135.
9. Cf. St. Ambrose, *De virginibus*, lib. III, c. 4, nn. 18-20; P.L. XVI, 225.
10. Cf. St. Alphonsus de Liguori, *Practica di amar Gesu Cristo*, c. 17, nn. 7-16.
11. PO 18.

CELIBACY AND LONELINESS

The priest by reason of his celibacy is a solitary: that is true, but his solitude is not emptiness because it is filled with God and the brimming riches of His kingdom. Moreover, for this solitude, which should be an internal and external plenitude of charity, he has prepared himself, if he has chosen it with full understanding, and not through any proud desire to be different from the rest of men, or to withdraw himself from common responsibilities, or to alienate himself from his brothers, or to show contempt for the world. Though set apart from the world, the priest is not separated from the People of God, because he has been appointed to act on behalf of men (Heb 5:1), since he is consecrated completely to charity (cf. 1 Cor 14:4ff.) and to the work for which the Lord has chosen him.[1]

At times loneliness will weigh heavily on the priest, but not for that reason will he regret having generously chosen it. Christ, too, in the most tragic hours of His life was alone — abandoned by the very ones whom He had chosen as witnesses to, and companions of, His life, and whom He had loved unto the end (Jn 13:1); but He stated, "I am not alone, for the Father is with me" (Jn 16:22). He who has chosen to belong completely to Christ will find, above all, in intimacy with Him and in His grace, the power of spirit necessary to banish sadness and regret and to triumph over discouragement. He will not be lacking the protection of the Virgin Mother of Jesus nor the motherly solicitude of the Church, to whom he has given himself in service. He will not be without the kindly care of his father in Christ, the bishop; nor will the fraternal companionship of his fellow priests and the comfort of the entire People of God be lacking to him. And if hostility, lack of confidence and the indifference of his fellowmen make his solitude quite painful, he will thus be able to share, with dramatic clarity, the very experience of Christ, as an apostle who is not above Him by whom he has been sent (cf. Jn 13:16; 14:18), as a friend admitted to the most painful and most glorious secret of his divine Friend who has chosen him to bring forth the mysterious fruit of life in his own life, which is only apparently one of death (cf. Jn 15:15-16, 20). — SCl 58, 59.

1. PO 3.

A SIGN TO ALL MEN

The kingdom of God which is not of this world (Jn 18:36) is present here on earth in mystery, and will reach her perfection with the glorious coming of the Lord Jesus.[1] The Church here below constitutes the seed and the beginning of this kingdom. And as she continues to grow slowly but surely, she longs for the perfect kingdom and desires vehemently with all her energy to unite herself with her King in glory.[2]

The pilgrim People of God, as seen in history, is on a journey toward its true homeland (Phil 3:20), where the divine sonship of the redeemed (1 Jn 3:2) will be fully revealed and where its splendor will be definitively attained by the transformed loveliness of the Spouse of the Lamb of God.[3]

Our Lord and Master has said that "in the resurrection they neither marry nor are given in marriage, but are like angels in heaven" (Mt 22:30). In the world of man, so deeply involved in earthly concerns and too often enslaved by the desires of the flesh (cf. 1 Jn 2:16), the precious divine gift of perfect continence for the kingdom of heaven stands out precisely as "a singular sign of the blessings of heaven" [4]; it proclaims the presence on earth of the final stages of salvation (cf. 1 Cor 7:29-31) with the arrival of a new world; and in a way it anticipates the fulfillment of the kingdom as it sets forth its supreme values which will one day shine forth in all the children of God. This continence, therefore, stands as a testimony to the necessary progress of the People of God toward the final goal of their earthly pilgrimage, and as a stimulus for all to raise their eyes to the things above, where Christ sits at the right hand of the Father and where our life is hidden in Christ with God until He appears in glory (Col 3:1-4). — SCl 33, 34.

Within modern culture, in which spiritual values are to a great extent obscured, the celibate priest indicates the presence of the absolute God, who invites us to be renewed in His image. Where the value of sexuality is so exaggerated that genuine love is forgotten, celibacy for the sake of the kingdom of Christ calls men back to the sublimity of faithful love and reveals the ultimate meaning of life.

Furthermore, one rightly speaks of the value of celibacy as an eschatological sign. By transcending every contingent human value, the celibate priest associates himself in a special way with Christ as the final and absolute good and shows forth, in anticipation, the freedom of the children of God. While the value of the sign and holiness of Christian marriage is fully recognized, celibacy for the sake of the kingdom nevertheless more clearly displays that spiritual fruitfulness or generative power of the New Law by which the apostle knows that in Christ he is the father and mother of his communities.

From this special way of following Christ, the priest draws greater strength and power for the building up of the Church; and this power can be preserved and increased only by an intimate and permanent union with Christ's Spirit. The faithful People of God wish to see in their pastors this union with Christ, and they are able to recognize it.

Through celibacy, priests are more easily able to serve God with undivided heart and spend themselves for their sheep, and as a result they are able more fully to be promoters of evangelization and of the Church's unity. For this reason, priests, even if they are fewer in number, but are resplendent with this outstanding witness of life, will enjoy greater apostolic fruitfulness.

Priestly celibacy, furthermore, is not just the witness of one person alone, but by reason of the special fellowship linking members of the presbyterium it also takes on a social character as the witness of the whole priestly order enriching the People of God. —Ministerial Priesthood, Nov. 1971, Synod Document.

Yes, venerable and well-beloved brothers in the priesthood, whom We cherish "with the affection of Christ Jesus" (Phil 1:8), it is truly this world in which we live, tormented by the pains of growth and change, justly proud of its human values and human conquests, which urgently needs the witness of lives consecrated to the highest and most sacred spiritual values. This witness is necessary in order that the refined and incomparable light, radiating from the most sublime virtues of the spirit, may not be wanting to our times. —SCl 46.

1. GS 39.
2. LG 5.
3. *Ibid.*, 48.
4. PC 12.

> For priests, who have the Lord as their "portion and heritage" (Num 18:20) temporal goods should be used only towards ends which are licit according to the doctrine of Christ and the direction of the Church. — PO 17.

Poverty: Glory of Christ's Followers

DETACHMENT AND THE SPIRIT OF CHRIST

SEARCH FOR AUTHENTIC POVERTY

THE POOR: A SACRAMENT OF CHRIST

DETACHMENT AND THE
SPIRIT OF CHRIST

Priests are invited to embrace voluntary poverty by which they are more manifestly conformed to Christ and become eager in the sacred ministry. For Christ, though He was rich, became poor on account of us, that by His need we might become rich (cf. 2 Cor 8:9). And by their example the apostles witnessed that a free gift of God is to be freely given (cf. Acts 8:18-25), with the knowledge of how to sustain both abundance and need (cf. Phil 4:12). A certain common use of goods, similar to the common possession of goods in the history of the primitive Church (cf. Acts 2:42-47), furnishes an excellent means of pastoral charity. By living this form of life, priests can laudably reduce to practice that spirit of poverty commended by Christ. — PO 17.

The Council described the spirit of poverty as "the glory and sign of the Church of Christ."[1] It is the task of the moment, the commitment to which you all are called. It is the evidence given by all who are today laboring, working, suffering, of all who are suffering in inequality and lack of hope, but who have the right to expect something from Christians, especially from priests. The spirit of poverty is the proclamation of the gospel to the world of today, which is not satisfied with words, but wants action; is not content with statements, but penetrates intentions with discernment and recognizes sincerity.

We spoke of this explicitly in Our first encyclical letter *Ecclesiam suam*, when We asked pastors and faithful to educate their speech and their conduct at the school of poverty, and to have the same mind as was in Christ (cf. Phil 2:5). We also recalled "those guiding principles which ought to found our trust more on God's help and on the goods of the spirit than on temporal means." We emphasized that "we should limit and subordinate possession and use of the latter to their usefulness for suitable exercise of our apostolic mission."[2]

For its part, the Council's decree on the ministry and the priestly life clearly exhorted priests to have the spirit of poverty and to practice it, because in that way "they can conform themselves to Christ in a more evident way and be in a position to carry out their sacred ministry with greater readiness."[3]

You, dearest priests, chaplains of labor, have the inspiring responsibility and the incomparable honor of representing Christ among your workers, among artisans, craftsmen and laborers, and you will one day have to render an account to God for their salvation.

Take care that they [workers] may be able to perceive Christ, through the translucent garment of your poverty, your gentleness, your understanding, your availability, in everything that makes a priest's life the life of a crucified man. May they in this way discover Christ's face and Christ's love, so that they may be able to open themselves to Him, receive Him into their souls as into their homes, and do Him honor through the way they live. — Pope Paul VI, to chaplains of labor (ONARMO), 6-25-69.

Certainly in advising holy poverty, We do not wholly wish, venerable brothers, in any way to approve the misery to which the ministers of the Lord in some cases are reduced in the cities and in the country. Commenting on the exhortation of the Lord regarding the detachment from the goods of this world, Venerable Bede warns us precisely against any abusive interpretation: "One must not believe," he wrote, "that the saints are commanded not to keep money for themselves or for the poor; since one reads that the Lord Himself had money in order to establish His Church...but let no one serve God because of it, nor deny justice for fear of poverty." — SNP.

As those dedicated to the service of God and the fulfillment of the office entrusted to them, priests deserve to receive an equitable remuneration, because "the laborer is worthy of his hire" (Lk 10:7),[4] and "the Lord directed that those who preach the gospel should have their living from the gospel" (1 Cor 9:14). Wherefore, insofar as an equitable remuneration of the priests would not be provided otherwise, the faithful themselves — that is, those in whose behalf the priest labors — are truly obliged to see to it that they can provide what help is necessary for the honorable and worthy life of the priests. — PO 20.

In their friendly and brotherly dealings with one another and with other men, priests are able to learn and appreciate human values and esteem created goods as gifts of God. By living in the world, let priests know how not to be of the world, according to the word of our Lord and Master (cf. Jn 17:14-16). By using the world as those who do not use it (cf. 1 Cor 7:31), let them achieve that freedom whereby they are free from every inordinate concern and become docile to the voice of God in their daily life. From this freedom and docility grows spiritual discretion in which is found the right relationship to the world and earthly goods. Such a right relationship is of great importance to priests, because the mission of the Church is fulfilled in the midst of the world and because created goods are altogether necessary for the personal development of man. Let them be grateful, therefore, for all that the heavenly Father has given them to lead a full life rightly; but let them see all that comes to them in the light of faith, so that they might correctly use goods in response to the will of God and reject those which are harmful to their mission. —PO 17.

1. GS 88.
2. AAS 56 (1964), p. 634.
3. PO 17
4. Cf. Mt 10:10; 1 Cor 9:7; 1 Tim 5:18.

SEARCH FOR AUTHENTIC POVERTY

Pius XI, taking modern society into consideration, addressed this grave warning to priests: "While one sees men selling and negotiating everything for money, may they proceed disinterestedly through the attractions of vice and may they reject with saintliness the unworthy cupidity of gain, may they not seek pecuniary advantages but rather the benefit of souls, and may they desire and ask for the glory of God and not theirs."

These words must be carved in the hearts of all priests. If there are some among them who lawfully possess personal means, may they not be attached to them. —SNP.

Ecclesiastical goods, properly so called, according to their nature and ecclesiastical law, should be administered by priests with the help of

capable laymen as far as possible and should always be
employed for those purposes in the pursuit of which it is
licit for the Church to possess temporal goods—namely,
for the carrying out of divine worship, for the procuring
of honest sustenance for the clergy, and for the exercise of
the works of the holy apostolate or works of charity, especially in behalf of the needy.[1]

Those goods which priests and bishops receive for
the exercise of their ecclesiastical office should be used
for adequate support and the fulfillment of their office and
status, excepting those governed by particular laws.[2] That
which is in excess they should be willing to set aside for
the good of the Church or for works of charity. Thus they
are not to seek ecclesiastical office or the benefits of it
for the increase of their own family wealth.[3] Therefore, in
no way placing their heart in treasures,[4] they should avoid
all greediness and carefully abstain from every appearance
of business. —PO 17.

Desire for riches entails a
whole series of temporal cares and earthly ties which occupy great and overwhelming space in the heart. Let us
not forget the gospel story of the rich young man. He was
given the chance of following Christ and therefore abandoning his riches. He preferred his wealth to the following
of Christ. The Lord "looked upon him and loved him" (Mk
10:21), but still had to watch him go sadly away.

But, even more than to the practice of the personal
virtue of poverty, the Council called us back to search after,
to practice another kind of poverty—ecclesial poverty,
that which the Church ought to practice as the Church,
as the assembly gathered together in the name of Christ.

One passage in the Council's documents on this matter is a great passage, and We choose it for quotation from
among very many others on the subject to be found in those
documents. The passage is as follows: "The spirit of poverty

and of charity are the glory and the testimony of the Church of Christ."[5]

These are luminous and vigorous words. They arose from an ecclesial conscience which was becoming fully awake, was hungry for truth and authenticity and desired to free itself from historical habits which had now been clearly revealed as causing deformations in the Church's evangelical genius and apostolic mission. There is imperative need for critical, historical and moral examination of conscience, so as to give the Church her genuine and modern features, in which the present generation desires to be able to recognize those of Christ.

Those who spoke in the Council on this matter dwelt particularly on this function of ecclesial poverty, that is, on its function of illustrating the Church's proper appearance.[6] Cardinal Lercaro spoke especially in this way at the close of the Council's first session (December 6, 1962). He emphasized a certain "aspect" which the Church of today ought to show people of our time in a particular way, the aspect with which Christ's mystery was revealed. That aspect is the moral one of poverty; it is also the sociological aspect, namely, that the Church rises by preference from among the poor.

We can all see what a power for reform there is in exalting the principle that the Church ought to be poor. The Church should also be seen to be poor.

We note with watchful attention that, in this period of ours, which is all absorbed in gaining, possessing, enjoying economic goods, a desire is apparent in public opinion both inside and outside the Church, to see evangelical poverty practiced. It is almost a need. People want to see it most where the gospel is preached and represented. —Pope Paul VI, to a general audience, 6-24-70.

From Our first encyclical, *Ecclesiam suam*, We have spoken of it [the spirit of poverty], insisting on the duty that is Ours "to make suitable decisions and regulations binding on the Church, so that we may base our confidence more on the help of God and on spiritual values, than on fallible, human means,"[7] and setting forth in the encyclical *Populorum progressio*, as an ideal to be pursued, the turning towards the spirit of poverty.[8] Those who desire the Church's renewal also speak of it.

We must take advantage of these dispositions, so favorable to the Church's poverty and to the formation of the modern Christian towards the spirit of poverty. At a time when the economic riches of the world are growing immensely, let us, the Church, return to being more faithful disciples of the poverty of Christ. Not to protest against the world in the matter of its progress, but for two purposes: first of all to remind ourselves that we must put our trust only in spiritual forces, in grace, in imitation of Christ, following the gospel admonition: "Beware of all covetousness; for a man's life does not consist in the abundance of his possessions" (Lk 12:15); and, secondly, to employ ourselves in making good use of riches, which must be used for bread for the poor, for better distribution of temporal goods, and for the service of man: this means in short, as Our predecessor John XXIII happily expressed it, "permanent disposition to pass on to others all that is best in ourselves."[9]

The thought becomes greater, it becomes more complex: poverty, in the history of the world, was strictly bound to working conditions, especially of the more humble, disdained, those exposed to arbitrary will and abuse. It is a mysterious law, a consequence of the first sin, by which physical pain entered the world, with manual labor, the sweat of the brow, distress — spiritual and material. Now, although He was the Son of God, Christ did not wish to escape from that law: in this too He was truly "the Son of Man." Under the tutelage of St. Joseph, Christ was a workman: He suffered, He sweated. He toiled during the thirty years of His hidden life. But with this acceptance of work by Him, the old condition of mortification and fatigue was transformed; and labor, although retaining the double element of healthy activity and painful fatigue, can thus — if regarded in the light of the new economy of grace — be referred to in its old function of collaboration with God, enabling us also to participate in the feelings of Christ and to follow His example. — Pope Paul VI, to new cardinals, 5-8-69.

1. Council of Antioch, canon 25; Mansi 2, 1328; *Decree of Gratian*, c. 23, C. 12 q. 1. (Friedberg, I), pp. 684-685.

2. This is to be understood especially with regard to the laws and customs prevailing in the Eastern Churches.

3. Council of Paris a, 829, can. 15: M.G.H., Sect. III, *Concilia*, t. 2, para. 6622; Council of Trent, Session XXV, *De Reform.*, chapter 1.

4. Ps 62:11 (Vulgate 61).

5. GS 88.

6. Cf. Congar, *Pour une Eglise servante et pauvre*, p. 107.

7. AAS 56 (1964), p. 643.

8. 21; AAS 59 (1967), p. 267.   9. PT; AAS 55 (1963), p. 226.

THE POOR: A SACRAMENT OF CHRIST

Although they have obligations towards all men, priests have a special obligation to the poor and weak entrusted to them, for our Lord Himself showed that He was united to them (cf. Mt 25:34-45), and their evangelization is mentioned as a sign of messianic activity. — PO 6.

Led by the Spirit of the Lord, who anointed the Savior and sent Him to evangelize the poor (cf. Lk 4:18), priests and also bishops, should avoid everything which in any way could turn the poor away. Before the other followers of Christ, let priests set aside every appearance of vanity in their possessions. Let them arrange their homes so that they might not appear unapproachable to anyone, lest anyone, even the most humble, fear to visit them. — PO 17.

We must love poverty, because it was loved by Christ, who "though he was rich, yet for your sake [he] became poor, so that by his poverty you might become rich" (2 Cor 8:9). We must put it into practice, making ourselves poor and empty before God — for He "has filled the hungry with good things, and the rich he has sent empty away" (cf. Lk 1:53) — by detaching ourselves from worldly goods, and giving what we do not need to those in want (cf. Lk 11:41).

We must love the poor, who in a certain way are a sacrament of Christ, for with them — the hungry, the thirsty, the exiles, the naked, the sick, and those in prison — He has seen fit to identify Himself in a mystical fashion (cf. Mt 25:31-46); we must come to their aid, suffer with them, and also follow them, for poverty is the surest path to the full possession of the kingdom of God. — Pope Paul VI, to new cardinals, 5-8-69.

Persevere in your mission of religious assistance, of moral counsel, of Christian friendship, of human comprehension, of the living presence — the gift of yourselves....

It is the testimony — not merely verbal, rhetorical, casual, nor purely demonstrative — but the real, living, suffering, indisputable interest, indeed love, that the Church professes for the working classes. We would say more; it is that same love that the Church has for the poor, who still "hunger and thirst after righteousness," and to whom the gospel promises preference in the kingdom of heaven.

You are the friends of the humble; in a certain way you are colleagues in their heavy toil. You are the elder brothers, who can understand, guide, and teach. You are the advocates of the justice that they—by natural, if not by legal right—await with increasing awareness and impatience. You are the bearers of human and superhuman hope; hope whose treasures only Christianity possesses, for those who in a state of hope suffer, live and die.

The human, social and moral reality in which your pastoral activities are exercised is so great, and in many situations still so crude, so much in need of understanding and charity, that the priest engaged in this work is given a mission of primary importance, in addition to that of his sacramental ministry, his evangelical mission. You need not be afraid if you preserve—as a tree preserves its roots—the contemplative, loving communion with the mystery of the presence, the truth, the obedience and grace proper to the Catholic priesthood. —Pope Paul VI, to chaplains of Italian Christian Workers Association, 4-24-68.

LITURGICAL
DIMENSION

Through the ministry of the priests, the spiritual sacrifice of the faithful is made perfect in union with the sacrifice of Christ. He is the only mediator who in the name of the whole Church is offered sacramentally in the Eucharist and in an unbloody manner until the Lord Himself comes (cf. 1 Cor 11:26). The ministry of priests is directed to this goal and is perfected in it. Their ministry, which begins with the evangelical proclamation, derives its power and force from the sacrifice of Christ. Its aim is that "the entire commonwealth of the redeemed and the society of the saints be offered to God through the High Priest who offered Himself also for us in His passion that we might be the body of so great a Head."[1] — PO 2.

Exercising the Priestly Office of Christ

PASTORAL-LITURGICAL ACTIVITY
MINISTERS OF THE WORD

PASTORAL-LITURGICAL ACTIVITY

The liturgy is the summit toward which the activity of the Church is directed; at the same time it is the font from which all her power flows. For the aim and object of apostolic works is that all who are made sons of God by faith and baptism should come together to praise God in the midst of His Church, to take part in the sacrifice, and to eat the Lord's supper.

The liturgy in its turn moves the faithful, filled with "the paschal sacraments," to be "one in holiness."[2] It prays that "they may hold fast in their lives to what they have grasped by their faith"[3]; the renewal in the Eucharist of the covenant between the Lord and man draws the faithful into the compelling love of Christ and sets them on fire. From the liturgy, therefore, and especially from the Eucharist, as from a font, grace is poured forth upon us; and the sanctification of men in Christ and the glorification of God, to which all other activities of the Church are directed as toward their end, is achieved in the most efficacious possible way. — SC 10.

Christ is always present in His Church, especially in her liturgical celebrations. He is present in the sacrifice of the Mass, not only in the person of His minister, "the same now offering, through the ministry of priests, who formerly offered Himself on the cross,[4] but especially under the eucharistic species. By His power He is present in the sacraments, so that when a man baptizes it is really Christ Himself who baptizes.[5] He is present in His word, since it is He Himself who speaks when the holy scriptures are read in the Church. He is present, lastly, when the Church prays and sings, for He promised: "Where two or three are gathered together in my name, there am I in the midst of them" (Mt 18:20).

Christ indeed always associates the Church with Himself in this great work wherein God is perfectly glorified and men are sanctified. The Church is His beloved Bride who calls to her Lord and through Him offers worship to the eternal Father.

Rightly, then, the liturgy is considered as an exercise of the priestly office of Jesus Christ. In the liturgy the sanctification of the man is signified by signs perceptible to the senses, and is effected in a way which corresponds with each of these signs; in the liturgy the whole public worship is performed by the Mystical Body of Jesus Christ, that is, by the Head and His members.

From this it follows that every liturgical celebration, because it is an action of Christ the Priest and of His Body which is the Church, is a sacred action surpassing all others; no other action of the Church can equal its efficacy by the same title and to the same degree. — SC 7.

The bishops and their assistants in the priesthood should relate their entire pastoral ministry ever more closely to the liturgy. In this way the faithful may derive the divine life in abundance from the perfect participation in the sacred celebrations and, made the ferment of Christ and the salt of the earth, will proclaim the divine life and communicate it to others. — IOE 8.

The power of pastoral-liturgical activity rests in this, that the Christian life may express the paschal mystery in which the Son of God, incarnate and made obedient even to the death of the cross, is so exalted in His resurrection and ascension that He may share His divine life with the world. By this life men, dead to sin and conformed to Christ, "may live no longer for themselves but for him who died for them and rose again" (2 Cor 5:15).

This is done through faith and through the sacraments of faith, that is, chiefly through Baptism[6] and the most sacred mystery of the Eucharist.[7] Around the Eucharist are ranged the other sacraments and the sacramentals[8] and the cycle of celebrations by which the paschal mystery of Christ is unfolded in the Church during the course of the year.[9]

Therefore, even if the liturgy does not exhaust the entire action of the Church,[10] nevertheless the greatest attention must be paid to the necessary connection between pastoral works and the sacred liturgy, so that pastoral-liturgical action is not exercised as if separate and abstract, but as intimately joined to other pastoral activities.

It is especially necessary that there be a close union between the liturgy and catechesis, religious formation, and preaching. —IOE 6, 7.

1. St. Augustine, *De Civitate Dei*, 10, 6; P.L. 41, 284.
2. Postcommunion for both Masses of Easter Sunday.
3. Collect of the Mass for Tuesday of Easter Week.
4. Council of Trent, Session XXII, Doctrine on the Holy Sacrifice of the Mass, C. 2.
5. cf. St. Augustine, *Tractatus in Ioannem*, VI, n. 7.
6. cf. SC 6.
7. cf. SC 47.
8. cf. SC 61.
9. cf. SC 102-107.
10. cf. SC 9.

MINISTERS OF THE WORD

The People of God are joined together primarily by the word of the living God. And rightfully they expect this from their priests. Since no one can be saved who does not first believe, priests, as co-workers with their bishops, have the primary duty of proclaiming the gospel of God to all.[1] In this way they fulfill the command of the Lord: "Going therefore into the whole world preach the gospel to every creature" (Mk 16:15),[2] and they establish and build up the People of God. Through the saving word the spark of faith is lit in the hearts of unbelievers and fed in the hearts of the faithful. This is the way that the congregation of faithful is started and grows, just as the Apostle describes: "Faith comes from hearing, and hearing through the word of Christ" (Rom 10:17). — PO 4.

In a sense, the apostolate and preaching are the same. Preaching is the primary apostolate. Our apostolate, venerable brothers, is above all, the ministry of the word. We know this very well, but it seems good to remind ourselves of it now, so as to direct our pastoral activities aright. We must go back to the study, not of human eloquence or empty rhetoric, but of the genuine art of the sacred word.

We must search for the laws of its simplicity and clarity, for its power and authority, so as to overcome our natural lack of skill in the use of the great and mysterious spiritual instrument of speech and to enable us worthily to compete with those who today exert so much influence through their words by having access to the organs of public opinion. We must beg the Lord for the great and uplifting gift of speech (cf. Jer 1:6), to be able to confer on faith its practical and efficacious principle (cf. Rom 10:17), and to enable our words to reach out to the ends of the earth (cf. Ps 18:5; Rom 10:18).

And may the catechetical teaching of the faith to the Christian people, and to as many others as possible, be marked by the aptness of its language, the wisdom of its method, the zeal of its exercise supported by the evidence of real virtues; and may it strive ardently to lead its hearers to the security of the faith, to a realization of the intimate connection between the divine word and life, and to the illumination of the living God. — EcS.

Although the pedagogy of faith demands that man be gradually initiated into the Christian life, the Church must nevertheless always proclaim to the world the gospel in its entirety. Each priest shares in the special responsibility of preaching the whole of the word of God and of interpreting it according to the faith of the Church.

The proclamation of the word of God is the announcement in the power of the Spirit of the wonders performed by God and the calling of men to share the paschal mystery and to introduce it as a leaven into concrete human history. It is the action of God in which the power of the Holy Spirit brings the Church together interiorly and exteriorly. The minister of the word by evangelization prepares the ways of the Lord with great patience and faith, conforming himself to the various conditions of individuals' and peoples' lives, which are evolving more or less rapidly.

Impelled by the need to keep in view both the personal and social aspects of the announcement of the gospel, so that in it an answer may be given to all the more fundamental questions of men,[3] the Church not only preaches conversion to God to individual men, but also, to the best of her ability, as the conscience of humanity, she addresses society itself and performs a prophetic function in society's regard, always taking pains to effect her own renewal.

As regards the experiences of life—whether of men in general or of priests—which must be kept in mind and always interpreted in the light of the gospel, these experiences cannot be either the sole or the principal norm of preaching. —Ministerial Priesthood, Nov., 1971, Synod Document.

To all men, priests are debtors that the truth of the gospel[4] which they have may be given to others. And so, whether by entering into profitable dialogue they bring people to the worship of God,[5] whether by openly preaching they proclaim the mystery of Christ, or whether in the light of Christ they treat contemporary problems, they are relying not on their own wisdom for it is the word of Christ they teach, and it is to conversion and holiness that they exhort all men.[6] But priestly preaching is often very difficult in the circumstances of the modern world. In order that it might more effectively move men's minds, the word of God ought not to be explained in a general and abstract way, but rather by applying the lasting truth of the gospel to the particular circumstances of life.

The ministry of the word is carried out in many ways, according to the various needs of those who hear and the special gifts of those who preach. In areas or communities of non-Christians, the proclaiming of the gospel draws men to faith and to the sacraments of salvation.[7] In the Christian community, especially among those who seem to understand and believe little of what they practice, the preaching of the word is needed for the very ministering of the sacraments. They are precisely sacraments of faith, a faith which is born of and nourished by the word. —PO 4.

Let priests who are bound by their office to procure the eternal salvation of the faithful, after they have themselves by diligent study perused the sacred pages and made them their own by prayer and meditations assiduously distribute the heavenly treasures of the divine word by sermons, homilies and exhortations; let them confirm the Christian doctrine by sentences from the Sacred Books and illustrate it by outstanding examples from sacred history and in particular from the gospel of Christ our Lord; and — avoiding with the greatest care those purely arbitrary and far-fetched adaptations, which are not a use, but rather an abuse of the divine word — let them set forth all this with such eloquence, lucidity and clearness that the faithful may not only be moved and inflamed to reform their lives, but may also conceive in their hearts the greatest veneration for the Sacred Scripture. — DAS 50.

As they [priests] seek how they may better teach others what they have learned,[8] they will better understand "the unfathomable riches of Christ" (Eph 3:8) and the manifold wisdom of God (cf. Heb 3:9-10). If they keep in mind that it is God who opens hearts (Acts 16:14), and that power comes not from themselves but from the might of God (cf. 2 Cor 4:7), in the very fact of teaching God's word they will be brought closer to Christ the Teacher and led by His Spirit. — PO 13.

All the clergy must hold fast to the Sacred Scriptures through diligent sacred reading and careful study, especially the priests of Christ and others, such as deacons and catechists who are legitimately active in the ministry of the word. This is to be done so that none of them will become "an empty preacher of the word of God outwardly, who is not a listener to it inwardly"[9] since they must share the abundant wealth of the divine word with the faithful committed to them, especially in the sacred liturgy. — DV 25.

1. Cf. Rev 19:10; LG 35: AAS 57 (1965), pp. 40-41.

2. Council of Trent, 23rd Session, chapter 1, canon 1: Denzinger 957 and 961 (1764 and 1771).

3. Cf. CD 13.

4. Cf. Jn 20:21; LG 22: AAS 57 (1965) pp. 21-28.

5. Cf. LG 22: AAS 57 (1965), pp. 33-36.

6. Cf. *ibid.*

7. Cf. Roman Pontifical "Ordination of a Priest," preface. These words are already found in the Verona Sacramentary (ed. L.C. Moehlberg, Rome, 1956, p. 122); also in Frankish Missal (ed. L.C. Moehlberg, Rome, 1957, p. 9) and in the Book of Sacramentaries of the Roman Church (ed. L.C. Moehlberg, Rome, 1960, p. 25) and Roman German Pontificals (ed. Vogel-Elze, Vatican City, 1963, vol. I, p. 34).

8. Cf. St. Thomas *Summa Theol.* II-II, q. 188, a. 7.

9. First Vatican Council, Dogmatic Constitution on Catholic Faith, Chapter 3, "On Faith" Denzinger 1789 (3008).

The most blessed Eucharist contains the entire spiritual wealth of the Church,[1] that is, Christ Himself, our pasch and living bread, by the action of the Holy Spirit through His very flesh vital and vitalizing, giving life to men who are thus invited and encouraged to offer themselves, their labors and all created things, together with Him. In this light, the Eucharist shows itself as the source and the apex of the whole work of preaching the gospel. —PO 5.

Ministers of the Eucharist

LIVING AND LIFE-GIVING

THE DAILY PASCH

FORCES OF GRACE

LIVING AND LIFE-GIVING

In the measure in which they participate in the office of the apostles, God gives priests a special grace to be ministers of Christ among the people. They perform the sacred duty of preaching the gospel, so that the offering of the people can be made acceptable and sanctified by the Holy Spirit (cf. Rom 15:16, Greek). Through the apostolic proclamation of the gospel, the People of God are called together and assembled. All belonging to this people, since they have been sanctified by the Holy Spirit, can offer themselves as "a sacrifice, living, holy, pleasing to God" (Rom 12:1). —PO 2.

By means of the eucharistic sacrifice Christ our Lord willed to give to the faithful a striking manifestation of our union among ourselves and with our divine Head, wonderful as it is and beyond all praise. For in this sacrifice the sacred minister acts as the vicegerent not only of our Savior but of the whole Mystical Body and of each one of the faithful. In this act of sacrifice through the hands of the priest, by whose word alone the immaculate Lamb is present on the altar, the faithful themselves, united with him in prayer and desire, offer to the eternal Father a most acceptable victim of praise and propitiation for the needs of the whole Church. And as the divine Redeemer, when dying on the cross, offered Himself to the eternal Father as Head of the whole human race, so "in this clean oblation" (cf. Jn 1:18) He offers to the heavenly Father not only Himself as Head of the Church, but in Himself His mystical members also. — MC 82.

Just as Christ was sent by the Father, so also He sent the apostles, filled with the Holy Spirit. This He did, that by preaching the gospel to every creature (cf. Mk 16:15), they might proclaim that the Son of God, by His death and resurrection, had freed us from the power of Satan (cf. Acts 26:18) and from death, and brought us into the kingdom of His Father. His purpose also was that they might accomplish the work of salvation which they had proclaimed, by means of sacrifice and sacraments, around which the entire liturgical life revolves.

Thus by Baptism men are plunged into the paschal mystery of Christ: they die with Him, are buried with Him, and rise with Him[2]; they receive the spirit of adoption as sons "in which we cry: Abba, Father" (Rom 8:15), and thus become true adorers whom the Father seeks (cf. Jn 4:23). In like manner, as often as they eat the supper of the Lord they proclaim the death of the Lord until He comes (cf. 1 Cor 11:26). For that reason, on the very day of Pentecost, when the Church appeared before the world, "those who received the word" of Peter "were baptized." And "they continued steadfastly in the teaching of the apostles and in the communion of the breaking of bread and in prayers...praising God and being in favor with all the people" (Acts 2:41-47).

From that time onwards the Church has never failed to come together to celebrate the paschal mystery: reading those things "which were in all the scriptures concerning him" (Lk 24:27), celebrating the Eucharist in which "the victory and triumph of His death are again made present,"[3] and at the same time giving thanks "to God for his unspeakable gift" (2 Cor 9:15) in Christ Jesus, "in praise of his glory" (Eph 1:12), through the power of the Holy Spirit. —SC 6.

Tirelessly promote the cult of the Eucharist, the focus where all other forms of piety must ultimately emerge.

May the faithful, thanks to your efforts, come to realize and experience ever more perfectly the truth of these words: "He who desires life finds here a place to live in and the means to live by. Let him approach, let him believe, let him be incorporated so that he may receive life. Let him not refuse union with the members, let him not be a corrupt member, deserving to be cut off, nor a disfigured member to be ashamed of. Let him be a grateful, fitting and healthy member. Let him cleave to the body, let him live by God and for God. Let him now labor here on earth, that he may afterwards reign in heaven."[4]

For if the sacred liturgy holds the first place in the life of the Church, the eucharistic mystery stands at the heart and center of the liturgy, since it is the font of life by which we are cleansed and strengthened to live not for ourselves but for God, and to be united in love among ourselves. —MF.

It is through the Eucharist that "the Church continually lives and grows. This Church of Christ is truly present in all legitimate local congregations of the faithful which, united with their pastors are called churches in the New Testament. These are, each in its own region, the new People, called by God in the Holy Spirit and in all fullness (cf. 1 Thes 1:5). In them the faithful are gathered by the preaching of Christ's gospel and the mystery of the Lord's Supper is celebrated, 'so that through the body and blood of the Lord the whole brotherhood is united.'[5] Every gathering around the altar under the sacred ministry of the bishop"[6] or of a priest who takes the place of the bishop[7] "is a sign of that charity and 'unity of the Mystical Body, without which there can be no salvation.'[8] In these communities, though they may often be small and poor or living among the 'diaspora,' Christ is present, by whose power the one, holy, catholic and apostolic Church is united. For 'the partaking of the body and blood of Christ has no less an effect than to change us into what we have received.'[9]"[10] —EM 7.

What is the apostolic work of the priest, considered in its essential action, if not to gather around the altar, wherever the Church lives, people united in faith, regenerated and purified? Precisely then the priest, by virtue of the powers he alone has received, offers the divine sacrifice in which Jesus Himself repeats the one and only immolation performed on Calvary for the redemption of the world and for the glorification of His Father. It is then through the priest that Christians gathered together offer to the heavenly Father the divine Victim and learn how to immolate themselves as a "sacrifice, living, holy, pleasing to God" (Rom 12:1).

It is there that the people of God, enlightened by the preaching of the Faith, nourished with the body of Christ, find their life, their growth and, if it is necessary, strengthen their unity. In one word, it is there that, from generation to generation, and everywhere in the world, there is built in charity the Mystical Body of Christ, which is the Church. —SNP.

1. Cf. St. Thomas, *Summa Theol*. III, q. 65, a. 3, ad 1; q. 79, a. 1, c. and ad, 1.
2. Cf. Rom 6:4; Eph 2:6; Col 3:1; 2 Tm 2:11.
3. Council of Trent, Session XIII, *Decree on the Holy Eucharist*, c. 5.
4. St. Augustine, *In Ioann. Tract.* 26, 13 P.L. 35, 1613.
5. Mozarabic Prayer—P.L. 96, 759 B.
6. LG 26—AAS 57 (1965), p. 31.
7. Cf. SC 42—AAS 56 (1964), pp. 111-112.
8. Cf. St. Thomas Aquinas, *Summa Theol*. III, q. 73, a. 3.
9. St. Leo the Great, *Serm. 63*, 7:P.L. 54, 357C.
10. LG 26; AAS 57 (1965), pp. 31-32.

THE DAILY PASCH

"In the mystery of the eucharistic sacrifice, in which the priest exercises his highest function, the work of our redemption is continually accomplished. Daily celebration of Mass, therefore, is most earnestly recommended, since, even if the faithful cannot be present, it remains an action of Christ and the Church,"[1] an action in which the priest is always acting for the salvation of the people. —EM 44.

In the celebration of the Eucharist, priests also are deputed to perform a specific function by reason of a special sacrament, namely Holy Orders. For they too "as ministers of the sacred mysteries, especially in the Sacrifice of the Mass...act in the person of Christ in a special way."[2] It is, therefore, fitting that, by reason of the sign, they participate in the Eucharist, by exercising the order proper to them,[3] by celebrating or concelebrating the Mass and not by limiting themselves to communicating like the laity. —EM 43.

It should be made clear that all who gather for the Eucharist constitute that holy people which, together with the ministers, plays its part in the sacred action. It is indeed the priest alone, who, acting in the person of Christ, consecrates the bread and wine, but the role of the faithful in the Eucharist is to recall the passion, resurrection and glorification of the Lord, to give thanks to God, and to offer the immaculate Victim not only through the hands of the priest, but also together with him; and finally, by receiving the body of the Lord, to perfect that communion with God and among themselves which should be the product of participation in the Sacrifice of the Mass.[4] For the faithful achieve a more perfect participation in the Mass when, with proper disposition, they receive the body of the Lord sacramentally in the Mass itself, in obedience to His words, "take and eat."[5]

Like the passion of Christ itself, this sacrifice, though offered for all, "has no effect except in those united to the passion of Christ by faith and charity.... To these it brings a greater or lesser benefit in proportion to their devotion."[6] —EM 12.

When the faithful adore Christ present in the sacrament, they should remember that this presence derives from the sacrifice and is directed toward both sacramental and spiritual Communion.

In consequence, the devotion which leads the faithful to visit the Blessed Sacrament draws them into an ever deeper participation in the Paschal Mystery. It leads them to respond gratefully to the gift of Him who through His humanity constantly pours divine life into the members of His body.[7] Dwelling with Christ our Lord, they enjoy His intimate friendship and pour out their hearts before Him for themselves and their dear ones, and pray for the peace and salvation of the world. They offer their entire lives with Christ to the Father in the Holy Spirit, and receive in this wonderful exchange an increase of faith, hope and charity. Thus they nourish those right dispositions which enable them with all due devotion to celebrate the memorial of the Lord and receive frequently the bread given us by the Father.

The faithful should therefore strive to worship Christ our Lord in the Blessed Sacrament, in harmony with their way of life. Pastors should exhort them to this, and set them a good example.[8] —EM 50.

Since "it is clear that the frequent or daily reception of the Blessed Eucharist increases union with Christ, nourishes the spiritual life more abundantly, strengthens the soul in virtue and gives the communicant a stronger pledge of eternal happiness, parish priests, confessors and preachers will frequently and zealously exhort the Christian people to this holy and salutary practice."[9] — EM 37.

Concelebration of the Eucharist aptly demonstrates the unity of the sacrifice and of the priesthood. Moreover, whenever the faithful take an active part, the unity of the People of God is strikingly manifested,[10] particularly if the bishop presides.[11]

Concelebration both symbolizes and strengthens the brotherly bond of the priesthood, because "by virtue of the ordination to the priesthood which they have in common, all are bound together in an intimate brotherhood."[12]

Therefore, unless it conflicts with the needs of the faithful which must always be consulted with the deepest pastoral concern, and although every priest retains the right to celebrate alone, it is desirable that priests should celebrate the Eucharist in this eminent manner. This applies both to communities of priests and to groups which gather on particular occasions, as also to all similar circumstances. Those who live in community or serve the same church should welcome visiting priests into their concelebration. — EM 47.

1. PO 13; AAS 58 (1966), pp. 1011-1012; cf. MF, AAS 57 (1965), p. 762.

2. PO 13; AAS 58 (1966), p. 1011; cf. LG 28, AAS 57 (1965), pp. 33-36.

3. SC 28; AAS 56 (1964), p. 107.

4. Cf. SC 48, 106, AAS 56 (1964), pp. 113, 126.

5. Cf. *ibid.*, 55, AAS 56 (1964), p. 115.

6. St. Thomas Aquinas, *Summa. Theol.* III, q. 79, as. 7, ad. 2.

7. PO 5, AAS 58 (1956), pp. 997-999.

8. Cf. *ibid.*, 18, AAS (1966), pp. 1018-1019.

9. SC; Decree on the daily reception of Communion, 20.xii., 1905, n. 6, AAS 38 (1905-1906), pp. 401f.; MD, AAS 39 (1947), p. 565.

10. SC 57, AAS 56 (1964), pp. 115-116; S.C.R., General Decree, *Ecclesiae semper*, 7. iii. (1965), AAS 57 (1965), pp. 410-412.

11. SC 41, AAS 56 (1964), p. 111; LG 28, AAS 57 (1965), pp. 33-36; PO 7, AAS 58 (1966), 1001-1003.

12. LG 28, AAS 57 (1965), p. 35; cf. PO 8, AAS 58 (1966), pp. 1003-1005.

FORCES OF GRACE

In the liturgy priests continue to carry on Christ's priestly office by the action of His Spirit.[1] By Baptism men are truly brought into the People of God; by the sacrament of Penance sinners are reconciled to God and His Church; by the Anointing of the Sick, the ill are given solace; and especially by the celebration of Mass they offer sacramentally the Sacrifice of Christ. In administering all sacraments, as St. Ignatius Martyr[2] has borne witness from the early days of the Church, priests by various titles are bound together hierarchically with the bishop. And so in a certain way they make him present in every congregation.[3] — PO 5.

The sacraments are celebrated in conjunction with the proclamation of the Word of God and thus develop faith by strengthening it with grace. They cannot be considered of slight importance, since through them the Word is brought to fuller effect, namely communion in the mystery of Christ.

Let priests then perform their ministry in such a way that the faithful will "have recourse with great eagerness to the sacraments which were instituted to nourish the Christian life."[4]

An enduring evangelization and a well-ordered sacramental life of the community demand, by their nature, a *diaconia* of authority, that is, a serving of unity and a presiding over charity. Thus the mutual relationship between evangelization and the celebration of the sacraments is clearly seen in the mission of the Church. A separation between the two would divide the heart of the Church to the point of imperilling the faith, and the priest, who is dedicated to the service of unity in the community, would be gravely distorting his ministry.

Unity between evangelization and sacramental life is always proper to the ministerial priesthood and must carefully be kept in mind by every priest. And yet the application of this principle to the life and ministry of individual priests must be made with discretion, for the exercise of the priestly ministry often in practice needs to take different forms in order better to meet special or new situations in which the gospel is to be proclaimed. — Ministerial Priesthood, Nov., 1971, Synod Document.

[**Regarding the new** pastorate of the sacraments] the renewal is chiefly derived from liturgical reform. You know what that is. But, apart from the purely ritual aspect, two other aspects contribute to this renewal: one concerns theological consistency, the other pastoral fruitfulness. Theological rethinking is clearly desirable, indeed necessary, above all because of the concept of sacrament itself, which is a divine action accomplished through a human action; the former is the principal cause of grace, the latter is its instrument and condition.[5]

This mysterious meeting of God's transcendent activity with man's ministerial activity deserves to be continually meditated upon and regarded with ever fresh wonder and constant lively feeling. Its existential character and the fact that it is always being repeated demand an ever watchful attention, and an attitude of ever new discovery, otherwise the sacramental action will be debased into an exterior and almost superstitious formalism.

Secondly, this doctrinal reflection is demanded by the nature of the sacrament, for we know that a sacrament is a symbol, a sign of an intervention and of efficacious conferring of divine grace. A sign is a language. This means that through the element perceptible to the senses the sacrament presents the theme chosen by Christ, that the inexhaustible meditation, leading to a meeting with a divine thought by means of which Christ desires to make us understand something of the mystery to which He wishes to associate us.

So this means that in regard to sacramental life our mentality ought to be one of continual effort to enter into the meaning of the sacramental symbol. Take Baptism, for example. St. Paul exhorts us to pass from the exterior experience of the sensible sign to the understanding of its meaning, which is actualized in a specific conferring of grace, that is of the mysterious divine Life, into our humble human life. "Do you not know," he asked, "that as many of us as were baptized into Jesus Christ were baptized into his death? Therefore we are buried with him through baptism into death, so that, just as Christ was raised up from the dead by the glory of the Father, so we also should walk in newness of life" (Rom 6:3-4).

What thoughts about the deep and stupendous supernatural truths are aroused in us by the eucharistic symbol of bread and wine! The chief of such truths is the unity of the Mystical Body.[6] To what thoughts of fullness of love does matrimony stir us, since it has been made the sign of the charity which links Christ and the Church for which He immolated Himself! (Eph 5:25) And so on.

This means that the new mentality with which we ought to celebrate the sacraments consists in an extremely worthy manner of celebration, one in which the minister's reverent and happy faith should shine through. (Is it always so in practice?) Apart from that, it consists in appropriate instruction for each sacrament. It may be said that in our usual religious practice and habits, only First Communion receives such care.

Renewed pastoral efforts should therefore be directed towards applying much more careful methods to preparation for the other sacraments also. Sacramental pedagogy needs to be more developed in pastoral work. The efficacious cause of grace is first and above all God working in the sacramental act itself (*ex opere operato,* as the theologians say), but the instrumental and conditioning cause of this mysterious divine action depends on man (*ex opere operantis*). It depends on the minister of the sacrament and on the recipient, as well as on the ecclesial community, which participates in celebration and conferment of the sacraments.[7]

So, what is required, that the pastorate of the sacraments may be renewed? Better catechetical and spiritual preparation is desirable, more perfect ritual and community celebration by both ministers and faithful, and more conscientious adoption of the sacramental fact into our lives, for the sacrament tends to have permanent moral effects. You know all this quite well. —Pope Paul VI, First Convention of Roman Presbytery, 10-28-70.

1. Cf. SC 7; MC: AAS 35 (1943), p. 230.
2. St. Ignatius Martyr, "Smyrn.," 8, 1-2 (ed. F.X. Funk, p. 282, 6-15); "Constitutions of the Apostles," VIII, 12,. 3 (ed. F.X. Funk, p.. 496); VIII, 29, 2, p. 532.
3. LG 28: AAS 57 (1965), pp. 33-36.
4. SC 59.
5. Cf. A. Ciappi, OP, *De sacramentis in communi,* (Berruti, 1957).
6. *Summa Theol.* 73, 3.
7. Cf. PO 13.

Let priests take care
to foster a knowledge of and facility in the liturgy,
that by their own liturgical ministry Christian
communities entrusted to their care may ever more
perfectly give praise to God, the Father, and Son,
and Holy Spirit. — PO 5.

Formation To Worship

**AN ACTIVE PARTICIPATION
EUCHARISTIC INSTRUCTION**

AN ACTIVE PARTICIPATION

Mother Church earnestly desires that all the faithful should be led to that full, conscious, and active participation in liturgical celebrations which is demanded by the very nature of the liturgy. Such participation by the Christian people as "a chosen race, a royal priesthood, a holy nation, a redeemed people" (1 Pt 2:9; cf. 2:4-5), is their right and duty by reason of their Baptism.

In the restoration and promotion of the sacred liturgy, this full and active participation by all the people is the aim to be considered before all else; for it is the primary and indispensable source from which the faithful are to derive the true Christian spirit; and therefore pastors of souls must zealously strive to achieve it, by means of the necessary instruction, in all their pastoral work. — SC 14.

Pastors of souls shall strive diligently and patiently to carry out the command of the constitution concerning the liturgical formation of the faithful and their active participation, both internal and external, "according to their age and condition, their way of life, and standard of religious culture."[1] They should be especially concerned about the liturgical formation and the active participation of those who are engaged in religious associations of the laity, since it is the latter's duty to share more intimately in the life of the Church

155

and also to assist the pastors of souls in properly promoting the liturgical life of the parish.[2] —IOE 19.

In order that the liturgy may be able to produce its full effects, it is necessary that the faithful come to it with proper dispositions, that their minds should be attuned to their voices, and that they should cooperate with divine grace lest they receive it in vain (cf. 2 Cor 6:1). Pastors of souls must therefore realize that, when the liturgy is celebrated, something more is required than the mere observation of the laws governing valid and licit celebration; it is their duty also to ensure that the faithful take part fully aware of what they are doing, actively engaged in the rite, and enriched by its effects. —SC 11.

The more clearly the faithful understand the place they occupy in the liturgical community and the part they have to play in the eucharistic action, the more conscious and fruitful will be the active participation which is proper to that community.[3]

Catechetical instruction should therefore explain the doctrine of the royal priesthood to which the faithful are consecrated by rebirth and the anointing of the Holy Spirit.[4]

Moreover there should also be further explanation of the role in the celebration of the Eucharist of the ministerial priesthood which differs from the common priesthood of the faithful in essence and not merely in degree.[5] The part played by others who exercise a ministry in the Eucharist should also be explained.[6] —EM 11.

1. SC 19.
2. Cf. SC 42.
3. Cf. SC 14, 26, 30, 38, AAS 56 (1964), pp. 104, 107, 108, 110.
4. Cf. LG 10, AAS 57 (1965), pp. 14-15; PO 2, AAS 58 (1966), pp. 991-993; MF, AAS 57 (1965), p. 761.
5. Cf. LG 10, AAS 57 (1965), pp. 14-15; PO 2, 5, AAS 58 (1966), pp. 991-993, 997-999.
6. Cf. SC 28-29, AAS 56 (1964), pp. 107-108.

EUCHARISTIC INSTRUCTION

In exercising their office of sanctifying, bishops should be mindful that they have been taken from among men and appointed their representative before God in order to offer gifts and sacrifices for sins.

They should, therefore, constantly exert themselves to have the faithful know and live the Paschal Mystery more deeply through the Eucharist and thus become a firmly-knit body in the unity of the charity of Christ.[1] "Intent upon prayer and the ministry of the word" (Acts 6:4), they should devote their labor to this end that all those committed to their care may be of one mind in prayer (cf. Acts 1:14; 2:46) and through the reception of the sacraments may grow in grace and be faithful witnesses to the Lord. —CD 15.

The eucharistic action, over which the priest presides, is the very heart of the congregation. So priests must instruct their people to offer to God the Father the divine Victim in the Sacrifice of the Mass, and to join to it the offering of their own lives. In the spirit of Christ the Shepherd, they must prompt their people to confess their sins with a contrite heart in the sacrament of Penance, so that, mindful of His words: "Repent for the kingdom of God is at hand" (Mt 4:17), they are drawn closer to the Lord more and more each day. Priests likewise must instruct their people to participate in the celebrations of the sacred liturgy in such a way that they become proficient in genuine prayer. They must coax their people on to an ever more perfect and constant spirit of prayer for every grace and need. They must gently persuade everyone to the fulfillment of the duties of his state of life, and to greater progress in responding in a sensible way to the evangelical counsels. Finally, they must train the faithful to sing hymns and spiritual songs in their hearts to the Lord, always giving thanks to God the Father for all things in the name of our Lord Jesus Christ (cf. 1 Cor 9:19-23, Vg.). — PO 5.

Suitable catechesis is essential if the mystery of the Eucharist is to take deeper root in the minds and lives of the faithful.

To convey this instruction properly, pastors should not only bear in mind the many aspects of the Church's teaching, as contained in the documents of the magisterium, but in their hearts and in their lives they must be open to the spirit of the Church in this matter.[2] Only then will they readily perceive which of the many facets of this mystery best suits the needs of the faithful at any one time.

The catechesis of the eucharistic mystery should aim to help the faithful to realize that the celebration of the Eucharist is the true center of the whole Christian life both for the universal Church and for the local congregations of that Church. For "the other sacraments, as indeed every ministry of the Church and every work of the apostolate, are linked with the Eucharist and are directed toward it. For the Eucharist contains the entire spiritual good of the Church, namely Christ Himself, our Passover and living bread, offering through His flesh, living and life-giving in the Spirit, life to men who are thus invited and led on to offer themselves, their labors and all created things together with Him."[3] — EM 5, 6.

In order that they should achieve a deeper understanding of the mystery of the Eucharist, the faithful should be instructed in the principal ways in which the Lord is present to His Church in liturgical celebrations.[4]

He is always present in a body of the faithful gathered in His name (cf. Mt 18:20). He is present too in His word, for it is He who speaks when the Scriptures are read in the Church.

In the sacrifice of the Eucharist He is present both in the person of the minister, "the same now offering through the ministry of the priest who formerly offered Himself on the cross,"[5] and above all under the species of the Eucharist.[6] For in this sacrament Christ is present in a unique way, whole and entire, God and man, substantially and permanently. —EM 9.

Try with your constant zeal to have all the faithful attend the Eucharistic Sacrifice from which they may obtain abundant and salutary fruit; and carefully instruct them...so that they may devoutly participate in it. The Mass is the chief act of divine worship; it should also be the source and center of Christian piety. Never think that you have satisfied your apostolic zeal until you see your faithful approach in great numbers the celestial banquet which is a sacrament of devotion, a sign of unity and a bond of love (cf. Heb 13:17).

By means of suitable sermons and particularly by periodic conferences and lectures, by special study weeks and the like, teach the Christian people carefully about the treasures of piety contained in the sacred liturgy so that they may be able to profit more abundantly by these supernatural gifts.

Never be discouraged by the difficulties that arise, and never let your pastoral zeal grow cold. "Blow the trumpet in Sion...call an assembly, gather together the people, sanctify the Church, assemble the ancients, gather together the little ones and them that suck at the breasts", (cf. Gn 4:10), and use every help to get the faithful everywhere to fill the churches and crowd around the altars so that they may be restored by the graces of the sacraments and joined as living members to their divine Head, and with

Him and through Him celebrate together the august sacrifice that gives due tribute of praise to the eternal Father.
— MC 201, 202, 204.

1. MD, AAS 39 (1947), pp. 97ff.; MF.

2. SC 14, 17-18, AAS 56 (1964), pp. 104, 105.

3. PO 5, AAS 58 (1966), p. 997.

4. SC 7, AAS 56 (1964), pp. 100-101.

5. Council of Trent, Session XXII, Decree on the Mass, chapt. 11, Denz. 940 (1743).

6. Cf. SC 7, AAS 56 (1964), pp. 100-101.

ECCLESIAL
DIMENSION

Christic the Lord, Son of the living God, came that He might save His people from their sins (cf. Mt 1:21) and that all men might be sanctified. Just as He Himself was sent by the Father, so He also sent His apostles (cf. Jn 20:21). Therefore, He sanctified them, conferring on them the Holy Spirit, so that they also might glorify the Father upon earth and save men, "to the building up of the body of Christ" (Eph 4:12), which is the Church. —CD 1.

Strength in Unity

STRENGTHEN YOUR BRETHREN

COLLEGIALITY: A SURE CHARISM OF TRUTH

DEFEND THE DEPOSIT OF FAITH

UNITED IN A SPIRIT OF TRUST

THAT THEY MAY BE ONE

STRENGTHEN YOUR BRETHREN

For the nurturing and constant growth of the People of God, Christ the Lord instituted in His Church a variety of ministries, which work for the good of the whole body. For those ministers, who are endowed with sacred power, serve their brethren so that all who are the People of God—and therefore enjoy a true Christian dignity, working toward a common goal freely and in an orderly way—may arrive at salvation.

This Sacred Council, following closely in the footsteps of the First Vatican Council, with that Council teaches and declares that Jesus Christ, the eternal Shepherd, established His holy Church, having sent forth the apostles as He Himself had been sent by the Father (cf. Jn 20:21); and He willed that their successors, namely the bishops, should be shepherds in His Church even to the consummation of the world. And in order that the episcopate itself might be one and undivided, He placed Blessed Peter over the other apostles, and instituted in him a permanent and visible source and foundation of unity of faith and communion.[1] And all this teaching about the institution, the perpetuity, the meaning and reason for the sacred primacy of the Roman Pontiff and of his infallible magisterium, this Sacred Council again proposes to be firmly believed by all the faithful. Continuing in that same undertaking, this Council is resolved to declare and proclaim before all men the doctrine concerning bishops, the successors of the apostles, who together with the successor of Peter, the Vicar of Christ,[2] the visible Head of the whole Church, govern the house of the living God. — LG 18.

The unity of government in the Catholic Church is obvious to all. For just as the faithful are subject to their priests, and the priests to their bishops, whom "the Holy Spirit has placed...to rule the Church of God" (Acts 20:28), so each and all the bishops are subject to the Roman Pontiff, who is regarded as the successor of St. Peter, whom Christ our Lord set as the rock and foundation of His Church (cf. Mt 16:18), and to whom alone in a special manner He gave the power of binding and loosing whatever is on earth (cf. Mt 16:19), and of strengthening his brethren (cf. Lk 22:32), and of feeding the whole flock (cf. Jn 21:15-17). — APC.

In this Church of Christ the Roman Pontiff, as the successor of Peter, to whom Christ entrusted the feeding of His sheep and lambs, enjoys supreme, full, immediate, and universal authority over the care of souls by divine institution. Therefore, as pastor of all the faithful, he is sent to provide for the common good of the universal Church and for the good of the individual churches. Hence, he holds a primacy of ordinary power over all the churches. — CD 1.

The successors of Peter, mortal like other men, die like them, more or less quickly. But the primacy of Peter will last forever, thanks to the special assistance promised to him when Jesus charged him to confirm his brethren in the faith (Lk 22:32). What matters the name, the face, the human origins of each Pope? It is always Peter who lives in him; it is Peter who guides and directs him; it is Peter above all who teaches and who spreads through the world the light of the truth which sets men free. This fact has made one great sacred orator exclaim that God has established at Rome an eternal chair: "Peter will live in his successors; Peter will speak forever from his chair."[3] —Pius XII, allocution, 1-17-40.

You see in the Pope, whoever he may be, the representative of God here below, the Vicar of Jesus Christ, the successor of Peter, of Peter whom our Lord made the visible head of His Church when He gave him the keys of the kingdom of heaven and the power to bind and loose (Mt 16:18-19). The senses, so to speak, here second faith: what you see and hear strengthens within you what you must believe.

Certainly, it is not Jesus Christ in person who appears to you now, as the multitudes saw Him on the shore of the Lake of Tiberias in Palestine (cf. Jn 6:1-2), or Martha and Mary in their house at Bethany (cf. Jn 11:1). At the same time, when you approach the Pope you have the impression of being taken back twenty centuries, into the presence of the Divine Nazarene. It seems to you that you hear in the voice of the Pope the voice of the Redeemer, that voice of which the Pope has always been the echo through the centuries. When he raises his hand to bless you, you know that this poor hand transmits to you, so to speak, heavenly help and favors.

Finally, when you feel the heart of the Pope beat close to your own, you are not at all mistaken in believing that you see in the attitude, the words, the deeds which the Lord inspires in him, something of the beating and the intimate emotions of the heart of Jesus. This is true because Christ gave His Vicar when He said to him, "Feed my lambs, feed my sheep" (cf. Jn 21:15-17), something of His

own redemptive and compassionate love for souls. — Pope
Pius XII, allocution, 4-17-40.

The most important qualities
[of a Roman Pontiff] are the zeal and solicitude of the
Good Shepherd, who must always be ready to undertake
the most arduous tasks, and be distinguished by prudence,
rectitude, constancy; nor may he draw back before the
supreme sacrifice. "The Good Shepherd lays down his
life for his sheep" (Jn 10:11). How beautiful is the Church
of Christ, "the fold of the sheep." The Shepherd "goes
before his sheep," all of whom follow Him. And to defend
them He does not fear to engage in combat with the raven-
ing wolf.

But then the mind is turned to wider considerations:
"And other sheep I have which are not of this fold, them
also I must bring, and they will hear my voice, and there
will be one flock and one shepherd" (Jn 10:16). In these
words you see expressed in all its extent and its nobility
the problem of the missions. Certainly, this is the first, if
it is not the only, care of the Roman Pontiff: for it is joined
to many other anxieties of no less importance. — Pope
John XXIII, homily to bishops, 11-4-58.

By virtue of sacramental con-
secration and hierarchical communion with the head and
members of the college, bishops are constituted as members of the episcopal body.[4] "The order of bishops is the
successor to the college of the apostles in teaching and pastoral direction, or rather, in the episcopal order, the apostolic body continues without a break. Together with its
head, the Roman Pontiff, and never without this head it
exists as the subject of supreme, plenary power over the
universal Church. But this power cannot be exercised
except with the agreement of the Roman Pontiff."[5] — CD 4.

This institution [World Synod of Bishops] has arisen from the teaching and spirit of the recent Ecumenical Council, and is intended, not to produce power rivalry or difficulties for ordered and effective government within the Church, but rather as a mutual inclination of Pope and episcopate for greater communion and organic collaboration.

For Our part, We intend to bring all this to realization, while respecting fully and heartily the duties and responsibilities of Our brothers in the episcopate, whether individually or in lawful canonical assemblies. Obviously, We will do so without, however, at any time renouncing in Our turn Our specific duties and responsibilities, which are imposed on Us both by the charism of the primacy conferred by Christ Himself on Peter—whose most lowly, yet authentic successor We are—and by the obligation, rather than the right, of exercising that primacy faithfully.

The Pope must be the Church's heart, to make charity circulate, charity which comes from the heart and goes to the heart. He must be a crossroads for charity, receiving all and loving all, because Christ left us Peter as "the Vicar of His love."[6] —Pope Paul VI, Close of Bishops' Synod, 11-6-69.

The college or body of bishops has no authority unless it is understood together with the Roman Pontiff, the successor of Peter as its head. The Pope's power of primacy over all, both pastors and faithful, remains whole and intact. In virtue of his office, that is as Vicar of Christ and pastor of the whole Church, the Roman Pontiff has full, supreme and universal power over the Church. And he is always free to exercise this power. The order of bishops, which succeeds to the college of apostles and gives this apostolic body continued existence, is also the subject of supreme and full power over the universal Church, provided we understand this body together with its head the Roman Pontiff and never without this head.[7] This power can be exercised only with the consent of the Roman Pontiff. For our Lord placed Simon alone as the rock and the bearer of the keys of the Church (cf. Mt 16:18-19), and made him shepherd of the whole flock (cf. Jn 21:15ff.); it is evident, however, that the power of binding and loosing, which was given to Peter (Mt 16:19), was granted also to the college of apostles, joined with their head (Mt 18:18; 28:16-20).[8] — LG 22.

1. Cf. Vatican Council I, Session IV, Dogmatic Const. *Pastor aeternus* (Denz., 1821), p. 3050f.

2. Cf. Conc. Flor., *Decretum pro Graecis*, 694 (Denz., 1307) et Conc. Vat I, *ibid.* (Denz., 1826) p. 3059.

3. Bossuet, *Sermon on the Unity of the Church*, I.

4. LG 22, AAS 57 (1965), pp. 25-27.

5. *Ibid.*

6. St. Ambrose, *Exp. in Luc.* I 175; PL 15 (1942).

7. Cf. *Relatio officialis Zinelli*, in Conc. Vat. I: Mansi 52, 1109 C.

8. Cf. Conc. Vat. I, Schema Const. Dogm. II, *De Ecclesia Christi*, c. 4: Mansi 53, 310. Cf. *Relatio Kleutgen de Schemate Reformato:* Mansi 3, 321 B—322 B *"et declaratio Zinelli":* Mansi 52, 1110 A. *Vide etiam* S. Leonem M., *Serm.* 4, 3: PL 54, 151 A.

COLLEGIALITY: A SURE CHARISM OF TRUTH

Let us reflect: there exists between us, who have been chosen to succeed the apostles, a special bond, the bond of collegiality. What is collegiality if not a communion, a solidarity, a brotherhood, a charity that is fuller and more binding than the relationship of Christian love among the faithful and among the followers of Christ associated in various other classes? Collegiality is charity.

If belonging to the Mystical Body of Christ makes Saint Paul say: "If one member suffers, all suffer together; if one member is honored, all rejoice together" (1 Cor 12:26), what should be the spiritual thrill of common sensitiveness for the general interest and also the particular interest of the Church within those who have greater duties in the Church? Collegiality is co-responsibility.

And what clearer manifestation of the character of authentic disciples of His did the Lord will should be possessed by the group of the apostles seated at the supper of the last farewell if not that of mutual love: "By this all men will know that you are my disciples, if you have love for one another"? (Jn 13:35) Collegiality is an evident love which the bishops must nourish among themselves.

And, as collegiality inserts each of us into the circle of the apostolic structure destined for the edification of the Church in the world, it obliges us to a universal charity. Collegial charity has no confines. To whom, in the end, other than to the faithful apostles, did the Lord address His last recommendations, raised in the ecstatic prayer which concludes the final discourses of the Last Supper: "That they may be one"? (Jn 17:23) Collegiality is unity. —Pope Paul VI, to Synod bishops, 10-16-69.

The authentic and acknowledged hierarchical system gives to the Church the consciousness of its stability, fraternity, concord, peace, and its ability to renew itself continually in the evangelical efficiency, in its capacity to fulfill its own particular mission in the world. —Pope Paul VI, at St. Peter's Square, 10-16-69.

Bishops are preachers of the faith, who lead new disciples to Christ, and they are authentic teachers, that is, teachers endowed with the authority of Christ, who preach to the people committed to them the faith they must believe and put into practice, and by the light of the Holy Spirit illustrate that faith. They bring forth from the treasury of Revelation new things and old (cf. Mt 13:52), making it bear fruit and vigilantly warding off any errors that threaten their flock (cf. Tm 4:1-4).

Bishops, teaching in communion with the Roman Pontiff, are to be respected by all as witnesses to divine and Catholic truth. In matters of faith and morals, the bishops speak in the name of Christ and the faithful are to accept their teaching and adhere to it with a religious assent. This religious submission of mind and will must be shown in a special way to the authentic magisterium of the Roman Pontiff, even when he is not speaking ex cathedra; that is, it must be shown in such a way that his supreme magisterium is acknowledged with reverence, the judgments made by him are sincerely adhered to, according to his manifest mind and will. His mind and will in the matter may be known either from the character of the documents, from his frequent repetition of the same doctrine, or from his manner of speaking. — LG 25.

It is of course true that the shepherds of the Church have always had this duty of handing on the faith in its fullness and in a manner suited to men of their time. That means trying to use a language easily accessible to them, answering their questions, arousing their interest and helping them to discover, through poor human speech, the whole message of salvation brought to us by Jesus Christ. It is in fact the episcopal college which, with Peter and under his authority, guarantees the authentic handing on of the deposit of faith, and for that purpose it has received, as St. Irenaeus expressed it, "a sure charism of truth."[1] The faithfulness of its witness, rooted in Sacred Tradition and Holy Scripture and nourished by the ecclesial life of the whole People of God is what empowers the Church, through the unfailing assistance of the Holy Spirit, to teach without ceasing the word of God and to make it progressively unfold. — Pope Paul VI, Apostolic Exhortation to All Bishops, 12-8-70.

All of us who through the laying on of hands have received the responsibility of keeping pure and entire the faith entrusted to us and the mission of proclaiming the gospel unceasingly, are called upon to witness to the obedience we all give the Lord. It is an inalienable and sacred right of the people in our charge to receive the word of God, the whole word of God, of which the Church has not ceased to acquire deeper comprehension. It is a grave and urgent duty for us to proclaim it untiringly, that the people may grow in faith and understanding of the Christian message and may bear witness throughout their lives to salvation in Jesus Christ.

...Certainly, faith is always an assent given because of the authority of God Himself. But the teaching office of the bishops is for the believer the sign and channel which enable him to receive and recognize the word of God. Each bishop, in his diocese, is united by his office with the episcopal college which, in succession to the apostolic college, has been entrusted with the charge of watching over the purity of faith and the unity of the Church. — Pope Paul VI, Apostolic Exhortation to All Bishops, 12-8-70.

Above all We think that our first attitude toward our Episcopal vocation must be faith, as in the Magi, as in every believer, a pure and complete faith towards the revealed truth, a coherent and magnificent fidelity towards the duties which it involves.

This is not an original attitude because it concerns every Christian. But in us teachers, in us pastors and bishops, this attitude must be perfect and exemplary. If orthodoxy must characterize a member of the Church, then by us first of all and by us above all orthodoxy must be clearly and strongly professed.

Today, as each one of you realizes, orthodoxy, that is, purity of doctrine, does not seem to take first place in the minds of Christians. How many things, how many truths have been questioned and doubted; how many liberties are taken with the true heritage of Catholic doctrine, not only in order to study its riches, to deepen the understanding of it and to explain it to modern man, but sometimes to subject it to the relativism in which profane thought experiments with its insecurity and seeks a new expression, or to adapt it by adjusting it to modern tastes and to the receptive capacities of the current mentality.

Brothers, let us be faithful, and let us have confidence that to the degree of our fidelity to Catholic dogma, neither the aridness of our teaching, nor the deafness of the present generation will hinder our word, but that its fruitfulness, its liveliness, its capacity of penetrating will find its proper and marvellous power (cf. Heb 4:12; 2 Cor 10:5).
— Pope Paul VI, to newly-consecrated bishops, 1-6-69.

Let us not be reduced to silence for fear of criticism, which is always possible and may at times be well-founded. However necessary the function of theologians, it is not to the learned that God has confided the duty of authentically interpreting the faith of the Church: that faith is borne by the life of the people whose bishops are responsible for them before God. It is for the bishops to tell the people what God asks them to believe.

This demands much courage of each one of us; for, even though we are assisted by exercising this responsibility in community, within the framework of the synods of bishops and the episcopal conferences, it is nonetheless a question of a personal and absolutely inalienable responsibility for us to meet the immediate daily needs of the People of God. This is not the time to ask ourselves, as some would have us do, whether it is really useful, opportune and necessary to speak; rather it is the time for us to take the means to make ourselves heard. For it is to us bishops that St. Paul's exhortation to Timothy is addressed: "Before God and before Christ Jesus who is to be judge of the living and the dead, I put this duty to you, in the name of his appearing and of his kingdom: proclaim the message and, welcome or unwelcome, insist on it. Refute falsehood, correct error, call to obedience — but do all with patience and with the intention of teaching. The time is sure to come when, far from being content with sound teaching, people will be avid for the latest novelty and collect themselves a whole series of teachers according to their own tastes; and then, instead of listening to the truth, they will turn to myths. Be careful always to choose the right course; be brave under trials; make the preaching of the Good News your life's work, in thoroughgoing service" (2 Tm 4:1-5). — Pope Paul VI, Apostolic Exhortation to All Bishops, 12-8-70.

Let us rejoice, we who are so much inclined to speak badly of our times, because the principle establishing that authority is a service, is no longer questioned by anyone, and meets with unanimous consent in the Church of God, even when certain customary forms, which are gradually giving way to a new ecclesial style, evoke other concepts of arbitrary power, personal utility, ostentatious prestige, hereditary superiority, which the history of past times accredited as legitimate but then handed down as if they were inherent in the nature and exercise of authority.

Contemporary history demands the recognition of a different reality: the Church is service. And if authority in the Church is still, and always, necessary, because it is willed by Christ and derives from Him (Mt 16:8-10), and therefore keeps its indispensable constitutional and mystical value, as vehicle of the mysteries of God (1 Cor 4:1) and as interpreter of the truth (Lk 10:16) and of Christ's will in His Church (Jn 21:15ff.), nevertheless it is assuming, in a more obvious way, attributes that are peculiar to it, pastoral and evangelical ones; and it manifests itself as service, therefore as love, as a sacrifice courageously consummated for the good of others, for the good of Christ's flock, for the whole Church (cf. Jn 10:11). — Pope Paul VI, to a general audience, 10-9-68.

...**The vocation** of service, which in the ministerial priesthood becomes a complete mission, does not change in any way the prerogatives of the functions of the hierarchy, of its doctrinal, jurisdictional and sanctifying powers, as if they derived on a democratic basis from the ecclesial community, from the People of God, as some people are wrongly affirming today. They derive from God, from Christ, from the sacred order and the mandate of those who form the hierarchy in the Church.

They are destined, on the other hand, for the good of the People of God. And if today this destination takes on its original importance, and entails, in the exercise of authority, forms more and more in keeping with its spiritual nature and its pastoral purpose — that is with the service that justifies it and requires it to be full of humility and love — all the more so does it wish to reflect the image of Christ living in those persons in the Church who represent, promote and perpetuate her mission of salvation. — Pope Paul VI, to a general audience, 10-17-68.

1. *Adversus haereses* IV, 26:2; PG 7, 1053.

DEFEND THE DEPOSIT OF FAITH

That divine mission entrusted by Christ to the apostles will last until the end of the world (cf. Mt 28:20), since the gospel they are to teach is for all time the source of all life for the Church. And for this reason the apostles, appointed as rulers in this society, took care to appoint successors.

For they not only had helpers in their ministry,[1] but also, in order that the mission assigned to them might continue after their death, they passed on to their immediate cooperators, as it were, in the form of a testament, the duty of confirming and finishing the work begun by themselves,[2] recommending to them that they attend to the whole flock in which the Holy Spirit placed them to shepherd the Church of God (cf. Acts 20:28).—LG 20.

The bishops themselves having been appointed by the Holy Spirit, are successors of the apostles as pastors of souls.[3] Together with the supreme Pontiff and under his authority they are sent to continue throughout the ages the work of Christ, the eternal pastor.[4] Christ gave the apostles and their successors the command and the power to teach all nations, to hallow men in the truth, and to feed them. Bishops, therefore, have been made true and authentic teachers of the faith, pontiffs, and pastors through the Holy Spirit, who has been given to them.[5]

...They exercise this office individually in reference to the portions of the Lord's flock assigned to them, each one taking care of the particular church committed to him, or sometimes some of them jointly providing for certain common needs of various churches.—CD 2, 3.

In the bishops for whom priests are assistants, our Lord Jesus Christ, the Supreme

High Priest, is present in the midst of those who believe. For sitting at the right hand of God the Father, He is not absent from the gathering of His high priests,[6] but above all through their excellent service He is preaching the word of God to all nations, and constantly administering the sacraments of faith to those who believe; by their paternal functioning (cf. 1 Cor 4:15) He incorporates new members in His Body by a heavenly regeneration, and finally by their wisdom and prudence He directs and guides the People of the New Testament in their pilgrimage toward eternal happiness. These pastors, chosen to shepherd the Lord's flock of the elect, are servants of Christ and stewards of the mysteries of God (cf. 1 Cor 4:1), to whom has been assigned the bearing of witness to the gospel of the grace of God (cf. Rom 15:16; Acts 20:24), and the ministration of the Spirit and of justice in glory (cf. 2 Cor 3:8-9).

For the discharging of such great duties, the apostles were enriched by Christ with a special outpouring of the Holy Spirit coming upon them (cf. Acts 1:8; 2:4; Jn 20:22-23), and they passed on this spiritual gift to their helpers by the imposition of hands (cf. 1 Tm 4:14; 2 Tm 1:6-7), and it has been transmitted down to us in episcopal consecration.[7] And the sacred Council teaches that by episcopal consecration the fullness of the sacrament of Orders is conferred, that fullness of power, namely, which both in the Church's liturgical practice and in the language of the Fathers of the Church is called the high priesthood, the supreme power of the sacred ministry.[8] But episcopal consecration, together with the office of sanctifying, also confers the office of teaching and of governing, which, however, of its very nature, can be exercised only in hierarchical communion with the head and the members of the college. —LG 21.

The shepherds of Christ's flock must holily and eagerly, humbly and courageously carry out their ministry, in imitation of the eternal high Priest, the Shepherd and Guardian of our souls. They ought to fulfill this duty in such a way that it will be the principal means also of their own sanctification. Those chosen for the fullness of the priesthood are granted the ability of exercising the perfect duty of pastoral charity by the grace of the sacrament of Orders. This perfect duty of pastoral charity[9] is exercised in every form of episcopal care and service, prayer, sacrifice and preaching. By this same sacramental grace, they are given the courage necessary to lay down their lives for their sheep, and the ability of promoting greater holiness in the Church by their daily example, having become a pattern for their flock (cf. 1 Pt 5:3). — LG 41.

What has actually taken place by means of the imposition of hands and the formula of consecration? What has happened is that these newly-elected ones [bishops] have been invested with an extraordinary outpouring of the Holy Spirit. An incomparable dignity — much more interior, indeed, than external — has transfigured them. A fearful power has been conferred upon them; a virtue which comes from on high, and is ratified in heaven (cf. Lk 24:49; Jn 20:23), has been communicated to them; a new and deeper assimilation to Christ has stamped upon them a superior personality.[10]

...In the bishop, our Lord Jesus Christ is among us. In a word, it is the communication of the fullness of the one supreme priesthood of Christ Himself, now appropriated to the bishop, which must occupy our attention, our admiration, our exultation. This is a grandeur which confounds us, for God alone is its cause (cf. Lk 1:48), and because God gives it to whom He wills, generally choosing the most humble (cf. 1 Cor 1:27). Yet it is a grandeur which exacts reverence, and which no one can despise with impunity (cf. Ti 2:15; Lk 10:16). Let us recognize Christ in the bishop, and let us praise the Lord!

For what reason, however, is this preference given to the bishop by Christ? We know this (and it is Our second consideration today): Christ has so favored the bishop in order to make him an apostle. The bishops, you know, are the successors of the apostles. And who are the apostles? They are those whom the Lord chose, and separated, and segregated for a mission in favor of the people (cf. Heb 5:1). They are those whom He sends forth (cf. Jn 15:16; Mt 19:29; Lk 18:29; Gal 1:15; Rom 1:1; Acts 13:2). Apostle means one sent forth. The apostles, and hence also the bishops, their successors, are the representatives, or, rather, the vehicles and instruments of the love of Christ for men. The episcopal ministry is a sign and an instrument of salvation (cf. Mt 9:38; Lk 6:13; Jn 20:21). In the ordinary divine economy of salvation, men do not save themselves by themselves. The Church is the visible sacrament of the saving love of God.[11]

The ministerial priesthood is indispensable[12] and finds its full expression in the episcopate. There must, in fact, be someone who brings men the Word of God[13]; there must be someone who distributes to them the mysteries of grace (cf. 1 Cor 4:1-2); there must be someone who guides them in the paths of the Lord[14]; there must be someone who unites them in Christ through the gospel (Rom 10:8; 1 Cor 4:1-2; Ti 1:7; 1 Pt 4:10; etc.).

In a word, the bishops are ministers, they are servants; they are not for themselves but for others.[15] They exist for the Church. It is for the Church that the bishops have the right and duty to exercise the functions of teachers, priests and shepherds.[16] They are for the Church, and to the Church they offer all their life (2 Cor 12:15). — Pope Paul VI, African Episcopal Ordination, 8-1-69.

We are logically and happily led to consider in you, venerable and beloved brethren — whom today We have assumed into the episcopal order and joined to the episcopal college—the mystery of the Epiphany, the plan of revelation. You are the heirs of this treasure of revealed truth, you are the custodians of the "deposit" (1 Tm 6:20), you are qualified representatives of Christ, you are the ministers of His magisterial, priestly and pastoral powers; and with respect to the Church you represent the Lord in the authentic and fullest form.

"Where the bishop is, there the community is assembled,[17] just as where Jesus Christ is, there is the Catholic Church." You are its rulers, and as such you are responsible for her, and to such a high and demanding degree that in the bishop charity has its most perfect evangelical expression, and it qualifies him as one who dedicates all his life to identifying himself with that love which gives itself (cf. Jn 15:13), and which makes of the following of Christ the salient and determining norm of existence (cf. Jn 21:19, 22).

Thus you, more than any others, are consecrated to the service of the Church. This is the recurring idea in Tradition, in every discourse on the episcopate. Among the many voices let Us recall one, that of Origen, who said of the bishop: "he who is called to the service of the whole Church."[18] Augustine never tired of repeating: "Be pleased not so much to preside as to be of help."[19] — Pope Paul VI, to newly-consecrated bishops, 1-6-69.

We must mention the manifold relationship which exists between the apostle, his successor, and divine revelation. No one, more than he, receives it, listens to it, meditates upon it, makes it his own. The words of Christ at the Last Supper teach us this and repeat it to us (Jn 15:14, etc.; Mk 4:11). You [bishops] are the disciples par excellence of revelation. No one more than you is the custodian of this heritage of divine truth, custodian of its exact words (1 Tm 6:20) and custodian of its practical fulfillment (Lk 11:28; Jn 14:15; 21:23). And to you, more than to any others in the Church of God is promised a particular outpouring of the Holy Spirit, which gives understanding and opens up the depths of revelation (Jn 14:26; 15:26). And from being privileged hearers you have become teachers of the divine doctrine.

The teaching office is one of the greatest powers specifically entrusted by Christ to His apostles and to those who will succeed them in the spreading of the message of truth and salvation, which is the gospel (Mt 28:20). And with the teaching office there must be a witnessing.

The doctrine of the faith does not impose itself like the truths of the rational order which as soon as announced are accepted and spread because of their intrinsic evidence. The doctrine of the faith is based on the word of God and of Christ and of him who is a faithful witness to it (cf. Lk 24:48; Acts 1:8, etc.; 10:39), an authoritative and decisive witness.[20] This witnessing involves danger and risk, the choice of the divine truth if need be at the risk of one's own life (cf. Jn 16:2; Heb 10:20ff.; 11:1ff.). — Pope Paul VI, to newly-consecrated bishops, 1-6-69.

You have become with Us, with all the Catholic episcopate, brothers, beloved ministers, and witnesses of Christ (cf. Acts 26:16), the defenders of the gospel (Phil 1:16) set apart in order to serve the gospel (Rom 1:1), the confessors of the gospel (cf. Rom 1:16). The word of God must so penetrate our lives as to establish a living relation of spiritual kinship with Christ (Lk 11:28); we are the imitators, the followers, the living images of the Lord (cf. 1 Cor 4:16, 11:1; 1 Pt 5:3); we must in a certain way personify, we must incarnate in our humble lives the Word of God, so that His revelation, through our ministry and our example, will continue to shine in the Church of God and in the world.

Ours is a great destiny, a grave destiny. We are, as Christ said, the light of the world (Mt 5:14); this light cannot and must not be extinguished. This is the meaning, this is the value of the sacramental act now fulfilled in your persons. We have made of you an ardent flame of the truth and the charity of the Master. Oh! that you may always burn and be consumed in this way, glowing and spreading the Easter light of Christ.

Our discourse ends with the confirmation of the bishop's function in the order of protecting and spreading the message of revelation. In seeking to recognize that function as willed by Christ, We will thank God "for giving such power to men" (Mt 9:8). We will pay it honor, perceiving how necessary and beneficial it is, since it is a ministry of truth and charity, indispensable for our advancement on the way of salvation. We bishops, who have been invested with so sublime an office, will do all to exercise it in humility of service, in fidelity of interpretation, and in the virtue that belongs to the word of God. In spreading this divine word among the People of God, we will take care to obtain from Him docility in listening and the comfort which our mission can receive from Himself, favored by the sentiment of faith. We will not heed the destiny, good or perilous though it be, which can result from our preaching (cf. 2 Tm 2:9; Jn 15:20-21). No, we will heed only the genuineness of our witness "lest the cross of Christ be made void" (1 Cor 1:17ff.). "To him be glory and power for ever and ever. Amen" (Rev 1:6). —Pope Paul VI, to newly-consecrated bishops, 1-6-69.

A bishop, since he is sent by the Father to govern His family, must keep before his eyes the example of the Good Shepherd, who came not to be ministered to but to minister (cf. Mt 20:28; Mk 10:45), and to lay down His life for His sheep (cf. Jn 10:11). Being taken from among men, and himself beset with weakness, he is able to have compassion on the ignorant and erring (Heb 5:1-2). Let him not refuse to listen to his subjects, whom he cherishes as his true sons and exhorts to cooperate readily with him. As having one day to render an account for their souls (Heb 13:17), he takes care of them by his prayer, preaching, and all the works of charity, and not only of them but also of those who are not yet of the one flock, who also are commended to him in the Lord. Since, like Paul the Apostle, he is debtor to all men, let him be ready to preach the gospel to all (Rom 1:14-15), and to urge his faithful to apostolic and missionary activity. But the faithful must cling to their bishop, as the Church does to Christ, and Jesus Christ to the Father, so that all may be of one mind through unity,[21] and abound to the glory of God (cf. 2 Cor 4:15). —LG 27.

This duty we have as bishops to proclaim the message of divine revelation is very serious and may seem above our powers. However, it is here that another attitude completes the moral psychology of the herald of the gospel. If fortitude is one of the characteristic virtues of the bishops—especially in these times filled with difficulties for the authorized exercising of the ministry nowadays often contested, and of the teaching office which is also today frequently weakened by criticism, doubt and doctrinal whim—the good pastor must not be afraid. He must perfect with psychological sensitivity (cf. Mt 11:16; Jn 2:25), with humility (cf. Mt 11:29), and with a spirit of sacrifice (cf. Jn 10:15; 2 Cor 12:15) his art of guiding men, sons and brothers, and of making them love that obedience within whose sphere the whole economy of salvation is unfolded (cf. Phil 2:8; Heb 13:17).

But he must not fear. The bishop is not alone; Christ is with him (Jn 14:9; Mt 28:20). He is assisted by a charism of the Spirit (Mt 10:20; Jn 15:18ff.). The habitual exercise of mastering himself and the awareness of the spiritual reality in which he has been called to live, will be that of confidence in the Lord and abandonment to His will and His Providence (cf. Lk 22:35). And finally We remind you, Our brothers, and those who are listening to Us today, of the warning of Jesus: "In the world you will have trouble, but be brave, I have conquered the world" (Jn 16:35). — Pope Paul VI, to new bishops, 1-6-69.

The individual bishops, who are placed in charge of particular churches, exercise their pastoral government over the portion of the People of God committed to their care, and not over other churches nor over the universal Church. But each of them, as a member of the episcopal college and legitimate successor of the apostles, is obliged by Christ's institution and command to be solicitous for the whole Church,[22] and this solicitude, though it is not exercised by an act of jurisdiction, contributes greatly to the advantage of the universal Church. For it is the duty of all bishops to promote and to safeguard the unity of faith and the discipline common to the whole Church, to instruct the faithful to love for the whole Mystical Body of Christ, especially for its poor and sorrowing members and for those who are suffering persecution for justice' sake (cf. Mt 5:10) and finally to promote every activity that is of interest to the whole Church, especially that the faith may take increase and the light of full truth appear to all men. And this also is important, that by governing well their own church as a portion of the universal Church, they themselves are effectively contributing to the welfare of the whole Mystical Body, which is also the body of the churches.[23] — LG 23.

It is God's plan that the Christian calling and the economy of salvation should be universal. It is also a demand that will become an active power in him who has the singular destiny to be chosen for the gospel, in the superior grade of that election, the election to the episcopate. "I chose you," says the Lord, "and I commissioned you to go out and to bear fruit" (Jn 15:16). It is part of God's intention for Revelation that it should shine in the darkness of the world, not only without any preconceived discrimination, but with the widest diffusion possible.

But this diffusion demands a service entrusted to men commissioned for it. Revealed truth demands a qualified doctrinal ministry (cf. Rom 10:14ff.); it demands brothers; it demands pastors; it demands teachers who will carry the gospel message of salvation to men; it demands apostles; it demands bishops. You have been entrusted with this service of the truth and for the faith: a service that makes responsible before God, Christ, the Church, and the world, him to whom it has been committed.

"It is a duty which has been laid on me," cries St. Paul, "I should be punished if I did not preach the gospel!" It demands zeal, courage, the spirit of initiative, the daring of preaching: "Though you be of slight voice and tardy tongue, give yourself to the word of God." [24] — Pope Paul VI, to newly-consecrated bishops, 1-6-69.

We do not think we are wronging you [bishops] if We suppose that you, too, like anyone in the Church of God today, need pastoral courage. The more important and heavy the office that a member of the Church fills — to testify to the faith and to serve the ecclesial community — the greater is this need of courage. "Conflicts without and anxieties within" (2 Cor 7:5).

We are going through a difficult hour. Everything is moving, everything seems to be breaking away from religion, faith and moral law. Everything, We were saying, has become a problem. The psychology of the world is in evolution, and we often have great difficulty in understanding its phenomena, fallacies and resources. Restlessness, intolerance, defection often arise from within the Church, from her dearest sons. It is a stormy time. The breathless invocation of the disciples to Jesus, sleeping at the bottom of the boat, would sometimes come to our lips: "Lord, save us! we are perishing!" (Mt 8:25)

But we all remember, in this connection, the Lord's reassuring rebuke: "Why are you fearful, O you of little faith?" (Mt 8:26)

There is no need for Us to remind you masters of Christian life how and where to get this courage, of which poor Don Abbondio said that "one cannot give it to one-self."[25] We all know what the sources of pastoral courage are: confidence, almost to the point of rashness, in divine assistance: "In the world you will have affliction. But take courage, I have overcome the world" (Jn 16:33); and love for the flock entrusted to us, for whose sake it seems normal to face every difficulty and every danger: "The good shepherd lays down his life for his sheep" (Jn 10:11). —Pope Paul VI, to Italian bishops, 6-19-71.

1. Cf. Acts 6:2-6; 11:30; 13:1; 14:23; 20:17; 1 Thes 5:12-13; Phil 1:1; Col 4:11, *et passim.*

2. Cf. Acts 20:25-27; 2 Tm 4:6 s. coll. c. 1 Tm 5:22; 2 Tm 2:2; Ti 1:5; S. Clem. Rom, *Ad Cor.* 44:3; (ed. Funk, 1, p. 156).

3. Cf. Vat. I fourth session, part I of Dogmatic Const. on the Church of Christ, c. 3, Denz. 1828 (3061).

4. Cf. Vat. I fourth session, Introduction to Dogmatic Constitution on the Church of Christ, Denz. 1821 (3050).

5. Cf. LG 21, 24, 25; AAS 57 (1965), pp. 24-25, 29-31.

6. St. Leo M, *Serm.* 5:3; PL 54, 154.

7. Conc. Trid., Sess. 23, cap. 3, *citat verba* 2 Tm 1:6-7, *Ut demonstrat Ordinem esse verum sacramentum:* Denz. 959 (1766).

8. In *Trad. Apost.* 3, ed. Botte, *Sources Chr.,* pp. 27-30, *Episcopo tribuitur "primatus sacerdotii."* Cf. *Sacramentarium Leonianum,* ed. C. Moehlberg, *Sacramentarium Veronense,* Romae, 1955, p. 119: *"ad summi sacerdotii ministerium.... Comple in sacerdotibus tuis mysterii tui summam" ...Idem, Liber Sacramentorum Romanae Ecclesiae,* Romae, 1960, pp. 121-122: *"Tribuas eis, Domine, cathedram episcopalem ad regendam Ecclesiam tuam et plebem universam."* Cf. PL 78, 224.

9. Cf. S. Thomas, *Summa Theol.* 11-11, q. 184, a. 5 et 6. *De perf. vitae spir.,* c. 18. Origines, *In is.* Hom. 6, 1: PG 13, 239.

10. Cf. Lk 10:16; Gal 2:20; LG 21.

11. LG 9.

12. *Ibid.,* 10.

13. DV 10.

14. Cf. Jn 21:15; LG 19-20.

15. Cf. Lk 22:26; Rom 1:14; LG 20.

16. Cf. 1 Pt 4:11; Pontificale Romanum 18; CD 12-16.

17. S. Ignatius of Antioch, *Smyrn* 8, 2.

18. *In Is.* Hom 6, 1; PG 13, 239.
19. Serm. 140, 1; P.L. 38, 1484.
20. Cf. Gal 1:8; DV 10; Denz. Sch. 3884-3887 (2313-2315).
21. Cf. S. Ignatius M., *Ad Ephes.* 5, 1 (ed. Funk, I, p. 216, n. 28).
22. Cf. Pius XII, Litt. Encyc. *Fidei Donum,* 4-21-57: AAS (1957), p. 237.
23. Cf. S. Hilarius Pict., *In Ps.* 14, 3: PL 9, 206; CSEL 22, p. 86, — S. Gregorius M., *Moral,* IV, 7, 12: PL 75, 643 C. Ps. — Basilius, *In Is.* 15, 296: PG 30, 637 C.
24. Origen.
25. A. Manzoni, *I Promessi Sposi,* chap. XXV.

UNITED IN A SPIRIT OF TRUST

Priests are always present in Our heart, in Our remembrance. They are equally present in Our esteem, in Our trust. They are present in the concrete vision of the activity of the Church: they are your [bishops'] first and indispensable collaborators, they are the most direct and the most committed "dispensers of the mysteries of God" (1 Cor 4:1), that is, of the word, of grace, of pastoral charity; they are the living models of the imitation of Christ; they are with us the first sharers in the sacrifice of the Lord; they are our brothers, our friends (cf. Jn 15:15): we must love them very much. Love them more.

If a bishop were to concentrate his most constant, understanding, patient and cordial attention on the formation, the assistance, the listening to, the guidance, the instruction, the exhortation and the encouragement of his clergy, he would have well employed his time, his heart and his activity. — Pope Paul VI, to Latin American bishops, 9-5-68.

There is an irreplaceable and very effective means to ensure for our dear priests an easier and happier way of being faithful to their obligations, and it is one which they have the right and duty to find in you, venerable brother bishops. It was you who called them and destined them to be priests; it was you who placed your hands on their heads; with you they are one in sharing the honor of the priesthood by virtue of the sacrament of Orders; it is you whom they make present in the community of the faithful; with you they are united in a spirit of trust and magnanimity since, insofar as is compatible with their order, they take upon themselves your duties and care.[1] In choosing a life dedicated to celibacy they follow the ancient examples of the prelates of the East and the West; this provides a new motive for union between bishop and priest and a sound hope that they will live together more closely.

The affection which Jesus had for His apostles showed itself very clearly when He made them ministers of His real and Mystical Body (cf. Jn 13-17); and even you in whose person "our Lord Jesus Christ, the supreme high Priest, is present in the midst of those who believe"[2] know that you owe the best part of your hearts and pastoral care to your priests and to the young men preparing to be priests.[3] In no other way can you better show this conviction than in the conscious responsibility and sincere and unconquerable love with which you preside over the education of your seminarians, and help your priests in every way possible to remain faithful to their vocation and their duties.

It is your fraternal and kindly presence and deeds that must fill up in advance the human loneliness of the priest, which is so often the cause of his discouragement and temptations.[4] Before being the superiors and judges of your priests, be their masters, fathers, friends, their good and kind brothers always ready to understand, to sympathize and to help. In every possible way encourage your priests to be your personal friends and to be very open with you. This will not weaken the relationship of juridical obedience; rather it will transform it into pastoral love so that they will obey more willingly, sincerely and securely.

If they are your devoted friends and if they have a filial trust in you, your priests will be able in time to open up their souls and to confide in you their difficulties in the certainty that they can rely on your kindness to be protected from eventual defeat, without a servile fear of punishment, but in the filial expectation of correction, pardon and help, which will inspire them to resume their difficult journey with a new confidence.

Venerable brothers, all of you are certainly convinced that to restore to the soul of a priest joy in and enthusiasm for his vocation, interior peace and salvation, is an urgent and glorious ministry which has an incalculable influence on a multitude of souls. There will be times when you must exercise your authority by showing a just severity towards those few who, after having resisted your kindness, by their conduct cause scandal to the People of God; but you will take the necessary precautions to ensure their seeing the error of their ways. Following the example of our Lord Jesus, the Pastor and Bishop of our souls (1 Pt 2:25), do not crush the bruised reed nor quench the smoking flax (Mt 12:20); like Jesus, heal their wounds (cf. 9:12), save what was lost (cf. Mt 18:11), with eagerness and love go in search of the lost sheep and bring him back to the warmth of the sheepfold (cf. Lk 15:4ff.) and, like Him, try until the end (cf. Lk 22:48) to call back the faithful friend.

We are certain, venerable brothers, that you will leave nothing undone to foster, by your teaching, prudence and pastoral zeal, the ideal of consecrated celibacy among your clergy. We are sure too that you will never neglect those priests who have strayed from the house of God, their true home, no matter where their painful odyssey has led them, since they still remain your sons. — SCl 93-95.

They [**bishops**] should be solicitous for the spiritual, intellectual and material welfare of the priests so that the latter can live holy and pious lives and fulfill their ministry faithfully and fruitfully. Therefore, they should encourage institutes and hold special meetings in which priests might gather from time to time both for the performance of longer exercises and the renewal of their spiritual life and for the acquisition of deeper subjects, especially Sacred Scripture and theology, the more important social questions, and the new methods of pastoral activity.

With active mercy bishops should pursue priests who are involved in any danger or who have failed in certain respects. — CD 16.

To you, venerable brothers, who bear the responsibility of the sanctification of your priests, We recommend that you help them in the difficulties, sometimes very serious of their personal life and of their ministry. What can a bishop not do who loves his priests, if he has won their confidence, if he knows them, follows them closely and guides them with a firm and always paternal authority? As pastors of the whole diocese, be pastors above all in a particular manner for those who collaborate so closely with you and to whom you are bound by such sacred bonds. — SNP.

Priests, who resemble bishops to a certain degree in their participation of the sacrament of Orders, form the spiritual crown of the bishops.[5] They participate in the grace of their office and they should grow daily in their love of God and their neighbor by the exercise of their office through Christ, the eternal and unique Mediator. They should preserve the bond of priestly communion, and they should abound in every spiritual good and thus present to all men a living witness to God.[6]

All this they should do in emulation of those priests who often, down through the course of the centuries, left an outstanding example of the holiness of humble and hidden service. Their praise lives on in the Church of God. By their very office of praying and offering sacrifice for their own people and the entire People of God, they should rise to greater holiness.

Keeping in mind what they are doing and imitating the holiness of the things they handle,[7] these priests in their apostolic labors, rather than being ensnared by perils and hardships, should rather rise to greater holiness through these perils and hardships. They should ever nourish and strengthen their action from an abundance of contemplation, doing all this for the comfort of the entire Church of God.

All priests, and especially those who are called "diocesan priests," due to the special title of their ordination, should keep continually before their minds the fact that their faithful loyalty toward and their generous cooperation with their bishop is of the greatest value in their growth in holiness. — LG 41.

Priests, prudent cooperators with the episcopal order,[8] its aid and instrument, called to serve the People of God, constitute one priesthood[9] with their bishop although bound by a diversity of duties. Associated with their bishop in a spirit of trust and generosity, they make him present in a certain sense in the individual local congregations, and take upon themselves, as far as they are able, his duties and the burden of his care, and discharge them with daily interest. And as they sanctify and govern under the bishop's authority, that part of the Lord's flock entrusted to them, they make the universal Church visible in their own locality and bring an efficacious assistance to the building up of the whole body of Christ (cf. Eph 4:12). Intent always upon the welfare of God's children, they must strive to lend their effort to the pastoral work of the whole diocese, and even of the entire Church.

On account of this sharing in their priesthood and mission, let priests sincerely look upon the bishop as their father and reverently obey him. And let the bishop regard his priests as his co-workers and as sons and friends, just as Christ called His disciples now not servants but friends (cf. Jn 15:15). All priests, both diocesan and religious, by reason of Orders and ministry, fit into this body of bishops and priests, and serve the good of the whole Church according to their vocation and the grace given to them. — LG 28.

All priests, in union with bishops, so share in one and the same priesthood and ministry of Christ that the very unity of their consecration and mission requires their hierarchical communion with the order of bishops.[10] At times in an excellent manner they manifest this communion in liturgical concelebration as joined with the bishop when they celebrate the Eucharistic Sacrifice.[11] Therefore, by reason of the gift of the Holy Spirit which is given to priests in Holy Orders, bishops regard them as necessary helpers and counsellors in the ministry and in their role of teaching, sanctifying and nourishing the People of God.[12] Already in the ancient ages of the Church we find liturgical texts proclaiming this with insistence, as when they solemnly call upon God to pour out upon the candidate for priestly ordination "the spirit of grace and counsel, so that with a pure heart he may help and govern the People of God,"[13] just as in the desert the spirit of Moses was spread abroad in the minds of the seventy prudent men (Nm 11:16-25), "and using them as helpers among the people, he easily governed countless multitudes."[14]

...Priests, never losing sight of the fullness of the priesthood which the bishops enjoy, must respect in them the authority of Christ, the supreme Shepherd. They must therefore stand by their bishops in sincere charity and obedience.[15] — PO 7.

Priests will adhere more faithfully to their mission the more they know and show themselves to be faithful to ecclesial communion. Thus the pastoral ministry, which is exercised by bishops, priests and deacons, is an eminent sign of this ecclesial communion, in that they have received a special mandate to serve this communion.

But in order that this ministry may really become a sign of communion, the actual conditions in which it is exercised must be considered to be of the greatest importance.

The guiding principle expressed by the Second Vatican Council in the decree *Presbyterorum ordinis,* namely that the very unity of consecration and mission requires the hierarchical communion of priests with the order of bishops, is considered fundamental to a practical restoration or renewal, with full confidence, of the mutual relationship between the bishop and the presbyterium over which the bishop presides. This principle is more concretely to be put into practice especially by the diligence of the bishops.

The service of authority on the one hand and the exercise of not merely passive obedience on the other should be carried out in a spirit of faith, mutual charity, filial and friendly confidence and constant and patient dialogue. Thus the collaboration and responsible cooperation of priests with the bishop will be sincere, human and at the same time supernatural.[16]

Personal freedom, responding to the individual vocation and to the charism received from God, and also the ordered solidarity of all for the service of the community and the good of the mission to be fulfilled are two conditions which should shape the Church's proper mode of pastoral action.[17] The guarantee of these conditions is the bishop's authority, to be exercised in a spirit of service. —Ministerial Priesthood, Nov., 1971, Synod Document.

All presbyters, both diocesan and religious, participate in and exercise with the bishop the one priesthood of Christ and are thereby constituted prudent cooperators of the episcopal order. In the care of souls, however, the first place is held by diocesan priests who are incardinated or attached to a particular church, for they have fully dedicated themselves in the service of caring for a single portion of the Lord's flock. In consequence, they form one presbytery and one family whose father is the bishop.

The relationships between the bishop and the diocesan priests should rest most especially upon the bonds of supernatural charity so that the harmony of the wills of the priests with that of their bishop will render their pastoral activity more fruitful. Wherefore, for the sake of greater service to souls, let the bishop call the priests into dialogue, especially about pastoral matters. This he should do not only on a given occasion but at regularly fixed intervals insofar as this is possible.

Furthermore, all diocesan priests should be united among themselves and so should share a genuine concern for the spiritual welfare of the whole diocese. They should also be mindful that the benefits they receive by reason of their ecclesiastical office are closely bound up with their sacred work. Therefore they should contribute generously, as the bishop may direct and as their means permit, to the material needs of the diocese. — CD 28.

They [**bishops**] should gladly listen to their priests, indeed consult them and engage in dialogue with them in those matters which concern the necessities of pastoral work and welfare of the diocese. In order to put this into effect, there should be — in a manner suited to today's conditions and necessities,[18] and with a structure and norms to be determined by law — a body or senate[19] of priests representing all the priests. This representative body by its advice will be able to give the bishop effective assistance in the administration of the diocese. — PO 7.

The Council of Priests, which is of its nature something diocesan, is an institutional manifestation of the brotherhood among priests which has its basis in the sacrament of Orders.

The activity of this Council cannot be fully shaped by law. Its effectiveness depends especially on a repeated effort to listen to the opinions of all in order to reach a consensus with the bishop, to whom it belongs to make the final decision.

If this is done with the greatest sincerity and humility, and if all one-sidedness is overcome, it will be easier to provide properly for the common good.

The Priests' Council is an institution in which priests recognize, at a time when variety in the exercise of their ministry increases every day, that they are mutually complementary in serving one and the same mission of the Church.

It is the task of this Council, among other things, to seek out clear and distinctly defined aims, to suggest priorities, to indicate methods of acting, to assist whatever the Spirit frequently stirs up through individuals or groups, and to foster the spiritual life, whence the necessary unity may more easily be attained.

New forms of hierarchical communion between bishops and priests[20] must be found, to facilitate contacts between local Churches. A search must be made for ways whereby priests may collaborate with bishops in supra-diocesan bodies and enterprises.

The collaboration of religious priests with the bishop in the presbyterium is necessary, though their work is of valuable assistance to the universal Church. — Ministerial Priesthood, Nov., 1971, Synod Document.

As the Council says, priests fulfill "in the renewal of Christ's Church a role of the greatest importance and of ever-increasing difficulty." [21] Did you not receive this particular mission of sacred service of the gospel — the mission of proclaiming it to all nations (cf. Mt 28:19), and of sanctifying the People of God — as a share in the very function of the apostles, in subordination to the order of bishops? [22]

Be also men of the Church. The Church cannot be separated from Jesus Christ; she is the Body of Christ. It is in the Church, with the Church and for the Church that your spiritual life will develop fully and that your ministry will be fruitful, for it is through her that the life of Christ is given to the faithful.[23] Be therefore one with your bishops, not only in the observance of a hierarchical bond, but by a genuine attachment of mind and heart, as to the representative of Christ the supreme Shepherd.[24] — Pope Paul VI, to the clergy (Australia), 12-10-70.

Because it is impossible for the bishop always and everywhere to preside over the whole flock in his Church, he cannot do other than establish lesser groupings of the faithful. Among these the parishes, set up locally under a pastor who takes the place of the bishop, are the most important: for in some manner they represent the visible Church constituted throughout the world. — SC 42.

Pastors are cooperators of the bishop in a very special way, for as pastors in their own name they are entrusted with the care of souls in a certain part of the diocese under the bishop's authority.

In exercising this care of souls, pastors and their assistants should so fulfill their duty of teaching, sanctifying and governing that the faithful and the parish communities will truly realize that they are members both of the diocese and of the universal Church. For this reason, they should collaborate with other pastors and priests who exercise a pastoral office in the area (such as vicars forane and deans), as well as with those engaged in works of a supra-parochial nature. In this way the pastoral work in the diocese will be unified and made more effective.

Moreover, the care of souls should always be infused with a missionary spirit so that it reaches out as it should to everyone living within the parish boundaries. If the pastor cannot contact certain groups of people, he should seek the assistance of others, even laymen who can assist him in the apostolate.

To render the care of souls more efficacious, community life for priests—especially those attached to the same parish—is highly recommended. This way of living, while it encourages apostolic action, also affords an example of charity and unity to the faithful.—CD 30.

---

1. LG 28.
2. *Ibid.*, 21.
3. PO 7.
4. Decree cit., *ibid.*
5. Cf. S. Ignatius M., *Magn.* 13, 1 (ed. Funk, 1, p. 241).
6. Cf. St. Pius X, Exhort. *Haerent animo*, Aug. 4, 1908: AAS 41 (1908), p. 560f., *Cod. Iur. Can.*, con. 124. Pius XI, Encyclical *Ad catholici sacerdotii*, 12-20-35: AAS 28 (1936), p. 22ff.
7. *Ordo Consecrationis sacerdotalis*, in Exhortatione initiali.
8. *Ordo Consecrationis sacerdotalis*, in praefatione.
9. Cf. S. Ignatius M., *Philad.* 4 (ed. Funk, 1, p. 266). S. Cornelius 1, apud S. Cyprianum, *Epist.* 48, 2: Hartel, III, 2, 610.
10. Cf. LG 28; AAS 57 (1965), p. 35.
11. Cf. "Ecclesiastical Constitution of the Apostles," XVIII: (ed. Shermann, "Die allgemeine Kirchenordnung," 1, Paderborn 1914, p. 26; A. Harnack, T.U.U., 11, 4, p. 13, n. 18 and 19); Pseudo-Jerome, "The Seven Orders of the Church" (ed. A. W. Kalff, Wurzburg, 1937, p. 45); S. Isidore of Hispali, "Ecclesiastical Offices," c. VII (PL 83, 787).
12. Cf. "Didascalia," II, 28, 4 (ed. F.X. Funk, p. 108); "Constitutions of the Apostles," II, 28, 4: II, 34, 3 (*ibid.*, pp. 109 and 117).
13. "Constitutions of the Apostles," VIII, 16, 4 (ed. F. X. Funk, 1, p. 522, 13); cf. "Epitome of the Constitutions of the Apostles," VI

(*ibid.*, II, p. 80, 3-4); "Testamentum Domini," (transl. I.E. Rahmani, Moguntiae, 1899, p. 69). Also in "Trad. Apost." (ed. B. Botte, *La Tradition Apostolique*, Munster, I.W., 1963, p. 20).

14. Roman Pontifical on the ordination of a priest, preface: these words are also found in the Leonine Sacramentary and the Gregorian Sacramentary. Similar words can be found in the Oriental Liturgies; cf. "Trad. Apost.": (Ancient Latin version of Verona, ed. B. Botte, *La Tradition Apostolique de St. Hippolyte. Essai de reconstruction*, Munster, I.W., 1963, p. 20); "Constitutions of the Apostles," VIII, 16, 4 (ed. F.X. Funk, 1, p. 522, 16-17); "Epitome on the Constitutions of the Apostles," 6 (ed. F.X. Funk, II, p. 20, 5-7): "Testamentum Domini" (transl. I.E. Rahmani, Moguntiae, 1899, p. 69); "Euchologium Serapionis," XXVIII (ed. F.X. Funk, "Didascalia and Constitutions," II, p. 190, lines 1-7); Maronite Rite of Ordination (transl. H. Denzinger, *Rites of the Orientals*, II, Wurzburg, 1863, p. 161). Among the Fathers can be cited: Theodore of Mopsuestia, "On First Timothy," 3,8 (ed. Swete, II, pp. 119-121); Theodoretus, "Questions on Numbers," XVIII (p. 80, 372b).

15. Cf. Paul VI, allocution to the family heads of Rome and Lenten speakers, March 1, 1965, in the Sistine Hall: AAS 57 (1965), p. 326.

16. Cf. LG 28; CD 15; PO 7.

17. Cf. PO 7.

18. The Cathedral Chapter is already found in established law, as the "senate and assembly" of the bishop (Code of Canon Law, c. 391), or if there is not one, an assembly of diocesan consultors (Code of Canon Law, cc. 423-428). It is Our desire to give recognition to such institutions so that modern circumstances and necessities might better be provided for. As is evident, this synod of priests forms the pastoral "consilium" spoken of in the Decree *Christus Dominus*, 27, of which the laity can also be members, and whose function is mainly to map out a plan for pastoral work. Concerning priests as counselors of the bishops, one might refer to the "Didascalia," II, 28, 4 (ed. F.X. Funk, 1, p. 108); also "Constituions of the Apostles," II, 28, 4 (ed. F.X. Funk, 1, p. 109); St. Ignatius Martyr, "Magn." 6, 1 (ed. F.X. Funk, p. 234, 10-16); "Trall." 3, 1 (ed. F.X. Funk, p. 244, 10-12); Origen, "Against Celsus," 3, 39: "Priests are counselors or 'bouleytai'" (PG 11, 957 d-960 a).

19. St. Ignatius Martyr, "Magn." 6, 1: (ed. F.X. Funk, p. 234, 10-13); St. Ignatius Martyr, "Trall.," 3, 1: (*ibid.*, p. 244, 10-12); St. Jerome, "On Isaiah," 11, 3 (PL 24, 61 A).

20. Cf. PO 7.

21. PO 1.

22. Cf. PO 2.

23. Cf. LG 7.

24. Cf. PO 7.

THAT THEY MAY BE ONE

Since priests are bound together by an intimate sacramental brotherhood and by their mission, and since they work and plan together for the same task, some community of life or a certain association of life shall be encouraged among them and can take various forms, including non-institutional ones. This shall be allowed for by the law itself through opportune norms and by renewed or newly-discovered pastoral structures.

Priestly associations should also be fostered which in a spirit of ecclesial communion and being recognized by the competent ecclesiastical authority, "through an apt and properly approved rule of life and through brotherly assistance," [1] seek to advance the aims which belong to their function and "holiness in the exercise of the ministry." [2]

It is desirable that, as far as possible, ways be sought, even if they prove rather difficult, whereby associations which perhaps divide the clergy into factions may be brought back to communion and to the ecclesial structure.

There should be greater communication between religious priests and diocesan priests, so that true priestly fraternity may exist between them and that they may provide one another with mutual help, especially in spiritual matters. — Ministerial Priesthood, Nov. 1971, Synod Document.

Priestly chastity is increased, guarded and defended by a way of life, surroundings and activity suited to a minister of God. For this reason the "close sacramental brotherhood" [3] which all priests enjoy in virtue of their ordination must be fostered to the utmost. Our Lord Jesus Christ has taught the urgency of the new commandment of charity. He gave a wonderful example of it when He instituted the sacrament of the Eucharist and the Catholic priesthood (Jn 13:15, 34-35) and prayed to His heavenly Father that the love the Father bore for Him from all eternity should be in His ministers and that He too should be in them (Jn 17:26).

So the unity of spirit among priests should be perfect and they should be active in their prayers, friendship and help of all kinds for one another. One cannot sufficiently recommend to priests a life lived in common and directed entirely toward their sacred ministry; the practice of having frequent meetings with a fraternal exchange of ideas, counsel and experience with their brother priests; the movement to form associations which encourage priestly holiness.

Priests should reflect on the advice of the Council[4] which reminds them of their common sharing in the priesthood so that they may feel a lively responsibility for fellow priests troubled by difficulties which gravely endanger the divine gift they have. They should have a burning charity for those who have greater need of love, understanding and prayer, who have need of prudent but effective help, and who have a claim on their unbounded charity as those who are, and should be, their truest friends. — SCl 79-81.

Older priests should receive younger priests as true brothers and help them in their first undertakings and priestly duties. The older ones should likewise endeavor to understand the mentality of younger priests, even though it be different from their own, and follow their projects with good will. By the same token, young priests should respect the age and experience of their seniors; they should seek their advice and willingly cooperate with them in everything that pertains to the care of souls.

In a fraternal spirit, priests should extend hospitality (cf. Heb 13:1-2), cultivate kindliness and share their goods in common (cf. Heb 13:16). They should be particularly solicitous for the sick, the afflicted, those overburdened with work, the lonely, those exiled from their homeland, and those who suffer persecution (cf. Mt 5:10). They should gladly and joyfully gather together for recreation, remembering Christ's invitation to the weary apostles: "Come aside to a desert place, and rest awhile" (Mk 6:31).

And further, in order that priests may find mutual assistance in the development of their spiritual and intellectual life, that they may be able to cooperate more effectively in their ministry and be saved from the dangers of loneliness which may arise, it is necessary that some kind of common life or some sharing of common life be encouraged among priests. This, however, may take many forms, according to different personal or pastoral needs, such as living together where this is possible, or having a common table, or at least by frequent and periodic meetings.

One should hold also in high regard and eagerly promote those associations which, having been recognized by competent ecclesiastical authority, encourage priestly holiness in the ministry by the use of an appropriate and duly approved rule of life and by fraternal aid, intending thus to do service to the whole order of priests.—PO 8.

Pastoral charity requires that priests avoid operating in a vacuum (cf. Gal 2:2) and that they work in a strong bond of union with their bishops and brother priests. If this be their program, priests will find the coordination and unity of their own life in the oneness of the Church's mission. They will be joined with the Lord and through Him with the Father in the Holy Spirit. This will bring them great satisfaction and a full measure of happiness (cf. 2 Cor 7:4). — PO 14.

Assistant pastors, as cooperators with the pastor, make, under the authority of the pastor, an indispensable and active contribution to the pastoral ministry. Therefore, there should always be fraternal association, mutual charity and reverence between the pastor and his assistants. They should assist one another with counsel, help and example, providing a united will and common zeal in the service of the parish.—CD 30.

By reason of the same communion in the priesthood, priests should realize that they are obliged in a special manner towards those priests who labor under certain difficulties. They should give them timely help, and also, if necessary, admonish them discreetly. Moreover, they should always treat with fraternal charity and magnanimity those who have failed in some matters, offer urgent prayers to God for them, and continually show themselves as true brothers and friends.—PO 8.

1. PO 8.
2. *Ibid.*
3. PO 8.
4. Decree cit., *ibid.*

> Fidelity to Christ cannot be separated from faithfulness to His Church. —PO 14.

Fidelity of Love

THE BONDING FORCE OF LOYALTY

A LOVE THAT BUILDS

THE BONDING FORCE OF LOYALTY

To you, the priests of the holy Catholic Church, to you, dearest of all Our sons, whom holy Orders have made Our brothers and Our collaborators in the ministry of salvation as well as the brothers and collaborators of your respective pastors; to you, today, We address Ourself.

...Our words will be brief and simple, but they are intended for you alone. Many years have these words lain in Our heart; because We have always been your Confrère, ever since We too experienced the mysterious destiny of being ordained a priest and of feeling the new and profound solidarity with all Our colleagues, with all those selected to personify Christ in our gift to the will of God, to the sanctification, guidance, and service of the faithful, to the relationship of salvation with the world.

Never have We neglected the communion of reverence, sympathy and brotherhood with you priests. And when the Holy Church called Us to exercise the functions of pastor, first as bishop and later as Pope, the thought of the clergy became Our continual concern, rich with esteem, solicitude and charity. Frequently have We regreted not having spoken to you sufficiently, not having borne witness more often and more earnestly to the feeling which the Spirit of the Lord inspired and still inspires in Our heart for you: a feeling which rises from Our innermost being and is accompanied by many other thoughts and feelings; because, above all things and in all things, in the order of charity, you priests, together with the bishops, Our brothers, hold the first place.

That is why We speak to you today. We are not address-ing you with an Encyclical or an Instruction or a legal canonical decree, but rather with a simple outpouring of Our heart. "We are frank with you...our heart is wide open to you" (2 Cor 6:11). This anniversary of the memory of the Apostles who laid the foundations of the Church by their evangelical message and their own blood obliges Us to open Our heart to you for a moment.

This We do with great admiration and great affec-tion. We know well your faithfulness to Christ and to the Church. We know your dedication to your ministry, your concern for your apostolate. We also know the respect and gratitude which many of the faithful feel for your evan-gelical unselfishness and apostolic charity.

Nor are We unaware of the treasures of your spiritual life, your interior conversation with God, your sacrifice with Christ, your yearning for contemplation united with activity. To each of you We feel impelled to repeat the words of our Lord in the Book of Revelation: "I know your works and your labor and your patience" (2:2).

What emotion and joy We feel at such a spectacle! How grateful We feel! We thank you and We bless you, in the name of Christ, for everything you are and every-thing you do in the Church of God. Like your bishops, you are its best workers, its columns, its teachers and its friends, the direct dispensers of the mysteries of God (cf. 1 Cor 4:1; 2 Cor 6:4).

We wish to tell you this from the depths of Our heart so that each of you may know and feel that you are ap-preciated and loved, so that each of you may rejoice to be in communion with Us in the great design and the difficult undertaking of the apostolate. — Pope Paul VI, to priests, 6-30-68.

The priestly ministry, since it is the ministry of the Church itself, can only function in the hierarchical union of the whole body. Pastoral charity, therefore, urges priests, as they operate in the framework of this union, to dedicate their own will by obedience to the service of God and their fellow men. In a great spirit of faith, let them receive and execute whatever orders the Holy Father, their own bishop, or other superiors give or recommend. — PO 15.

Obedience is motivated by faith, develops into a school of evangelical humility, and links the obedient man to the wisdom, unity, constructiveness and charity by which the body of the Church is sustained. It confers upon him who imposes it and upon him who conforms himself to it the merit of being like Christ who was "made obedient unto death" (Phil 2:8).

By obedience, therefore, in the context of dialogue, We mean the exercise of authority in the full awareness of its being a service and ministry of truth and charity, and We mean the observance of canonical regulations and respect for the government of legitimate superiors in the spirit of untroubled readiness as becomes free and loving children. The spirit of independence, of criticism, of rebellion, ill accords with the charity which gives life to the Church's solidarity, concord and peace, and easily transforms the dialogue into argument, dispute and disagreement. This most regrettable attitude, so easy, alas, to produce, is condemned by the Apostle Paul in his warning words: "Let there be no divisions among you" (1 Cor 1:10). — EcS.

With a willing heart let them [priests] spend and even exhaust themselves (cf. 2 Cor 7:4) in whatever task they are given, even though it be menial and unrecognized. They must preserve and strengthen a necessary oneness with their brothers in the ministry, especially with those whom God has selected as visible rulers of His Church. For in this way they are laboring to build the Body of Christ which grows "through every gesture of service" (cf. Eph 4:11-16).

This obedience is designed to promote the mature freedom of the children of God; by its very nature it postulates that in the carrying out of their work, spurred on by charity, they develop new approaches and methods for the greater good of the Church. With enthusiasm and courage, let priests propose new projects and strive to satisfy the needs of their flocks. Of course, they must be ready to submit to the decisions of those who rule the Church of God. —PO 15.

It is all a matter of understanding what the Church is, what kind of formation she gives us, how fortunate we are to be her children, what is required in order to be loyal to her.

Our generation's great temptation is to grow weary of the truth we have received as a gift. Many who recognize the importance and usefulness of changes occurring in the scientific, technical and social fields, lose faith in speculative thought, in tradition, in the Church's magisterium. They distrust Catholic doctrine; they think of emancipating themselves from its dogmatic character. They no longer want definitions binding on all forever. They deceive themselves into thinking that they have found another liberty, and they no longer value the freedom they already possess. They alter the terms of doctrine sanctioned by the Church, or give it a new, arbitrary interpretation, with a display of erudition and even greater psychological intolerance.

Perhaps they dream of shaping a new kind of Church corresponding to their own ideas, which are sometimes noble and lofty. But it would not be the authentic Church, as Christ willed it, and as it developed and matured in the course of history.

So it happens that obedience grows lax; with it liberty—which is characteristic of the faithful believing and working in, with and for the Church—likewise decreases. It is replaced by an unnoticed submission to other obediences, which can become burdensome and contrary to the true freedom of a child of the Church. — Pope Paul VI, to a general audience, 1-28-70.

Another danger lies in personal claims of prophetic insight. Many who talk about the Church today say they are inspired by a prophetic spirit. They make risky and sometimes inadmissible assertions, and appeal to the Holy Spirit as if the divine Paraclete were at their service at all times; they sometimes do this, unfortunately, with an unspoken intention of freeing themselves from the Church's magisterium, which also enjoys the assistance of the Holy Spirit. The Holy Spirit's charisms are freely granted by Him to the whole People of God, and also to the ordinary believer[1]; but verification of them and exercise of them are subject to the authority of the hierarchical ministry.[2]

May God grant that this presumption of elevating a personal judgment or, as often happens, personal or momentary experience, into a rule or criterion of religious doctrine may not cause havoc. May God never allow that treating these private opinions as charismatic gifts and prophetic inspirations may lead astray so many good and well-meaning people.[3]

We should then have a new "free examination of conscience" and that would give rise to so many varied and most questionable opinions in doctrinal matters and church discipline; it would take certainty away from our faith, together with its uniting power; it would make personal liberty the immediate guide, though conscience is and ought to be just that.[4] Such a use of liberty would be contrary to its primary responsibility which is to seek for the truth from the supreme guide of the Church's magisterium.[5] — Pope Paul VI, to a general audience, 9-25-69.

With what strength Our last predecessors have denounced the grave dangers of the spirit of independence in the heart of the clergy, both because of doctrinal teaching and because of the methods of the apostolate and ecclesiastical discipline.

We do not wish to insist, however, on this point, but We prefer to exhort Our priest-sons to develop within themselves the filial sense of belonging to the Church, our Mother. Of the Curé of Ars it was said that he only lived in the Church and for the Church, like a bundle of straw placed on a burning brazier. Priests of Jesus Christ, we are immersed in the brazier vivified by the Holy Spirit by fire. We have received everything from the Church. Let us act in her name and by virtue of the powers she has conferred on us. Let us serve her within the bonds of unity and in a way in which she wishes to be served. —SNP.

1. Jn 3:8; 1 Cor 12:11; LG 12; AA 3.
2. Cf. 1 Cor 4:1 and 14:1ff.; CD 15; LG 7, etc.
3. Cf. 2 Pt 1:20; DV 8.   4. DH 2, 3.   5. Cf. DV 8.

A LOVE THAT BUILDS

There is no need for Us to tell you [Synod of Bishops] how important your voices are for our holy Church, one and catholic, voices which echo that of the apostles. Nor need We tell you how grave is our shared responsibility. You know this very well. But may the desire we all have for the Church not be vain: that, through the power of the Spirit of God "who speaks in you" (Mt 10:20), and through the intercession of Mary, the Mother of Christ according to the flesh and also the Mother, We can say, of His Mystical Body according to the Spirit on the day of Pentecost, the Church may be "built up" (cf. Eph 4:12) by the Synod which today takes its place in the pages of her centuries-old history.

The image of "building," so often used in Sacred Scripture, invites us today to work together, with all our strength, for the great purpose which is our life's one aim: to build up the Church on its unshakable foundation, Christ Himself, the way, the truth and the life.

Let us not permit ourselves to deviate in the slightest from this way: it is the only way. Let us not permit ourselves to be enticed by any other voice: truth is one. Let us not permit ourselves to be drawn toward any font other than that of the living and life-giving God.

This is our clearly outlined duty as pastors. May the Lord grant us to be faithful to it, following the example of the holy pastors who were able to guide the Church with courage and wisdom, down the centuries of its storm-tossed earthly pilgrimage, through the rocks toward the open sea, where Christ is calling it, that it may bring the good news of salvation to all.

Although We are weaker and more infirm than Simon, We have received from the same Lord the name and the office of Peter, and We are with you to give new increase to the mystical and invisible edifice, in order that it may, today as in the past, welcome within its well-built luminous walls the People of God, who now stand in need, above all else, of the true faith which does not deceive, the sure hope which does not mislead, and the love reborn which does not grow cold and die. — Pope Paul VI, to Synod of Bishops, 9-30-71.

This is a difficult time in the Church's life, yet it is also a time which God is blessing, a time rich in grace and full of hope. Today as yesterday, the Church is carrying out her mission of salvation throughout the world, and transmits the promises of redemption and everlasting life. The Church today may be groaning, as St. Paul said of every creature, by reason of the pains of giving birth, which go before exultation at the appearance of new life; yet the Church also bears the Spirit of God within herself, the Creator Spirit, the Spirit of love and charity.

The spirit of division may be at work as usual in the Father's field and is sowing cockle there (cf. Mt 13:25), but we were forewarned, and we will not allow ourselves to be taken in by its deceptions or discouraged by its intrusions. We will go on with our humble, modest, fervent and disinterested work, watching the signs of the times, in a genuine climate of sincere and loyal dialogue and fraternal conversation, inspired by prayer and nourished by charity.

The Lord's Spirit is also at work in His Church. He is not a spirit of contestation, but a Spirit of renewal and peacefulness. He is uninterruptedly stirring up fresh undertakings, those of the apostolate and of holiness.... We ought to make ourselves even more attentive to His voice, more docile to His inspirations, more fearless in responding to His urgings. He is launching us out into the deep, that is, toward the needs of the new age.

Let us meet these needs with love, with serious thought, and without giving in to the unwise tendencies of the secular world, without fearing the traps set by the evil one, but being certain of being in God's hands, of being carried along by His love. — Pope Paul VI, to Sacred College of Cardinals, 5-18-70.

We think that the need is the need of fidelity, of loyalty. In the first place, a practical and empirical loyalty, if you like, to the religious and Christian manner of life of which you are the heirs.... You have to take up that inheritance: it would be foolish to neglect it, to let it go to waste.

We know that such respect for tradition is not fashionable. Some say it is neither permitted nor is it reasonable. Life is changing in such a radical way today that we may no longer stick to forms which modeled life yesterday. That is right: we cannot and we ought not remain bound to the past. Indeed, it is our duty to take up all the good things which the new times have to offer us. We will say more: we ourselves ought to promote progress at every level, and hasten that development which prodigious modern civilization is offering man, so that he may be more man, that all may enjoy the benefits of a better world.

But this run forward gives us no right to leave the good way which past tradition has marked down for our track. That is to say that there is something in tradition to which we ought to be faithful, if we do not wish to become degenerate and unfaithful. It is one of the most delicate and complex of tasks to identify that "something" in the process of renewal going on in the Church today. It is a twofold problem: what of the old ought to be preserved, and what new things ought to be introduced.

And so we come to a second fidelity which is necessary for the Church today, the fidelity that is founded on authorized and responsible evaluation of those elements which are constituent in the Church or have been acquired in history and may not be arbitrarily thrown away by the Church herself, both in the institutional and in the doctrinal fields. Such appreciation must not be hasty and it must not be arbitrary. No one can invent a new Church according to his own judgments or personal tastes.

It is not uncommon nowadays to find people, good and religious people, especially young ones, who feel entitled to denounce the whole of the Church's historical past, particularly its post-Tridentine period, as unauthentic, obsolete and no good for our times. They go on to make use of terms which have become commonplace already but are extremely superficial and inexact: they declare that we have definitely finished with an epoch (the Constantinian epoch perhaps, the pre-conciliar epoch, the juridical epoch, an authoritarian epoch...) and we have begun another (which is free, adult, prophetic) and which must be set going at once, along lines laid down by these new and often amateur masters....

To be truly loyal to the Church today we shall have to be careful of dangers arising from the intention, perhaps from the temptation, to renew the Church with radical purposes and drastic methods that might overthrow her.

We will end by recalling a third kind of fidelity to the Church, the fidelity of love. The Church today has more need than ever of this loyalty. It is not passive obedience, professed through inertia or spiritual laziness, nor is it something worn more on the outside than kept in the heart, through fear of losing the esteem of others and suffering the troubles which sincerity meets with when it denies or betrays. Love does not conceal defects and needs, which a filial eye can discern in Holy Mother Church. On the contrary, the more it becomes aware of them and observes them, the more it suffers and thinks about remedies for them. But its eye is a clear one, a loving one, and it above all sees the good in the Church.

Can it be that there is no more good to be seen in the Church, because there is now so much to challenge and to offend? Can it be that her tradition, which is the most defamed part of our Church today, does not shine with great men and great deeds? Can it be that today she no longer gives us examples of wisdom and holiness?

To love the Church! That is what we need to do today — that is our duty. Criticisms and reforms can be useful and are possible, on condition that they are promoted by real love. To love her, as Christ did for the reason that Christ loved her, and sacrificed Himself for her (Eph 5:25) — to love her even with our own personal self-sacrifice. — Pope Paul VI, to a general audience, 9-25-69.

In his first apostolic letter
St. Peter himself admonishes us to be strong in faith:
"Resist him, steadfast in the faith" (5:9). That is, we should
not be able to call ourselves disciples and followers and
heirs and successors of St. Peter if our adhesion to the
saving message of the Christian revelation did not have
the interior firmness which makes it into a true and practical life principle. Rome ought to have this primacy
also, the primacy, We repeat, of fidelity, which translates
faith into life, into art, an art of holiness, the art of giving
the faith constant and coherent expression, a style of Christian authenticity.

And today, we promise this fidelity in our hearts,
and in the prayer to St. Peter we ask him for it. We ask
him as a man who experienced its difficulties and con-
tradictions but also as the man who, as head of the apostles
and of all who would be associated with him in the faith,
had from Christ the incomparable favor of a prayer, uttered
by Christ Himself so that he should be strong in faith:
"So that your faith may not fail." He also received the infallible mandate to confirm his brethren after the hour of
weakness: "Strengthen your brethren" (cf. Lk 22:31-32).

And We wish that this fidelity were considered by
us not only under its aspect of unmoving adhesion to the
truth, which we have received from Christ, which has been
developed and has been fixed by the Church's magisterium,
strengthened by Peter, but also under the aspect of its
intrinsic capacity to spread and be apostolic. In other
words it should not be fidelity static and motionless
in its historical and social language, so as to preclude
communication with others, and accessibility to others.
We desire a fidelity that shall find the inward impulse
for its evangelizing effort in its content's genuineness
(cf. 1 Cor 9:16, "Woe to me," St. Paul writes, "if I have
not preached the gospel").

In that also, fidelity should find its authority to have
itself accepted by others (cf. Gal 1:8, "Even if we," St. Paul

writes, "or an angel from heaven should preach a gospel
to you other than that which we have preached to you,
let him be anathema!"). In it again, we should wish that
fidelity shall find the charism of the Holy Spirit accom-
panying the gospel's voice (cf. Jn 15:20).

And we will ask St. Peter for another fidelity, which
is also superlatively his, the fidelity of love for Christ,
which pours itself out in concrete and generous pastoral
service (cf. Jn 21:15ff.). We here at Rome have great
duties, precisely because of the mission of Peter, which
was established here and radiates from here. We have
greater duties than any other Church. — Pope Paul VI,
to a general audience, 7-10-69.

The priest is not a solitary;
he is a member of an organized body, of the universal
Church, of a diocese, and typically and superlatively of
his parish. It is the whole Church which must be adapted
to the new needs of the world; having concluded the Council, the Church is completely committed to this spiritual,
organizational renewal. Let us help her by our collaboration, our consent, our patience.

Beloved brothers and sons, have confidence in the
Church. Love her greatly. She is the direct object of the love
of Christ: "Christ loved the Church" (Eph 5:25). Love her
even with her limitations and her defects. Not, of course,
because of her limitations and defects or perhaps even
of her guilt, but because only by loving her can we heal
her and reveal clearly her shining beauty as the spouse
of Christ.

It is the Church which will save the world, that Church
which is the same today as she was yesterday and as she
will be tomorrow, that Church which, guided by the
Spirit and helped by all her children, always discovers
the means of renewing herself, of growing young again,
and of giving a new answer to ever renewed demands.
— Pope Paul VI, Message to Priests, 6-30-68.

"**Where is** the Church going?" It is going, in time and in the midst of mankind, toward Christ, in the awareness—greater than ever since the Council—that it has no other goal to attain. The Church goes forward in joy and patience, experiencing now progress, now difficulties, and always sustained by its eschatological hope: the Church is going foward to meet the Lord Jesus.—Pope Paul VI, to College of Cardinals, 2-24-71.

APOSTOLIC
DIMENSION

> Priests must take the lead in seeking the things of Jesus Christ, not the things that are their own (cf. Phil 2:21). They must work together with the lay faithful, and conduct themselves in their midst after the example of their Master, who among men "came not to be ministered to, but to minister, and to give his life as redemption for many" (Mt 20:28). —PO 9.

Pastoral Life: A Total Dedication

A MAN FOR OTHERS

ECCLESIAL AWARENESS

IN THE WORLD, BUT NOT

OF THE WORLD

NECESSARY DISCERNMENT

A MAN FOR OTHERS

Let me, as the representative of Christ, give you two basic principles to guide your priestly life: look upon your priestly office and its holy powers always as a service — a service serious and responsible, yet beautiful and dignified, for the welfare of mankind. Be their leader, consoler and friend; and perform your service out of love for the Church. Do not be a hindrance but a help in leading mankind to God. — Pope Paul VI, to newly-ordained priests, 10-12-68.

This is evident to all: the priest is a man who does not live for himself, but for others. He is the man of the community. Today this is the aspect of the priesthood which is most easily understood. Some find therein a reply to aggressive questions about the survival of the priesthood in the modern world which even interrogates the priest's very *raison d'être*. The service he renders to society, and, in particular, to the ecclesial community amply justifies the existence of his priesthood. The world needs him. The Church needs him. When We say this, We review all the needs of the human race. What category of persons has no need of the Christian message of faith and grace, of someone who devotes himself unselfishly and lovingly to others? Are there any limits to pastoral charity? And is not the need of such charity even greater where there is least desire for it?

In fields such as the missions, youth, schools, the sick, and, especially insistent today, the world of workers — in all these there is a continual urgent call upon the priestly heart. Can we then entertain any doubt as to our lack of a place, a function, a mission in modern life? On the contrary, we ask ourselves: How can we reply to so many who have need of us? How can we elevate our personal sacrifice to the rising level of our pastoral and apostolic duties? Now, as perhaps never before, the Church realizes that she is the indispensable channel of salvation, now, as never before, the dynamism of her *"dispensatio"* excels. Shall we then foolishly postulate a world without the Church, a Church without properly prepared and specialized and consecrated ministers? By his very nature the priest is a sign of Christ's love for mankind, and a witness to the amplitude with which the Church seeks to make that love real, to the final measure of the cross. — Pope Paul VI, Message to Priests, 6-30-68.

As they direct and nourish the People of God, may [priests] be aroused by the example of the Good Shepherd that they may give their life for their sheep (cf. Jn 10:11), ready for the supreme sacrifice following the example of priests who, even in our own day, have not shrunk from giving their lives. As they are leaders in the faith and as they "enter the sanctuary with confidence, through the blood of Christ" (Heb 10:19), they approach God "with sincere hearts in the full assurance of the faith" (Heb 10:22), they set up a sure hope for their faithful (cf. 2 Cor 1:7), that they may comfort those who are depressed by the same consolation wherewith God consoles them (cf. 2 Cor 1:4). As leaders of the community they cultivate an asceticism becoming to a shepherd of souls, renouncing their personal convenience, seeking not what is useful to themselves but to many, for their salvation (cf. 1 Cor 10:33), always making further progress to do their pastoral work better and, where needful, prepared to enter into new pastoral ways under the direction of the Spirit of Love, which breathes where It will (cf. Jn 3:8). — PO 13.

The demands of our ministry require a total gift of self and sever us from every binding or ambiguous tie with the world. At the same time they make us realize that we have been set up *for* the world, for its raising up and sanctification, for its spiritual enlivening and consecration. Woe to the shepherd who should forget even one sheep, for he will be called to give an account of all: it is the tradition of Scripture, of the prophets and of the gospels that reminds us of this with frightening severity. Christ's love, which has conferred upon us the charism of pastoral authority, has granted us this charism for the sake of all men, and especially "for those who have strayed in any way from the path of truth or who are ignorant of the gospel of Christ and His saving mercy." [1]
—Pope Paul VI, to bishops, 2-13-72.

The priest with grace and peace in his heart will face with generosity the manifold tasks of his life and ministry. If he performs these with faith and zeal he will find in them new occasions to show that he belongs entirely to Christ and His Mystical Body, for his own sanctification and the sanctification of others. The charity of Christ which urges him on (2 Cor 5:14) will help him not to renounce his higher feelings but to elevate and deepen them in a spirit of consecration in imitation of Christ the High Priest, who shared intimately in the life of mankind, loved and suffered for them (Heb 4:15), and of Paul the Apostle who shared in the cares of all (1 Cor 9:22; 2 Cor 11:29), in order to bring the light and power of the gospel of God's grace to shine in the world (Acts 20:24). —SCl 76.

Love, if it really be that, immediately leads to its absolute expression: total giving of self, sacrifice. This is what Jesus said of Himself, and this is what He did. He offered Himself as an example for those in the pastoral office to follow: "The good shepherd gives his life for his sheep" (Jn 10:11).

A twofold sum of pastoral requisites is involved here. There are subjective ones, consisting of the virtues proper to whoever exercises the cure of souls. And how many there are! They include concern (remember St. Paul's "pressing anxiety" [2 Cor 11:28]), disinterestedness, humility, tenderness (cf. St. Paul again, in his moving address to the Christians of Miletus: Acts 20:19).

On the other hand there are the objective requisites for the pastoral art: study of and experience in the business of caring for souls (this has already reached the point where the pastoral function may be classified among the sciences derived from theology); then there is pastoral theology, among the treasures of which is psychology (take, for example, the third book of St. Gregory the Great's famous *Regula pastoralis).* And there is sociology, so much in fashion at the moment. These all have a rightful and dignified place in the sum of objective requisites for pastoral office.

We may conclude from all this that the pastorate is not just empiricism and good-fellowship applied to community relationships. Still less is it neglect to have recourse to doctrinal principles which are indispensable for energy and fruitfulness in the pastoral apostolate. On the contrary, it means concrete, existential application of theological truths and spiritual charisms to the apostolate, that apostolate which reaches both individual souls and communities of persons, and which, as We said, is called the cure of souls. — Pope Paul VI, to a general audience, 7-16-70.

We would like the awareness of being destined as a pastor to serve your neighbor never to be extinguished within you: We would like it to make you always sensitive to the ills, the needs and the sufferings which surround the life of a priest. All classes of people seem to stretch out their hands to him and to ask for his understanding, his compassion and his assistance:

children, young people, the poor, the sick, those who hunger for bread and for justice, the unfortunate, the sinners—all have need of the help of the priest. Never say that your lives are irrelevant and useless. "Who is weak," says St. Paul, "and I am not weak?" (2 Cor 11:29)

If you have this sensitivity to the physical, moral and social deficiencies of mankind, you will also find in yourselves another sensitivity, that to the potential good which is always to be found in every human being; for a priest, every life is worthy of love. This twofold sensitivity, to evil and to good in man, is the beating of Christ's heart in that of the faithful priest. It is not without something of the miraculous, a miracle that is psychological, moral and, if you like, mystical, while at the same time being very much a social one. It is a miracle of charity in the heart of a priest. —Pope Paul VI, to newly-ordained Filipino priests, 11-28-70.

Let us be attentive to the questions that are expressed through the life of men, especially of the young: "What father among you," Jesus says to us, "would hand his son a stone when he asked for bread?" (Lk 11:11) Let us listen willingly to the questionings that come to disturb our peace and quiet. Let us bear patiently the hesitations of those who are groping for the light. Let us know how to walk in brotherly friendship with all those who, lacking the light we ourselves enjoy, are nevertheless seeking through the mists of doubt to reach their Father's house. But, if we share in their distress, let it be in order to try to heal it. If we hold up to them Christ Jesus, let it be as the Son of God made man to save us and to make us sharers in His life and not as a merely human figure, however wonderful and attractive (cf. 2 Jn 7-9). —Pope Paul VI, Apostolic Exhortation to All Bishops, 12-8-72.

1. CD 11.

ECCLESIAL AWARENESS

How is the Church today? The question is natural and spontaneous, but it opens out upon too many varied and broad horizons. Perhaps it even impels our curiosity beyond the limits of our human vision which is transcended by the design of God for the development of the life of the Church—a development which may become evident only in the world beyond time.

Even if we limit our gaze to the immediate and actually experienced observation of the present condition of the Church, the answer to our question cannot embrace the whole reality, for that reality is so vast and complex. But respecting our obligation "to watch and pray so as not to enter into temptation" (cf. Mt 26:41), we can ask ourselves at any time: What is the condition of the Church today? "Watchman, how goes the night?" (Is 21:11) is the voice of Scripture that still resounds in our ears. That voice wakens in our heart, which is also stirred by the contemporary spirit of observation, the desire and the need to take note of how things are progressing.

...We all notice that, in the people who make up the Church, especially scholars and youth, the Church is to a great extent undergoing the influence of the culture and manner of life characteristic of the outside world. As a result, an often excessive yielding to the fashion of the moment inclines the Church's members towards a relativism which calls for vigilance and temperance. We do not want to refuse recognition to all the good, just and beautiful things which are offered to the Church too in its pilgrimage through time by the truly rich and in certain aspects astounding experience of our age. Neither do we want in any way to discourage the apostolic solicitude of those who try to make themselves "all things to all men" (cf. 1 Cor 9:22) in order to draw all to Christ.

Today, uniform acting and accessible language are very important for establishing contact with the world to which we want to bring our message. But there is the danger that, however praiseworthy in its intentions, such an attitude may find expression in superficial conformity, that is, in the abandonment of precious elements in our cultural and moral heritage. It may also give rise to the temptation to make Christianity excessively easy for ourselves and for those to whom we would like to communicate it, by removing from it what it cannot give up: the mystery of its dogmas, the scandal of its cross and the fundamental need for its hierarchical communion.

Thus, alongside the consoling advance of the Church's self-awareness and to its power to expand and to engage in missionary activity, the Church's present circumstances reveal certain sad and worrying losses and certain painful difficulties, both external and—this We say with greater regret—internal.

But let us take care at once to comprehend the secret of providence hidden in these trials. Let us try, that is, to understand what a spur for purification, penance and fervor is found in them for us all. Let us try to respond to the beneficial call to greater faith, greater hope and greater charity that these trials constitute for any one of us who really wishes to love the Lord and lovingly serve the neighbor whom our age presents to our mission. "Power is at its best in weakness.... For it is when I am weak that I am strong" (2 Cor 12:9-10).—Pope Paul VI, to College of Cardinals, 6-24-71.

By their vocation and ordination, the priests of the New Testament are indeed set apart in a certain sense within the midst of God's people. But this is so, not that they may be made distant from this people or from any man, but that they be totally dedicated to the work for which the Lord has raised them up."[1]

Priests thus find their identity to the extent that they fully live the mission of the Church and exercise it in different ways in communion with the entire People of God, as pastors and ministers of the Lord in the Spirit, in order to fulfill by their work the plan of salvation in history. "By means of their own ministry, which deals principally with the Eucharist as the source of perfecting the Church, priests are in communion with Christ the Head and are leading others to this communion. Hence they cannot help realizing how much is yet wanting to the fullness of that Body, and how much therefore must be done if it is to grow from day to day." [2] — Ministerial Priesthood, Nov. 1971, Synod Document.

Having before our eyes the joys of the priestly life, this holy Synod cannot at the same time overlook the difficulties which priests experience in the circumstances of contemporary life. For we know how much economic and social conditions are transformed, and even more how much the customs of men are changed, how much the scale of values is changed in the estimation of men. As a result, the ministers of the Church and sometimes the faithful themselves feel like strangers in this world, anxiously looking for the ways and words with which to communicate with it. For there are new obstacles which have arisen to the faith: the seeming unproductivity of work done, and also the bitter loneliness which men experience can lead them to the danger of becoming spiritually depressed.

The world which today is entrusted to the loving ministry of the pastors of the Church is that which God so loved that He would give His only Son for it (cf. Jn 3:16). Truly this world, indeed weighed down with many sins but also endowed with many talents, provides the Church with the living stones (cf. 1 Pt 2:5) which are built up into the dwelling place of God in the Spirit (cf. Eph 2:22). This same Holy Spirit, while impelling the Church to open new ways to go to the world of today, suggests and favors the growth of fitting adaptations in the ministry of priests. — PO 22.

There is need of love for the Church and for the world in which the Church is present as a sacrament of salvation. The holy Church, God's people making its way to heaven, the guardian of the revealed word of God and the means of redemption, the spouse of Christ, washed by His precious blood, expects from us the witness of this full fidelity.

It is our duty to serve her, protect her, present her to the world. She becomes one body made up of us who are human beings living in definite conditions of time and history; and therefore she is obscured by our weaknesses, doubts and fears, so that she does not shine as Christ wished her to shine — He who nonetheless "loved the Church and sacrificed himself for her to make her holy. He made her clean by washing her in water with a form of words" (Eph 5:25-26). We must therefore ever strive for perfection, in order that we may give honor to her who has need of our activity. Let us hold back from no sacrifice, in order to make her truly that "signal for a distant nation" (Is 5:26).

When we love the Church in this way, we shall have for the world the love which we owe it because of our vocation. The men of today are waiting for the word to free their minds which are in suffering and anxiety. They look towards the Church to find if she is still able to answer their expectation or if they must seek refuge elsewhere. We must strive with all our strength that men should have faith in us, especially by loving them with fatherly and fraternal affection. — Pope Paul VI, at the close of the Synod, 11-18-71.

1. PO 3.   2. AG 39.

IN THE WORLD, BUT NOT OF THE WORLD

[Priests] **cannot be** ministers of Christ unless they be witnesses and dispensers of a life other than earthly life. But they cannot be of service to men if they remain strangers to the life and conditions of men.[1] Their ministry itself, by a special title, forbids that they be conformed to this world (cf. Rom 12:2); yet at the same time it requires that they live in this world among men. They are to live as good shepherds that know their sheep, and they are to seek to lead those who are not of this sheepfold that they, too, may hear the voice of Christ, so that there might be one fold and one shepherd (cf. Jn 10:14-16). To achieve this aim, certain virtues, which in human affairs are deservedly esteemed, contribute a great deal: such as goodness of heart, sincerity, strength and constancy of mind, zealous pursuit of justice, affability, and others. The Apostle Paul commends them saying: "Whatever things are true, whatever honorable, whatever just, whatever holy, whatever loving, whatever of good repute, if there be any virtue, if anything is worthy of praise, think upon these things" (Phil 4:8).[2] — PO 3.

Priests are admonished by their bishop in the sacred rite of ordination that they "be mature in knowledge" and that their doctrine be "spiritual medicine for the People of God."[3] The knowledge of the sacred minister ought to be sacred because it is drawn from sacred sources and directed to a sacred goal. Especially is it drawn from reading and meditating on the Sacred Scriptures,[4] and it is equally nourished by the study of the holy Fathers and other Doctors and monuments of tradition. In order, moreover, that they may give apt answers to questions posed by men of this age, it is necessary for priests to know well the doctrines of the magisterium and the councils and documents of the Roman Pontiffs and to consult the best of prudent writers of theological science.

Since human culture and also sacred science has progressed in our times, priests are urged to suitably and without interruption perfect their knowledge of divine things and human affairs and so prepare themselves to enter more opportunely into conversation with their contemporaries. — PO 19.

All truly Christian undertakings are related to the salvation of mankind, which, while it is of an eschatological nature, also embraces temporal matters. Every reality of this world must be subjected to the lordship of Christ. This however does not mean that the Church claims technical competence in the secular order, with disregard for the latter's autonomy.

The proper mission entrusted by Christ to the priest, as to the Church, is not of the political, economic or social order, but of the religious order[5]; yet, in the pursuit of his ministry, the priest can contribute greatly to the establishment of a more just secular order, especially in places where the human problems of injustice and oppression are more serious. He must always, however, preserve ecclesial communion and reject violence in words or deeds as not being in accordance with the gospel.

In fact, the word of the gospel which he proclaims in the name of Christ and the Church, and the effective grace of sacramental life which he administers should free man from his personal and social egoism and foster among men conditions of justice, which would be a sign of the love of Christ present among us.[6] — Ministerial Priesthood, Nov., 1971, Synod Document.

With priestly ordination, in communion with your bishop, you have received an intimate and unrepeatable configuration with Christ Jesus, in order to continue His divine mandate in the world.

This is your first mission, your principal task, your essential occupation, from which all the others draw justification and food. As Christ lived for the glory of the Father, obtaining in this way the salvation of men His brothers, so the first attribution of the priestly ministry is in being delegated to represent God in Christ, and thus to save the world. All other duties of a temporal, social, contingent character, are derived from this and must be set on this plane. Woe betide the priest who tries to be everything, do everything, the politician, the sociologist, the expert, the consultant, the organizer and so on, but fails in the specific mission that makes him a priest: the glory of God in sacrifice for his brothers, to whom he must communicate divine life in the life-bringing contact with Christ. — Pope Paul VI, to young priests, 6-12-71.

It is inadmissable that there should be mediocrity, dissipation, slackness, that there should be the predicaments of certain profane and worldly experiences. For you must not believe that to know the world it is necessary to have deplorable experience of it: I mean blind, instinctive and disorderly experience. He who remains unblemished by such bad experience can get to know the world better—"blessed are the pure of heart because they shall see"—and it is the same with you: do not seek to have the evil that is in the world.

It is necessary, it is true, to know the things and the miseries of this life, but like the doctor, who studies and treats, without taking the disease. On the contrary, he tries to become immunized, and the more he is immunized the fitter he is to bend over the patient, treat him and cure him.

It is the same for us. We must be immune from this obtruding profanation, this contamination, this impurity, this assault of sensuality, which comes from all sides today. And if we are really able to become immunized, to be resolute and sagacious in our moral conduct, if we are able to give our spiritual timbre an energy of faithfulness, which is then marked by the sign of the cross, we will, by the grace of God, be able to do something worthy of our vocation, during our pilgrimage in time, towards the eternal hope. — Pope Paul VI, to students of a major seminary, 4-1-71.

The priest is not for himself, but he is for others: the priest is the one who must pursue man in order to make a believer of him and not simply await for man to come to him. If his church is empty, he must go out "into the streets and alleys of the town," in search of the poor, and then again "to the open roads and and the hedgerows" and persuade guests, picked up here and there, to come in (cf. Lk 14:21-23). This apostolic urgency weighs heavily upon the hearts of many priests, whose churches have become deserted. And when this is so, how could We help admiring them; how could We help supporting them?

But let us be on guard, precisely with relation to the experimental and positive nature of the apostolate. To begin with, it is not always like this. There are still communities of the faithful overflowing in numbers and eager for a normal observance. Why leave them? Why should we change for them the method of the ministry, when it is still authentic, valid and magnificently fruitful? Would we not do an injustice to the fidelity of many good Christians in order to undertake adventures whose outcome is uncertain? And secondly, when it is sufficient to open a new church and with loving care welcome the people who spontaneously hurry there, eager for the divine word and for sacramental grace, why should we devise new and strange forms of apostolate, of dubious outcome and perhaps of short duration?

Would it not be better, perhaps, to perfect the traditional ones, and make them flourish again — as the Council teaches us — with pastoral realism, with new beauty, and with new effectiveness, before attempting others which often are arbitrary and of doubtful result, or of a result restricted to particular groups detached from the communion of the faithful? — Pope Paul VI, "Priests Should Be in the World, but Not of the World," address of 2-17-69.

Oh! We will not forget the word of Jesus, who commands us to leave the ninety-nine sheep in the desert who are safe, to go after that which is lost (cf. Lk 15:4); and particularly if the ratio — as happens today in certain situations — were the reverse, in other words, that of a single sheep in safety while those lost are ninety-nine. However, the principle of unity and of the completeness of our flock, the principle of pastoral love and of our responsibility toward souls and of their inestimable value, will always give us guidance.

We must take heed. The need, in fact the duty, of an effective mission and a mission inserted into the reality of the social life, can produce other troubles, such as that of devaluating the sacramental and liturgical ministry, as though it were a curb and an obstacle to a direct evangelization of the modern world; or the wish, somewhat widespread today, to make a priest a man like any other, in dress, in secular professions, in attendance at theatrical performances, in world experience, in social and political commitments, in the establishment of a family of his own with renunciation of holy celibacy.

They talk of wanting, in this way, to integrate the priest in society. Is this how we should interpret the magisterial word of Christ, who wants us to be in the world but not of the world? Did He not call and select His disciples, those who had to spread and continue the announcement of the kingdom of God, distinguishing and even separating them from the common way of living, and calling them to leave all things to follow Him alone? The whole gospel speaks of this qualification, of this "specialization" of the disciples who had then to serve as apostles.

Jesus detached them, not without a radical sacrifice on their part, from their everyday occupations, from their legitimate and normal interests, from their assimilation in the social setting, from their sacrosanct affections: and He wished them to be devoted to Him, with the complete gift of themselves, a commitment forever; counting, yes, on their free and spontaneous answer, but expecting a total renunciation, an heroic immolation.

Let us listen once more to the catalogue of the things we must deprive ourselves of, from the very lips of Jesus: "And everyone who has left house, or brothers, or sisters, or father, or mother, or children, or lands, for my name's sake..." (Mt 19:29). And the disciples were aware of this personal and paradoxical condition of theirs: it is Peter who speaks: "Behold, we have left all and followed you" (*ibid.* 27).

Can the disciple, the apostle, the priest, the genuine minister of the gospel be a man socially like other men? He can be poor, yes, like others; he can be a brother, yes, to others; he can be a servant, yes, to others; a victim, yes, for others; though at the same time endowed with a very lofty and very special function: "You are the salt of the earth.... You are the light of the world!" —Pope Paul VI, "Priests Should Be in the World, but Not of the World," address of 2-17-69.

The priestly ministry, even if compared with other activities, not only is to be considered as a fully valid human activity but indeed as more excellent than other activities, though this great value can be fully understood only in the light of faith. Thus, as a general rule, the priestly ministry shall be a full-time occupation. Sharing in the secular activities of men is by no means to be considered the principal end nor can such participation suffice to give expression to priests' specific responsibility. Priests, without being of the world and without taking it as their model, must nevertheless live in the world,[7] as witnesses and stewards of another life.[8]

In order to determine in concrete circumstances whether secular activity is in accord with the priestly ministry, inquiry should be made whether and in what way those duties and activities serve the mission of the Church, those who have not yet received the gospel message and finally the Christian community. This is to be judged by the local bishop with his presbyterium, and if necessary in consultation with the episcopal conference.

When activities of this sort, which ordinarily pertain to the laity, are as it were demanded by the priest's very mission to evangelize, they must be harmonized with his other ministerial activities, in those circumstances where they can be considered as necessary forms of true ministry.[9] — Ministerial Priesthood, Nov., 1971, Synod Document.

Let priests be mindful of the laity's maturity, which is to be valued highly when it is a question of their specific role.

Leadership or active militancy on behalf of any political party is to be excluded by every priest unless, in concrete and exceptional circumstances, this is truly required by the good of the community, and receives the consent of the bishop after consultation with the priests' council and, if circumstances call for it, with the episcopal conference.

The priority of the specific mission which pervades the entire priestly existence must therefore always be kept in mind so that, with great confidence, and having a renewed experience of the things of God, priests may be able to announce these things efficaciously and with joy to the men who await them.

Together with the entire Church, priests are obliged, to the utmost of their ability, to select a definite pattern of action, when it is question of the defense of fundamental human rights, the promotion of the full development of persons and the pursuit of the cause of peace and justice; the means must indeed always be consonant with the gospel. These principles are all valid not only in the individual sphere, but also in the social field; in this regard priests should help the laity to devote themselves to forming their consciences rightly.

In circumstances in which there legitimately exist different political, social and economic options, priests like all citizens have a right to select their personal options. But since political options are by nature contingent and never in an entirely adequate and perennial way interpret the gospel, the priest, who is the witness of things to come, must keep a certain distance from any political office or involvement. — Ministerial Priesthood, Nov., 1971, Synod Document.

All pastors should remember that by their daily conduct and concern (cf. Phil 1:27) they are revealing the face of the Church to the world, and men will judge the power and truth of the Christian message thereby. By their lives and speech, in union with religious and their faithful, may they demonstrate that even now the Church by her presence alone and by all the gifts which she contains, is an unspent fountain of those virtues which the modern world needs the most. — GS 44.

1. EcS, AAS 56 (1964), pp. 627 and 638.
2. Cf. St. Polycarp, *Epist. ad Philippenses*, 6, 1 (ed. F. X. Funk, *Apostolic Fathers*, I, p. 303).
3. Roman Pontifical on the Ordination of Priests.
4. Cf. LG 65, AAS 57 (1965), pp. 64-65.
5. Cf. GS 42.
6. Cf. *op. cit.* 58.
7. Cf. PO 3, 17; Jn 17:14-16.
8. Cf. PO 3.
9. Cf. *op. cit.* 8.

NECESSARY DISCERNMENT

The diversity of functions is a constitutional principle in the Church of God. In the first place, it has reference to the ministerial priesthood: let us be careful not to lose this specific function because of a misunderstood purpose for assimilation, one of "democratization," as it is said today, in the environmental society: "But if the salt becomes tasteless, what can make it salty again? It is good for nothing and can only be thrown out to be trampled underfoot by men" (Mt 5:13).

These are words of the Lord, which should make us reflect on the discernment necessary in applying the formula recalled: to be in the world, but not of the world.

Lack of this discernment, of which the ecclesiastical education, ascetic tradition, canon law, have spoken so much to us, may bring about exactly the opposite effect to the one we had hoped to bring about when imprudently abandoning it: effectiveness, renewal, modernity.

The effectiveness of the priest's presence and action in the world can thus be done away with—the very effectiveness we wanted to achieve when we reacted imprudently to the separation of the priest from the rest of society. It can be wiped out—in the esteem and trust of the people, and by a practical demand to devote to profane occupations and to human affections: time, heart, freedom, superiority of spirit (cf. 1 Cor 2:15), which the priestly ministry alone wished to keep for itself. — Pope Paul VI, "Priests Should Be in the World, but Not of the World," address of 2-17-69.

The apostles, their successors and those who cooperate with them, are sent to announce to mankind Christ, the Savior. Their apostolate is based on the power of God, who very often shows forth the strength of the gospel on the weakness of its witnesses.

All those dedicated to the ministry of God's word must use the ways and means proper to the gospel which in a great many respects differ from the means proper to the earthly city. —GS 76.

A priest should ask himself: Am I really what I should be? Am I really where I should be? Am I really doing the work I ought to do? However, it seems to Us that these weighty questions can easily be answered and in this way: do well what the Church gives you to do. Give no credit to the novelties of the present day, they are often subversive. Do not think that you will find in them a better solution nor an easy actuation of the great choice the Lord has made in your persons.

Generally speaking, there are two recurring questions which lead to disquiet. One is to ascertain the authenticity of one's vocation. To this, we all agree. Certainly we must verify if we are true, authentic priests of Christ and of His Church. And the second question: we want to be close to the world; again, We can but praise this very lawful preoccupation, as long as those concerned in this way do not want to break through all the accepted structures and discard a discipline that the Church has created and is continually perfecting. In order to be nearer the world, some priests think that it is sufficient for them to change their habit, adopting the worldly ways of lay people and exercising a profession of their own. Beware of this casuistic behavior, because the salt of the earth will thus lose its flavor. How can worldly priests go out to a world that they must convert? This assimilation of the world may give them the illusion of a closer contact with souls, but take heed! It can be the means of deleting the specifically efficacious function which, as priests, we must fulfill, that which distinguishes us and places us at the very nerve center of the people, but does not incorporate us materially nor socially with them to whom we must address our message.

Willingly, We assure you of Our prayer, Our blessing, Our understanding and Our desire to help you to be genuine, operative, authentic instruments of the gospel of the Lord. We Ourself would like to be an example for you to follow. We would like to be with you, right in your ranks, to learn about the difficulties that beset you. We would like to say also to you that you will find the fruitfulness of your ministry on the thresholds of your presbyteries and churches.... The people are there, you have but to open your hearts to them, to understand them and to serve them. Hold fast to the certainty that the sacramental and ministerial mission entrusted to you, as priests, cannot be compared to any other. Whosoever lives his vocation in its integrity cannot but sense its total fullness, because he knows that he is the living instrument of the transmission of God's grace to souls. The efficaciousness of the priest's ministry is incomparable; no other means can take its place. Courage then, dear brothers..., courage!
— Pope Paul VI, to priests and seminarians, 12-26-68.

In addition to inexhaustible and supernatural sources of apostolic fortitude, we can find other natural sources, near to our inner reflection and to our human experience. One...is the study of the new relationships that arise between us, our ministry, and contemporary man. It is being carried out by everyone, moreover: research on the phenomenology of modern life. The latter, as we know, but perhaps not enough, is in the phase of change, or at least of becoming more knowable.

It is this mobility, it is this new knowledge that sometimes disconcerts us, frightens us, or at least intimidates us. We must observe modern life and get to know it; it is a new duty, which makes us emerge from habit (We do not mean tradition!), empiricism, customary formalism. We must become better judges of the souls, the spirits of our time.

There is the danger that this observation may prevail over the norm of faith and God's law; today relativism is a great temptation. But once this temptation is overcome, that is, once experimental data (statistics, psychological and sociological reviews, certain historical determinisms) have been given their relative and experimental value, the new knowledge of men and of the world (let us recall the Master's words: "I know mine" [Jn 10:14]), enables us to deal more courageously with the rising problems of new and threatening situations.

We will discover many things thanks to this vigilance, more necessary than ever in us pastors now. The two main ones are: the discovery of our truths as inalienable, never to be renounced in any way, faith above all; and the new possibilities that the human spirit presents to the initiative of our ministry.

Let us remember: the further away man is from us, that is, from our announcement of truth and hope, the more he needs us. It is a question of discovering, and if possible awakening, this secret need, and of offering him wisely our gift of charity and joy. He who loves, discovers; he who loves, invents the art of approaching souls and revealing Christ to them. And we believe that a new confidence must strengthen our ministry: confidence also in men who, fundamentally, when they are not consciously corrupt in thought and in morals, are often better than they seem — more unhappy than bad, more deluded than obstinate, more in need of truth and love than of abandonment and rejection. — Pope Paul VI, to Italian bishops, 6-19-71.

We are not unaware of the difficulty which a priest has when he has to find the way to transmit the message of salvation to modern man. He feels the weight of a society which says that Christian principles are its own principles — justice, respect for the human person, desire for peace and unity — but is perhaps profoundly estranged from God's mind, from Christ's mind.

For the Council to attain its purpose, it is necessary to know the concrete world in which our priestly ministry is exercised. This requires constant attention to the deficiencies, the miseries and above all the hopes which simmer about us. It requires a mind ready to go out to meet these things. This is how the Church can, through your service, achieve a lively dialogue with the world.

It also demands total commitment from you, and no nostalgia for the secular world, so that through your personal testimony the brethren may be able to think about your announcement of the gospel message, understand it, and imitate it. — Pope Paul VI, to Spanish bishops, 6-1-70.

Lord, help us to understand. We must learn to love men in this way, and then to serve them accordingly. It will cost us nothing to serve them, but it will be our honor, our aspiration. We will never feel separated from them socially just because in virtue of our office we are and must be distinct from them. We will never refuse to be their brothers and comforters, their teachers and servants. We will be enriched by their poverty, and we will be poor in the midst of their wealth. We will be able to understand their concerns and to transform them not into anger and violence but into the strong and peaceful force of constructive work. We will hold dear the fact that our service is silent (Mt 6:3) and disinterested (cf. Mt 10:8), sincere in fortitude, in love and in sacrifice, confident that Your power will one day make it efficacious (Jn 4:37). We will always have before us and within us Your one holy Catholic Church, on pilgrimage towards its eternal goal; and we will carry impressed in our memories and our hearts our apostolic motto: "On behalf of Christ, therefore we are acting as ambassadors" (2 Cor 5:20). — Pope Paul VI, to newly-ordained priests and deacons, 9-5-68.

In the building up of the Church, priests must treat all with exceptional kindness in imitation of the Lord. They should act towards men, not as seeking to please them (cf. Gal 1:10), but in accord with the demands of Christian doctrine and life. They should teach them and admonish them as beloved sons (cf. 1 Cor 4:14), according to the words of the Apostle: "Be urgent in season, out of season; reprove, entreat, rebuke with all patience and teaching" (2 Tm 4:2). [1] — PO 6.

Pastoral Care and Parish Response

SOUL OF THE PARISH

PRIESTHOOD OF THE FAITHFUL

A RIGHT SET OF VALUES

CREATING APOSTLES

CATECHESIS IN ACTION

SOUL OF THE PARISH

Priests have been placed in the midst of the laity to lead them to the unity of charity, "loving one another with fraternal love, eager to give one another precedence" (Rom 12:10). It is their task, therefore, to reconcile differences of mentality in such a way that no one need feel himself a stranger in the community of the faithful. They are defenders of the common good, with which they are charged in the name of the bishop. At the same time, they are strenuous assertors of the truth, lest the faithful be carried about by every wind of doctrine (cf. Eph 4:14). They are united by a special solicitude with those who have fallen away from the use of the sacraments, or perhaps even from the faith. Indeed, as good shepherds, they should not cease from going out to them. — PO 9.

In the exercise of their teaching office it is the duty of pastors to preach God's word to all the Christian people so that, rooted in faith, hope and charity, they will grow in Christ, and as a Christian community bear witness to that charity which the Lord commended (cf. Jn 13:35). It is also the duty of pastors to bring the faithful to a full knowledge of the mystery of salvation through a catechetical instruction which is consonant with each one's age. In imparting this instruction they should seek not only the assistance of religious but also the cooperation of the laity, establishing also the Confraternity of Christian Doctrine.

In discharging their duty of sanctifying their people, pastors should see to it that the celebration of the Eucharistic Sacrifice is the center and culmination of the whole life of the Christian community. They should labor without stint that the faithful are nourished with spiritual food through the devout and frequent reception of the sacraments and through intelligent and active participation in the liturgy. Pastors should also be mindful of how much the sacrament of Penance contributes to developing the Christian life and, therefore, should always make themselves available to hear the confessions of the faithful. If necessary, they should invite the assistance of priests who are experienced in various languages.

In fulfilling their office as shepherd, pastors should take pains to know their own flock. Since they are the servants of all the sheep, they should encourage a full Christian life among the individual faithful and also in families, in associations especially dedicated to the apostolate, and in the whole parish community. Therefore, they should visit homes and schools to the extent that their pastoral work demands. They should pay special attention to adolescents and youth. They should devote themselves with a paternal love to the poor and the sick. They should have a particular concern for workingmen. Finally, they should encourage the faithful to assist in the works of the apostolate. — CD 30.

Let the spiritual shepherds recognize and promote the dignity as well as the responsibility of the laity in the Church. Let them willingly employ their prudent advice. Let them confidently assign duties to them in the service of the Church, allowing them freedom and room for action. Further, let them encourage lay people so that they may undertake tasks on their own initiative. Attentively in Christ, let them consider with fatherly love the projects, suggestions and desires proposed by the laity (cf. 1 Thes 5:19 and 1:10, 4:1). However, let the shepherds respectfully acknowledge that just freedom which belongs to everyone in this earthly city.

A great many wonderful things are to be hoped for from this familiar dialogue between the laity and their spiritual leaders: in the laity a strengthened sense of personal responsibility, a renewed enthusiasm, a more ready application of their talents to the projects of their spiritual leaders. The latter, on the other hand, aided by the experience of the laity, can more clearly and more incisively come to decisions regarding both spiritual and temporal matters. In this way, the whole Church, strengthened by each one of its members, may more effectively fulfill its mission for the life of the world. —LG 37.

As educators in the faith, priests must see to it either by themselves or through others that the faithful are led individually in the Holy Spirit to a development of their own vocation according to the gospel, to a sincere and practical charity, and to that freedom with which Christ has made us free (cf. Gal 4:3; 5:1 and 13). Ceremonies however beautiful, or associations however flourishing, will be of little value if they are not directed towards the education of men to Christian maturity.[2] In furthering this, priests should help men to see what is required and what is God's will in the important and unimportant events of life.

Also, Christians should be taught that they live not only for themselves, but, according to the demands of the new law of charity; as every man has received grace, he must administer the same to others (cf. Pt 4:10ff.). In this way, all will discharge in a Christian manner their duties in the community of men. —PO 6.

At this hour of God, it is necessary to intensify pastoral and missionary work, as something essential and fundamental that gives a sense and perspective to all the other activities of Christians. Initiatives must be undertaken to promote priestly and religious vocations, and also to help improve the formation of future priests and of the priests already occupied in apostolic tasks, so that, endowed with real spiritual and human maturity, they may completely meet the needs of their great mission. Special attention and interest must be dedicated to the preparation of lay apostles who, impelled by a real living Christianity, will commit themselves actively and generously to the transformation of society. In particular, thought must go to the young, the protagonists of a future that is already beginning, so that they may really find in the Church the inspiration and the complete view of man that they are looking for in order to be able to change the face of the world and make it really just and fraternal! — Pope Paul VI, letter to C.E.L.A.M., 5-10-71.

Priests should remember that in performing their office they are never alone, but strengthened by the power of almighty God, and believing in Christ who called them to share in His Priesthood, they should devote themselves to their ministry with complete trust, knowing that God can cause charity to grow in them. — PO 22.

1. Cf. *Didascalia*, II, 34, 3; II, 46, 6; II, 47, 1 (ed. F.X. Funk, *Didascalia and Constitutions*, I, pp. 116, 142 and 143).
2. Cf. St. Jerome, *Epistles*, 58, 7 (PL 22, 584).

PRIESTHOOD OF THE FAITHFUL

Christ the Lord, High Priest taken from among men, (cf. Heb 5:1-5) made the new people "a kingdom and priests to God the Father" (cf. Rev 1:6; cf. 5:9-10). The baptized, by regeneration and the anointing of the Holy Spirit, are consecrated as a spiritual house and a holy priesthood, in order that through all those works which are those of the Christian man they may offer spiritual sacrifices and proclaim the power of Him who has called them out of darkness into His marvelous light (cf. 1 Pt 2:4-10). Therefore all the disciples of Christ, persevering in prayer and praising God (cf. Acts 2:42, 47), should present themselves as a living sacrifice, holy and pleasing to God (cf. Rom 12:1). Everywhere on earth they must bear witness to Christ and give an answer to those who seek an account of that hope of eternal life which is in them (cf. 1 Pt 3:15).

Though they differ from one another in essence and not only in degree, the common priesthood of the faithful and the ministerial or hierarchical priesthood are nonetheless interrelated: each of them in its own special way is a participation in the one priesthood of Christ.[1] The ministerial priest, by the sacred power he enjoys, teaches and rules the priestly people; acting in the person of Christ, he makes present the Eucharistic Sacrifice, and offers it to God in the name of all the people. But the faithful, in virtue of their royal priesthood, join in the offering of the Eucharist.[2] They likewise exercise that priesthood in receiving the sacraments, in prayer and thanksgiving, in the witness of a holy life, and by self-denial and active charity. — LG 10.

By the waters of Baptism, as by common right, Christians are made members of the Mystical Body of Christ the Priest, and by the "character" which is imprinted on their souls, they are appointed to give worship to God. Thus they participate, according to their condition, in the priesthood of Christ.

The fact, however, that the faithful participate in the Eucharistic Sacrifice, does not mean that they also are endowed with priestly power.

There are today those who, approximating to errors long since condemned,[3] teach that in the New Testament by the word "priesthood" is meant only that priesthood which applies to all who have been baptized and hold that the command by which Christ gave power to His apostles at the Last Supper to do what He Himself had done, applies directly to the entire Christian Church, and that thence, and thence only, arises the hierarchical priesthood. Hence they assert that the people are possessed of a true priestly power, while the priest only acts in virtue of an office committed to him by the community. Wherefore they look on the Eucharistic Sacrifice as a "concelebration," in the literal meaning of that term, and consider it more fitting that priests should "concelebrate" with the people present than that they should offer the sacrifice privately when the people are absent.

...The priest acts for the people only because he represents Jesus Christ, who is Head of all His members and offers Himself in their stead. Hence he goes to the altar as the minister of Christ, inferior to Christ but superior to the people.[4] The people, on the other hand, since they in no sense represent the divine Redeemer and are not a mediator between themselves and God, can in no way possess the sacerdotal power. — MD 82-84, 88.

1. Cf. Pius XII, Alloc. *Magnificate Dominum*, 11-2-54: AAS 46 (1954), p. 669. MD 20: AAS 39 (1947), p. 555.

2. Cf. Pius XI, Encycl. Letter *Miserentissimus Redemptor*, 5-8-28: AAS 20 (1928), p. 171f. Pius XII, Alloc. *Vous Nous Avez*, 9-22-56: AAS 48 (1956), p. 714.

3. Cf. Conc. Trid., Sess. XXIII, c. 4.

4. Cf. Robert Bellarmine, *De Missa*, II, cap. 4.

A RIGHT SET OF VALUES

The whole Church must work vigorously in order that men may become capable of rectifying the distortion of the temporal order and directing it to God through Christ. Pastors must clearly state the principles concerning the purpose of creation and the use of temporal things and must offer the moral and spiritual aids by which the temporal order may be renewed in Christ.—AA 7.

True though it is that the evils from which mankind suffers today come in part from economic instability and from the struggle of interests regarding a more equal distribution of the goods which God has given man as a means of sustenance and progress, it is no less true that their root is deeper and more intrinsic, belonging to the sphere of religious belief and moral convictions which have been perverted by the progressive alienation of the peoples from that unity of doctrine, faith, customs and morals which once was promoted by the tireless and beneficent work of the Church. If it is to have any effect, the re-education of mankind must be, above all things, spiritual and religious. Hence, it must proceed from Christ as from its indispensable foundation; it must be actuated by justice and crowned by charity.—SP.

Perhaps never before has the world had such need of spiritual values, and We are convinced, never has it been so disposed to welcome their proclamation. For the most affluent regions of the world are fast discovering for themselves that happiness does not consist in possessions; they are learning from a bitter "experience of emptiness" how true are our Lord's words:

"Not on bread alone does man live, but on every word that proceeds from the mouth of God" (Mt 4:4).

We must tell men, and keep on telling them that "the key, the focal point, and the goal of human history" is to be found in our Lord and Master.[1] We must tell them that this is true not only for believers, but also applies to everyone, for whom Christ died and whose ultimate vocation is to correspond to God's design: "to unite all things in him, things in heaven and things on earth" (Eph 1:10). — Pope Paul VI, message for Mission Sunday, 6-25-71.

The hour now striking on the clock of history demands great courage indeed from all the Church's children. In a very special way it calls for the *courage of truth*, that which the Lord in person recommended to His disciples, when He said, "Let your yes be yes, and your no, no" (Mt 5:37).

How often divine Scripture warns us about such things! Let us not listen to those who claim to be bringing us a different gospel (cf. Gal 1:8-9). How many *gnoses* have disappeared during the course of the centuries, even though in their own times they seemed to be much more intelligent things than the mystery of the cross and the name of Jesus the Savior (cf. 1 Cor 18:25).

Idols are always rising up again. But what would Christianity be if it sought to reduce itself to an ideology, to a naturalistic sociology? What would the Church be if it let itself break up into so many sects? No, Christ came to free man from all idols, above all from those idols which his own mind shapes from century to century: "with the savage energy of the passions and the destructive scepticism of human intelligence in religious matters...no truth, however sacred, can long resist it."[2]

The courage of truth is demanded from Christians more and more if they are to remain faithful to their vocation of animating this new world which is being sought.

May our faith in Christ never weaken in this age of ours which is distinguished, as was St. Augustine's, by real "poverty and penury of truth." [3] May everyone be ready *vitam impendere vero*, to pledge his life to truth! [4]

Courage to proclaim the truth is the first and indispensable charity which pastors of souls ought to exercise. Never, not even under the pretext of charity towards one's neighbor, let us permit a minister of the gospel to utter a purely human word. The salvation of mankind is at stake. Therefore, while the memory of Pentecost is still green, We appeal to all responsible pastors to raise their voices when necessary, with the strength of the Holy Spirit (cf. Acts 1:8) to cleanse what is dirty, to warm what is lukewarm, to strengthen what is weak, to enlighten what is dark.

More than at any other time this is the hour of clarity for the Church's faith. That faith calls on us to illuminate the darkness of human realities with the lightning of the gospel message, in search of that spiritual peace which arises from possession of the truth and from love of prayer, according to the great and beautiful saying of Our predecessor upon the Chair of the Church of Milan, St. Ambrose: Peace is good and necessary, so that no one shall be troubled by uncertainties or shaken by the storm of bodily passions, but that calm attention to worship of God shall continue in simplicity of faith and tranquillity of mind. [5] — Pope Paul VI, to College of Cardinals, 5-18-70.

The source and root of all evils which affect individuals, peoples and nations with a kind of poison and confuse the minds of many is this: ignorance of the truth — and not only ignorance, but at times a contempt for, and deliberate turning away from it.

This is the source of all manner of errors which, like contagious diseases, pass deep into minds and into the very bloodstream of human society, and turn everything upside down with serious damage to all individuals and to the whole human race....

If so much labor and care is expended today in the learning and mastery of human knowledge so that our generation boasts—and with perfect right—of the marvellous progress made in the field of scientific research, why do we not expend equal, or greater industry, skill and ingenuity in assimilating by some sure and safe method, doctrines which affect not earthly and mortal life, but the life in heaven which will have no end? Then alone, when we have reached the truth which has its source in the gospel, and which must be introduced into life's activities, then only, We say, will our minds find rest in peace and joy. This joy will far exceed that satisfaction which can arise from investigation into human affairs and from these wonderful inventions which we use today and which are daily extolled to the skies. —APC.

1. GS 10.
2. Cardinal John Henry Newman, *Apologia pro Vita Sua, A History of My Religious Opinions* (Longmans: London, 1902), Chapter 5.
3. Serm. 11, 11; *Miscellanea Agostiniana* (1930), p. 256.
4. Juvenal, *Sat.* IV, 91.
5. *De Spiritu Sancto* I, 12, 126; G.S.E.L., (ed. Faller, 79, 9, p. 69).

CREATING APOSTLES

The hierarchy should promote the apostolate of the laity, provide it with spiritual principles and support, direct the conduct of this apostolate to the common good of the Church, and attend to the preservation of doctrine and order.

The hierarchy entrusts to the laity certain functions which are more closely connected with pastoral duties, such as the teaching of Christian doctrine, certain liturgical actions, and the care of souls. By virtue of this mission, the laity are fully subject to higher ecclesiastical control in the performance of this work.

As regards works and institutions in the temporal order, the role of the ecclesiastical hierarchy is to teach and authentically interpret the moral principles to be followed in temporal affairs. Furthermore, they have the right to judge, after careful consideration of all related matters and consultation with experts, whether or not such works and institutions conform to moral principles and the right to decide what is required for the protection and promotion of values of the supernatural order.

Bishops, pastors of parishes, and other priests of both branches of the clergy should keep in mind that the right and duty to exercise this apostolate is common to all the faithful, both clergy and laity, and that the laity also have their own roles in building up the Church.[1] For this reason they should work fraternally with the laity in and for the Church and take special care of the lay persons in these apostolic works.[2]

Special care should be taken to select priests who are capable of promoting particular forms of the apostolate of the laity and are properly trained.[3] Those who are engaged in this ministry represent the hierarchy in their pastoral activity by virtue of the mission they receive from the hierarchy. Always adhering faithfully to the spirit and teaching of the Church, they should promote proper relations between laity and hierarchy. They should devote themselves to nourishing the spiritual life and an apostolic attitude in the Catholic societies entrusted to them; they should contribute their wise counsel to the apostolic activity of these associations and promote their undertakings. Through continuous dialogue with the laity, these priests should carefully investigate which forms make apostolic activity more fruitful. They should promote the spirit of unity within the association as well as between it and others. —AA 24, 25.

        Priests must sincerely acknowledge and promote the dignity of the laity and the part proper to them in the mission of the Church. And they should hold in high honor that just freedom which is due to everyone in the earthly city. They must willingly listen to the laity, consider their wants in a fraternal spirit, recognize their experience and competence in the different areas of human activity, so that together with them they will be able to recognize the signs of the times. While trying the spirits to see if they are of God (cf. 1 Jn 4:1), priests should uncover with a sense of faith, acknowledge with joy and foster with diligence the various humble and exalted charisms of the laity. Among the other gifts of God, which are found in abundance among the laity, those are worthy of special mention by which not a few of the laity are attracted to a higher spiritual life. Likewise, they should confidently entrust to the laity duties in the service of the Church, allowing them freedom and room for action; in fact, they should invite them on suitable occasions to undertake works on their own initiative. —PO 9.

        Today there is a phenomenon of spontaneous associative growth in certain sectors of the People of God. The fear that it may assume, with charismatic pretexts, closed and sometimes contesting forms, must not prevent us from looking carefully after these groups, which are often capable of spiritual intensity and bold initiatives of charity.

On the contrary, let us see with pleasure, and also with hope and admiration, in some cases, how young people belonging to similar groups are able to create initiatives in the field of social work that demand personal sacrifice. This on the part of the poor is a great sign of real Christian vitality, and deserves our esteem and support in itself. As charity to God produces charity to one's neighbor, we must hope that the latter in its turn will produce charity to God, and therefore to the whole family of God, the Church, a real school and family of Christians who wish to be, like the early Christians after Pentecost, one heart and one soul. —Pope Paul VI, to Italian bishops, 6-19-71.

The apostolate can attain its maximum effectiveness only through a diversified and thorough formation. This is demanded not only by the continuous spiritual and doctrinal progress of the lay person himself but also by the accomodation of his activity to circumstances varying according to the affairs, persons, and duties involved.

Since the laity share in their own way in the mission of the Church, their apostolic formation is specially characterized by the distinctively secular and particular quality of the lay state and by its own form of the spiritual life.

The formation for the apostolate presupposes a certain human and well-rounded formation adapted to the natural abilities and conditions of each lay person. Well-informed about the modern world, the lay person should be a member of his own community and adjusted to its culture.

However, the lay person should learn especially how to perform the mission of Christ and the Church by basing his life on belief in the divine mystery of creation and redemption and by being sensitive to the movement of the Holy Spirit who gives life to the People of God and who urges all to love God the Father as well as the world and men in Him. This formation should be deemed the basis and condition for every successful apostolate.

In addition to spiritual formation, a solid doctrinal instruction in theology, ethics, and philosophy adjusted to differences of age, status, and natural talents, is required. The importance of general culture along with practical and technical formation should also be kept in mind.

To cultivate good human relations, truly human values must be fostered, especially the art of living fraternally and cooperating with others and of striking up friendly conversation with them.

Since formation for the apostolate cannot consist in merely theoretical instruction, from the beginning of their formation the laity should gradually and prudently learn how to view, judge and do all things in the light of faith as well as to develop and improve themselves along with others through doing, thereby entering into active service of the Church.[4] This formation, always in need of improvement because of the increasing maturity of the human person and the proliferation of problems, requires an ever deeper knowledge and planned activity. In the fulfillment of all the demands of formation, the unity and integrity of the human person must be kept in mind at all times so that his harmony and balance may be safeguarded and enhanced.

In this way the lay person engages himself wholly and actively in the reality of the temporal order and effectively assumes his role in conducting the affairs of this order. At the same time, as a living member and witness of the Church, he renders the Church present and active in the midst of temporal affairs.[5] —AA 28, 29.

1. Cf. Pius XII, allocution to the second convention of laymen representing all nations on the promotion of the apostolate, 10-5-57: AAS 49 (1957), p. 927.
2. Cf. LG 37: AAS 57 (1965), pp. 442-443.

3. Cf. Pius XII, Apostolic Exhortation *Menti Nostrae*, 9-23-50: AAS 42 (1950), p. 660.

4. Cf. Pius XII, allocution to the first international Boy Scouts congress, 6-6-52: AAS 44 (1952), pp. 579-580; MM, AAS 53 (1961) p. 456.

5. Cf. LG, p. 33: AAS 57 (1965), p. 39.

CATECHESIS IN ACTION

Bishops should take pains that catechetical instruction — which is intended to make the faith, as illumined by teaching, a vital, explicit and effective force in the lives of men — be given with sedulous care to both children and adolescents, youths and adults. In this instruction a suitable arrangement should be observed as well as a method suited to the matter that is being treated and to the character, ability, age, and circumstances of the life of the students. Finally, they should see to it that this instruction is based on Sacred Scripture, tradition, the liturgy, magisterium, and life of the Church. — CD 14.

The training for the apostolate should start with the children's earliest education. In a special way, however, adolescents and young persons should be initiated into the apostolate and imbued with its spirit. This formation must be perfected throughout their whole life in keeping with the demands of new responsibilities. It is evident, therefore, that those who have the obligation to provide a Christian education also have the duty of providing formation for the apostolate. — AA 30.

The function entrusted to the catechist demands of him a fervent sacramental and spiritual life, a practice of prayer, and a deep feeling for the excellence of the Christian message and for the power it has to transform one's life; it also demands of him the pursuit of the charity, humility, and prudence which allow the Holy Spirit to complete His fruitful work in those being taught.

It is necessary that ecclesiastical authorities regard the formation of catechists as a task of the greatest importance.

This formation is meant for all catechists,[1] both lay and religious, and also for Christian parents, who will be able to receive therefrom effective help for taking care of the initial and occasional catechesis for which they are responsible. This formation is meant for deacons, and especially for priests, for "by the power of the sacrament of Orders, and in the image of the eternal High Priest (cf. Heb 5:1-10; 7:24; 9:11-28), they are consecrated to preach the gospel, shepherd the faithful, and celebrate divine worship as true priests of the New Testament."[2] Indeed, in individual parishes the preaching of the word of God is committed chiefly to the priests, who are obliged to open the riches of Sacred Scripture to the faithful, and to explain the mysteries of the faith and the norms of Christian living in homilies throughout the course of the liturgical year.[3]

Finally, the formation is meant for teachers of religion in public schools, whether these belong to the Church or to the state. To carry out a task of such great importance, only persons should be selected who are distinguished for talent, doctrine, and spiritual life.[4] —*Catechetical Directory* 115.

Since every important act in the Church participates in the ministry of the word, and since catechesis always has a relation to the universal life of the Church, it follows that catechetical action must necessarily be coordinated with the over-all pastoral action. The aim of this cooperation is to have the Christian community grow and develop in a harmonious and orderly fashion; for, surely, although it has distinct aspects because of the various functions, it nevertheless strives toward a single basic goal.

It is necessary, therefore, that catechesis be associated with other pastoral activities,[5] that is, with the biblical, liturgical, and ecumenical movements, with the lay apostolate and social action, and so on. Besides, it must be kept in mind that this cooperation is necessary from the very outset, that is, from the time that studies and plans for the organization of pastoral work are started. — *Catechetical Directory* 129.

Shepherds of souls should always keep in mind the obligation they have of safeguarding and promoting the enlightenment of Christian existence through the word of God for people of all ages and in all historical circumstances,[6] so that it may be possible to have contact with every individual and community in the spiritual state in which each one is.

They should also remember that catechesis for adults, since it deals with persons who are capable of an adherence that is fully responsible, must be considered the chief form of catechesis. All the other forms, which are indeed always necessary, are in some way oriented to it. In obedience to the norms of the Second Vatican Council, shepherds of souls should also strive "to re-establish or better adapt the instruction of adult catechumens."[7] — *Catechetical Directory* 20.

Those to be taught, especially if they are adults, can contribute in an active way to the progress of the catechesis. Thus, they should be asked how they understand the Christian message and how they can explain it in their own words. Then a comparison should be made between the results of that questioning and what is taught by the magisterium of the Church, and only those things which are in agreement with the Faith should be approved. In this way powerful aids can be found to hand on effectively the one true Christian message. —*Catechetical Directory* 75.

The goals to be attained in the field of pastoral action may differ in degree and style according to differences of place and of needs. Nevertheless, all must pertain to the growth of faith and morality among Christians and to a strengthening of their relationships with God and neighbor. They should, for example, have the objectives that adults achieve a mature faith, that Christian teaching reach scientific and technical groups, that the family be able to carry out its Christian duties, that the Christian presence exert an influence on the work of social transformation. —*Catechetical Directory* 104.

The theocentric-trinitarian purpose of the economy of salvation cannot be separated from its objective, which is this: that men, set free from sin and its consequences, should be made as much like Christ as possible.[8] As the incarnation of the Word, so every revealed truth is for us men and for our salvation. To view the diverse Christian truths in their relation to the ultimate end of man is one of the conditions needed for a most fruitful understanding of them.[9]

Catechesis must, then, show clearly the very close connection of the mystery of God and Christ with man's existence and his ultimate end. This method in no way implies any contempt for the earthly goals which men are divinely called to pursue by individual or common efforts; it does, however, clearly teach that man's ultimate end is not confined to these temporal goals, but rather surpasses them beyond all expectation, to a degree that only God's love for men could make possible. — *Catechetical Directory* 42.

The truths to be believed include God's love. He created all things for the sake of Christ and restored us to life in Christ Jesus. The various aspects of the mystery are to be explained in such a way that the central fact, Jesus, as He is God's greatest gift to men, holds first place, and that from Him the other truths of Catholic teaching derive their order and hierarchy from the educational point of view.[10] — *Catechetical Directory* 16.

God, who formerly spoke to the human race by revealing Himself through divine deeds together with the message of the prophets, of Christ, and of the apostles, even now still secretly directs, through the Holy Spirit, in sacred tradition, by the light and sense of the faith, the Church, His bride, and He speaks with her, so that the People of God, under the leadership of the magisterium, may attain a fuller understanding of revelation.

The Church's shepherds not only proclaim and explain directly to the People of God the deposit of faith which has been committed to them, but moreover they make authentic judgments regarding expressions of that deposit and the explanations which the faithful seek and offer. They do this in such a way that "in holding to, practicing, and professing the heritage of the faith, there results on the part of the bishops and faithful a remarkable common effort."[11]

From this it follows that it is necessary for the ministry of the word to set forth the divine revelation such as it is taught by the magisterium and such as it expresses itself, under the watchfulness of the magisterium, in the living awareness and faith of the People of God. In this way the ministry of the word is not a mere repetition of ancient doctrine, but rather it is a faithful reproduction of it, with adaptation to new problems and with a growing understanding of it. —*Catechetical Directory* 13.

1. Cf. AG 17, 26.
2. LG 28.
3. Cf. SC 51.
4. Cf. GS 5.
5. ES 17.
6. Cf. CD 14.
7. CD 14; cf. AG 14.
8. Cf. LG 39.
9. Cf. Vatican Council I, Dogmatic Constitution *Dei Filius*, Dz-Sch., 3016.
10. Cf. *Catechetical Directory* 43, 49.
11. DV 10.

The spiritual gift which priests receive at their ordination prepared them not for a sort of limited and narrow mission but for the widest possible and universal mission of salvation, "even to the ends of the earth" (Acts 1:8), for every priestly ministry shares in the universality of the mission entrusted by Christ to His apostles. —PO 10.

Reaching Out to Others

THE DESIRE FOR UNITY

A CHANGE OF HEART

DIALOGUE FOSTERS
           UNDERSTANDING

MISSIONARY IMPULSE

SHARING THE GOOD NEWS

THE DESIRE FOR UNITY

We think that it is a duty today for the Church to deepen the awareness that she must have of herself, of the treasure of truth of which she is heir and custodian and of her mission in the world. Even before proposing for study any particular question, and even before considering what attitude to assume before the world around her, the Church in this moment must reflect on herself to find strength in the knowledge of her place in the divine plan; to find again greater light, new energy and fuller joy in the fulfillment of her own mission; and to determine the best means for making more immediate, more efficacious and more beneficial her contacts with mankind to which she belongs, even though distinguished from it by unique and unmistakable characteristics. — EcS.

The ecclesial community by prayer, example, and works of penance, exercises a true motherhood towards souls who are to be led to Christ. The Christian community forms an effective instrument by which the path to Christ and His Church is pointed out and made smooth for non-believers. It is an effective instrument also for arousing, nourishing and strengthening the faithful for their spiritual combat.

In building the Christian community, priests are never to put themselves at the service of some human faction of ideology, but, as heralds of the gospel and shepherds of the Church, they are to spend themselves for the spiritual growth of the body of Christ. — PO 6.

Let Us now speak of that unity which We especially desire, and with which the pastoral office committed to Us by God is most closely linked. I mean the unity of the Church.

Of course, all know that the divine Redeemer founded a society which was to keep its unity till the end of time, according to the promise: "Behold I am with you all days even to the consummation of the world" (Mt 28:20); and that for this intention He prayed most fervently to His heavenly Father. But this prayer of Jesus Christ, which surely was heard, and granted for His reverence (Heb 5:7): "That they all may be one as you, Father, in me, and I in you, that they also may be one in us" (Jn 17:21), implants in Us a comforting hope and gives assurance that eventually all the sheep who are not of this fold will desire to return to it; consequently, in accordance with the words of the same divine Redeemer, "there will be one fold and one shepherd" (Jn 10:16). — APC.

It is beyond doubt that the divine Redeemer established His Church and endowed and strengthened it with a strong mark of unity. Otherwise — to use an absurd expression — if He had not done so, He would have done something completely transitory and at least in the future, contradictory to Himself, in much the same way as nearly all philosophies, which depend on the whim of men's opinion, come into existence one after another in the course of time, are altered, and pass away. But it is plain to all that this is opposed to the divine teaching authority of Jesus Christ who is "the way, the truth and the life" (Jn 14:6).

This unity, however, venerable brethren and dear children — which, as We said, ought not to be something frail, uncertain and unsteady, but something solid, firm and safe — if it is lacking in other groups of Christians, it is not lacking in the Catholic Church, as all who carefully examine the question can easily observe. It is a unity which is distinguished and adorned by these three marks: unity of doctrine, of government, of religious practice.

It is a unity which is clearly visible to the gaze of all so that all can recognize and follow it. It has this nature, We say, by the will of the divine Founder, so that within it all the sheep may be gathered together into one fold, under the guidance of one shepherd; so that all the children may be invited into the one Father's house, founded on the cornerstone of Peter; and so that as a result of it, efforts may be made to link all peoples by this bond of brotherhood to the one kingdom of God, whose citizens joined harmoniously together heart and soul while on earth, may eventually enjoy happiness in heaven. — APC.

A CHANGE OF HEART

There can be no ecumenism worthy of the name without a change of heart. For it is from renewal of the inner life of our minds (cf. Eph 4:24), from self-denial and an unstinted love that desires of unity take their rise and develop in a mature way. We should therefore pray to the Holy Spirit for the grace to be genuinely self-denying, humble, gentle in the service of others, and to have an attitude of brotherly generosity towards them. St. Paul says: "I, therefore, a prisoner for the Lord, beg you to lead a life worthy of the calling to which you have been called, with all humility and meekness, with patience, forbearing one another in love, eager to maintain the unity of the spirit in the bond of peace" (Eph 4:1-3). This exhortation is directed especially to those raised to sacred Orders precisely that the work of Christ may be continued. He came among us "not to be served but to serve" (Mt 20:28).

The words of St. John hold good about sins against unity: "If we say we have not sinned, we make him a liar, and his word is not in us" (1 Jn 1:10). So we humbly beg pardon of God and of our separated brethren, just as we forgive them that trespass against us.

All the faithful should remember that the more effort they make to live holier lives according to the gospel, the better will they further Christian unity and put it into practice. For the closer their union with the Father, the Word, and the Spirit, the more deeply and easily will they be able to grow in mutual brotherly love. — UR 7.

This change of heart and holiness of life, and along with public and private prayer for the unity of Christians, should be regarded as the soul of the whole ecumenical movement, and merits the name "spiritual ecumenism."

It is a recognized custom for Catholics to have frequent recourse to that prayer for the unity of the Church which the Savior Himself on the eve of His death so fervently appealed to His Father: "That they may all be one" (Jn 17:21).

In certain special circumstances, such as the pre-scribed prayers "for unity," and during ecumenical gatherings, it is allowable, indeed desirable that Catholics should join in prayer with their separated brethren. Such prayers in common are certainly an effective means of obtaining the grace of unity, and they are a true expression of the ties which still bind Catholics to their separated brethren. "For where two or three are gathered together in my name, there am I in the midst of them" (Mt 18:20).

Yet worship in common *(communicatio in sacris)* is not to be considered as a means to be used indiscriminately for the restoration of Christian unity. There are two main principles governing the practice of such common worship: first, the bearing witness to the unity of the Church, and second, the sharing in the means of grace. Witness to the unity of the Church very generally forbids common worship to Christians, but the grace to be had from it sometimes commends this practice. The course to be adopted, with due regard to all the circumstances of time, place, and persons, is to be decided by local episcopal authority, unless otherwise provided for by the Bishops' Conference according to its statutes, or by the Holy See. — UR 8.

Before the whole world let all Christians confess their faith in the triune God, one and three in the incarnate Son of God, our Redeemer and Lord. United in their efforts, and with mutual respect, let them bear witness to our common hope which does not deceive us. In these days when cooperation in social matters is so widespread, all men without exception are called to work together, with much greater reason all those who believe in God, but most of all, all Christians in that they bear the name of Christ. Cooperation among Christians vividly expresses the relationship which in fact already unites them, and it sets in clearer relief the features of Christ the Servant.

This cooperation, which has already begun in many countries, should be developed more and more, particularly in regions where a social and technical evolution is taking place be it in a just evaluation of the dignity of the human person, the establishment of the blessings of peace, the application of gospel principles to social life, the advancement of the arts and sciences in a truly Christian spirit, or also in the use of various remedies to relieve the afflictions of our times such as famine and natural disasters, illiteracy and poverty, housing shortage and the unequal distribution of wealth. All believers in Christ can, through this cooperation, be led to acquire a better knowledge and appreciation of one another, and so pave the way to Christian unity. — UR 12.

DIALOGUE FOSTERS UNDERSTANDING

We need to keep ever present the ineffable, yet real relationship of the dialogue, which God the Father, through Christ in the Holy Spirit, has offered to us and established with us, if we are to understand the relationship which we, i.e. the Church, should strive to establish and to foster with the human race.

The dialogue of salvation was opened spontaneously on the initiative of God: "He [God] loved us first" (1 Jn 4:10); it will be up to us to take the initiative in extending to men this same dialogue, without waiting to be summoned to it.

The dialogue of salvation began with charity, with the divine goodness: "God so loved the world as to give his only-begotten Son" (Jn 3:16); nothing but fervent and unselfish love should motivate our dialogue.

The dialogue of salvation was made accessible to all; it was destined for all without distinction (cf. Col 3:11); in like manner our own dialogue should be potentially universal, i.e. all-embracing and capable of including all, except him alone who would either absolutely reject it or insincerely pretend to accept it. — EcS.

...**The Church** must be ever ready to carry on the dialogue with all men of good will, within and without its own sphere. There is no one who is a stranger to its heart, no one in whom its ministry has no interest. It has no enemies, except those who wish to be such. Its name of catholic is not an idle title. Not in vain has it received the commission to foster in the world, unity, love and peace.

The Church is not unaware of the formidable dimensions of such a mission; it knows the disproportion in numbers between those who are its members and those who are not; it knows the limitations of its power; it knows, likewise, its own human weaknesses and failings. It recognizes, too, that acceptance of the gospel depends, ultimately, not upon any apostolic efforts of its own nor upon any favorable temporal conditions, for faith is a gift of God and God alone defines in the world the times and limits of salvation.

But the Church knows that it is the seed, the leaven, the salt and light of the world. It sees clearly enough the astounding newness of modern times, but with frank confidence it stands upon the paths of history and says to men: "I have that for which you search, and that which you lack." It does not thereby promise earthly felicity, but it does offer something—its light and its grace—which makes the attainment as easy as possible; and then it speaks to men of their transcendent destiny. In doing this it speaks to them of truth, justice, freedom, progress, concord, peace and civilization. These are words whose secret is known to the Church, for Christ has entrusted the secret to its keeping. And so the Church has a message for every category of humanity: for children, for youth, for men of science and learning, for the world of labor and for every social class, for artists, for statesmen and for rulers. Most of all, the Church has words for the poor, the outcast, the suffering and the dying: for all men. — EcS.

To what extent should the Church adapt itself to the historic and local circumstances in which its mission is exercised? How should it guard against the danger of a relativism which would falsify its moral and dogmatic truth? And yet, at the same time, how can it fit itself to approach all men so as to save all, according to the example of the Apostle: "I became all things to all men that I might save all"? (1 Cor 9:22) The world cannot be saved from the outside. As the Word of God became man, so must a man to a certain degree identify himself with the forms of life of those to whom he wishes to bring the message of Christ.

Without invoking privileges which would but widen the separation, without employing unintelligible terminology, he must share the common way of life — provided that it is human and honorable — especially of the most humble, if he wishes to be listened to and understood. And before speaking, it is necessary to listen, not only to a man's voice, but to his heart. A man must first be understood and, where he merits it, agreed with. In the very act of trying to make ourselves pastors, fathers and teachers of men, we must make ourselves their brothers. The spirit of dialogue is friendship and, even more, it is service. All this we must remember and strive to put into practice according to the example and commandment that Christ left to us (cf. Jn 13:14-17).

But the danger remains. The apostle's art is a risky one. The desire to come together as brothers must not lead to a watering-down or subtracting from the truth. Our dialogue must not weaken our attachment to our Faith. In our apostolate we cannot make vague compromises about the principles of faith and action on which our profession of Christianity is based. An immoderate desire to make peace and sink differences at all costs is fundamentally, a kind of scepticism about the power and content of the Word of God which we desire to preach. Only the man who is completely faithful to the teaching of Christ can be an apostle. And only he who lives his Christian life to the full can remain uncontaminated by the errors with which he comes into contact. — EcS.

The **dialogue** supposes that we possess a state of mind which we intend to communicate to others and to foster in all our neighbors: the state of mind of one who feels within himself the burden of the apostolic mandate, of one who realizes that he can no longer separate his own salvation from the endeavor to save others, of one who strives constantly to put the message of which he is custodian into the mainstream of human discourse.

The dialogue is, then, a method of accomplishing the apostolic mission; it is an example of the art of spiritual communication. Its characteristics are the following:

1) **Clearness** above all; the dialogue supposes and demands comprehensibility; it is an outpouring of thought; it is an invitation to the exercise of the highest powers which man possesses; this very claim would be enough to classify the dialogue among the best manifestations of human activity and culture; this fundamental requirement is enough to enlist our apostolic care to review every angle of our language to guarantee that it be understandable, acceptable, and well-chosen.

2) A second characteristic of the dialogue is its **meekness**, the virtue which Christ sets before us to be learned from Him: "Learn of me because I am meek and humble of heart" (Mt 1:29); the dialogue is not proud, it is not bitter, it is not offensive. Its authority is intrinsic to the truth it explains, to the charity it communicates, to the example it proposes; it is not a command, it is not an imposition. It is peaceful; it avoids violent methods; it is patient; it is generous.

3) **Trust,** not only in the power of one's words, but also in an attitude of welcoming the trust of the interlocutor; trust promotes confidence and friendship; it binds hearts in mutual adherence to the Good which excludes all self-seeking.

4) Finally, pedagogical **prudence,** which esteems highly the psychological and moral circumstances of the listener (cf. Mt 7:6), whether he be a child, uneducated, unprepared, diffident, hostile; prudence strives to learn the sensitivities of the hearer and requires that we adapt ourselves and the manner of our presentation in a reasonable way lest we be displeasing and incomprehensible to him.

In the dialogue, conducted in this manner, the union of truth and charity, of understanding and love is achieved.
— EcS.

The way and method in which the Catholic Faith is expressed should never become an obstacle to dialogue with our brethren. It is, of course, essential that the doctrine should be clearly presented in its entirety. Nothing is so foreign to the spirit of ecumenism as a false irenicism, in which the purity of Catholic doctrine suffers loss and its genuine and certain meaning is clouded.

At the same time, the Catholic Faith must be explained more profoundly and precisely, in such a way and in such terms as our separated brethren can also really understand.

Moreover, in ecumenical dialogue, Catholic theologians standing fast by the teaching of the Church and investigating the divine mysteries with the separated brethren must proceed with love for the truth, with charity, and with humility. When comparing doctrines with one another, they should remember that in Catholic doctrine there exists a "hierarchy" of truths, since they vary in their relation to the fundamental Christian Faith. Thus the way will be opened by which through fraternal rivalry all will be stirred to a deeper understanding and a clearer presentation of the unfathomable riches of Christ (cf. Eph 3:8).
— UR 11.

The principle that We are happy to make Our own is this: Let us stress what we have in common rather than what divides us. This provides a good and fruitful subject for our dialogue. We are ready to carry it out wholeheartedly. We will say more: on many points of difference regarding tradition, spirituality, canon law, and worship, We are ready to study how We can satisfy the legitimate desires of Our Christian brothers, still separated from us. It is Our dearest wish to embrace them in a perfect union of faith and charity.

But We must add that it is not in Our power to compromise with the integrity of the Faith or the requirements of charity. We foresee that this will cause misgiving and opposition, but now that the Catholic Church has taken the initiative in restoring the unity of Christ's fold, it will not cease to go forward with all patience and consideration. It will not cease to show that the prerogatives, which keep the separated brothers at a distance, are not the fruits of historic ambition or of fanciful theological speculation, but derive from the will of Christ and that, rightly understood, they are for the good of all and make for common unity, freedom and Christian perfection. The Catholic Church will not cease, by prayer and penance, to prepare herself worthily for the longed-for reconciliation. — EcS.

MISSIONARY IMPULSE

The priesthood of Christ, in which all priests really share. is necessarily intended for all peoples and all times, and it knows no limits of blood,

nationality or time, since it is already mysteriously pre-
figured in the person of Melchisedech (cf. Heb 7:3). Let
priests remember, therefore, that the care of all Churches
must be their intimate concern. Hence, priests of such
dioceses as are rich in vocations should show themselves
willing and ready, with the permission of their own or-
dinaries (bishops), to volunteer for work in other regions,
missions or endeavors which are poor in numbers of clergy.
—PO 10.

The spirit of the community
should be so fostered as to embrace not only the local
Church, but also the universal Church. The local community should promote not only the care of its own faithful, but, filled with a missionary zeal, it should prepare
also the way to Christ for all men. —PO 6.

Being examples to the flock
(1 Pt 5:3), [priests] must take charge of their local community and serve it in such a way that it may deserve to
be given the title of the Church of God (cf. 1 Cor 1:2;
2 Cor 1:1) which is the title that distinguishes the one
People of God in its entirety. They must be mindful of
their obligation truly *to show the face of the priest's and
pastor's ministry* to believers and unbelievers, to Catholics and non-Catholics, by their daily life and care; to
bear witness to all of truth and life; as good shepherds,
to search out even those (cf. Lk 15:4-7) "who after baptism
in the Catholic Church have fallen away from sacramental
practice, or worse still, from belief,"[1] that through their
tireless work "the Church as the universal sacrament of
salvation"[2] may shine out before all men and become the
sign of God's presence in the world.[3] "Together with the
religious and their faithful, they should show by their lives

and utterance that the Church, merely by its presence here with all that it has to offer, is an inexhaustible source of those virtues which the world needs today."[4] "A priest, however, has a duty not only to his own flock but to the whole community, to which he must strive to give a truly Christian character,"[5] which should be penetrated with a genuine missionary spirit and one of Catholic universality. —RF.

Love is light and strength. Love is communication. It was because of the driving force of love that the apostles went beyond the borders of their own land and journeyed to the frontiers of the Roman Empire and doubtless even further.

The missionary mandate, "Go, therefore, and make disciples of all nations" (Mt 28:19), is always relevant. Throughout the centuries Jesus Christ repeats to all classes of the baptized His missionary command: "As the Father sent me, so am I sending you" (Jn 20:21). Our missionary duty finds its origin in this order. It finds its source in the merciful love of the Father for all mankind, without distinction of persons. "Hence, prompted by the Holy Spirit, the Church must walk the same road which Christ walked," and the Church means all of us, joined together like a body receiving its life-giving influence from the Lord Jesus.[6] God chose to rely on men to be the bearers of His gospel, the stewards of His grace, and the builders of His kingdom. Who can claim that this is no concern of his? Since there is a variety of conditions of life, and, consequently, different ways of giving a response, every member of the Church is reached by this call which is directed to each and every one. The whole Church is missionary, for her missionary activity, as the recent Council so forcibly reminded us, is an essential part of her vocation. To forget it or to carry it out carelessly would be, on our part, a betrayal of our

Master. We are dealing with a fundamental impulse, a duty of the first order, one which we must all accept, without leaving any room for doubt or limitation. — Pope Paul VI, at the consecration of Australian bishops, 12-3-70.

Although every disciple of Christ, as far as in him lies, has the duty of spreading the Faith,[7] Christ the Lord always calls whomever He will from among the number of His disciples, to be with Him and to be sent by Him to preach to the nations (cf. Mk 3:13). Therefore, by the Holy Spirit, who distributes the charismata as He wills for the common good (1 Cor 12:11), He inspires the missionary vocation in the hearts of individuals, and at the same time He raises up in the Church certain institutes[8] which take as their own special task the duty of preaching the gospel, a duty belonging to the whole Church.

They are assigned with a special vocation who, being endowed with a suitable natural temperament, and being fit as regards talent and other qualities, have been trained to undertake mission work[9]; be they native or be they foreigners: priests, religious, or laymen. Sent by legitimate authority, they go out in faith and obedience to those who are far from Christ. They are set apart for the work for which they have been taken up (cf. Acts 13:2), as ministers of the gospel, "that the offering up of the gentiles may become acceptable, being sanctified by the Holy Spirit" (Rom 15:16). — AG 23.

Man must respond to God who calls, and in such a way, that without taking counsel with flesh and blood (cf. Gal 1:16), he devotes himself wholly to the work of the gospel. This response, however, can only be given when the Holy Spirit gives His inspiration and His power. For he who is sent enters upon the life and mission of Him who "emptied Himself, taking the nature of a slave" (Phil 2:7). Therefore, he must be ready to stay at his vocation for an entire lifetime, and to renounce himself and all those whom he thus far considered as his own, and instead to "make himself all things to all men" (1 Cor 9:22).

Announcing the gospel to all nations, he confidently makes known the mystery of Christ, whose ambassador he is, so that in Him he dares to speak as he ought (cf. Eph 6:19; Acts 4:31), not being ashamed of the scandal of the cross. Following in his Master's footsteps, meek and humble of heart, he proves that His yoke is easy and His burden light (cf. Mt 11:29ff.).

By a truly evangelical life,[10] in much patience, in long-suffering, in kindness, in unaffected love (cf. 2 Cor 6:4ff.), he bears witness to his Lord, if need be to the shedding of his blood. He will ask of God the power and strength, that he may know that there is an overflowing of joy amid much testing of tribulation and deep poverty (cf. 2 Cor 8:2). Let him be convinced that obedience is the hallmark of the servant of Christ, who redeemed the human race by His obedience. —AG 24.

The leaders of the People of God must walk by faith, following the example of faithful Abraham, who in faith "obeyed by going out into a place which he was to receive for an inheritance; and he went out not knowing where he was going" (Heb 11:8). Indeed, the dispenser of the mysteries of God can see himself in the man who sowed his field, of whom the Lord said: "then sleep and rise, night and day, and the seed should sprout without his knowing" (Mk 4:27). As for the rest, the Lord Jesus, who said: "Take courage, I have overcome the world" (Jn 16:33), did not by these words promise His Church a perfect victory in this world. Certainly this holy synod rejoices that the earth has been sown with the seed of the gospel which now bears fruit in many places, under the direction of the Holy Spirit who fills the whole earth and who has stirred up a missionary spirit in the hearts of many priests and faithful. Concerning all this, this holy synod gives fervent thanks to the priests of the entire world. "Now to him who is able to accomplish all things in a measure far beyond what we ask or conceive in keeping with the power that is at work in us—to him be glory in the Church and in Christ Jesus" (Eph 3:20-21). —PO 22.

1. LG 28.
2. *Ibid.*
3. Cf. AG 15.
4. GS 43.
5. PO 6.
6. Cf. AG 5.
7. LG 17.
8. "Institutes" refers to orders, congregations, institutions and associations which work in the missions.
9. Cf. Pius XI, *Rerum Ecclesiae* (AAS, 1926, 69-7); Pius XII, *Saeculo exeunte* (AAS, 1940, 256); *Evangelii praecones* (AAS, 1951, 506).
10. Cf. Benedict XV, *Maximum illud* (AAS, 1919, 449-450).

SHARING THE GOOD NEWS

The members of the Church are impelled to carry on missionary activity by reason of the love with which they love God and by which they desire to share with all men the spiritual goods of both this life and the life to come.

By means of this missionary activity, God is fully glorified, provided that men fully and consciously accept

His work of salvation, which He has accomplished in Christ. In this way and by this means, the plan of God is fulfilled—that plan to which Christ conformed with loving obedience for the glory of the Father who sent Him (cf. Jn 7:18; 8:30, 44, 50; 17:1), that the whole human race might form one People of God and be built up into one temple of the Holy Spirit which, being the expression of brotherly harmony, corresponds with the innermost wishes of all men.

And so at last, there will be realized the plan of our Creator, who formed man to His own image and likeness, when all who share one human nature, regenerated in Christ through the Holy Spirit and beholding the glory of God, will be able to say with one accord: "Our Father."[1] —AG 7.

Priests personally represent Christ, and are collaborators of the order of bishops in that threefold sacred task which by its very nature belongs to the mission of the Church.[2] Therefore, they should fully understand that their life is also consecrated to the service of the missions. Now because by means of their own ministry—which consists principally in the Eucharist which perfects the Church—they are in communion with Christ the Head and are leading others to this communion, they cannot help but feel how much is yet wanting to the fullness of that body, and how much therefore must be done that it may grow from day to day. They shall therefore plan their pastoral care in such a way that it will serve to spread the gospel among non-Christians.

In their pastoral activities, priests should stir up and preserve amid the faithful a zeal for the evangelization of the world, by instructing them in sermons and in Christian doctrine courses about the Church's task of announcing Christ to all nations, by enlightening Christian families about the necessity and the honor of fostering missionary vocations among their own sons and daughters, by promoting mission fervor in young people from the schools and Catholic associations so that among them there may arise future heralds of the gospel. Let priests teach the faithful to pray for the missions, and let them not be ashamed to ask alms of them for this purpose, becoming like beggars for Christ and for the salvation of souls.[3] — AG 39.

Christ's command to "go into the whole world; preach the gospel to every creature" (Mk 16:15) "was inherited from the apostles by the order of bishops, assisted by priests, and united with the successor of Peter."[4]

Christ could have asked His Father and He would have given Him at once "more than twelve legions of angels" (Mt 26:53) to announce His redemption to the world. Instead, Christ gave the task and the privilege to us; to us, "the very least of all the saints" (Eph 3:8), who are indeed unworthy to be called apostles (cf. 1 Cor 15:9). He deliberately left Himself with no voice but ours to tell the glad tidings to mankind. It is we to whom this grace is given: "to preach to the Gentiles the unsearchable riches of Christ" (Eph 3:8).

...Christ, who was Himself "anointed to preach the good news to the poor...to set at liberty those who are oppressed" (Lk 4:18), would not have *us* exclude the poor and underprivileged — or, for that matter, the men of any particular race, color, tribe or human condition whatever — from the joy of hearing the good news of His gospel.

True to His spirit, our missionaries have never, at any time, thought to separate the love of God from the love of mankind, much less to oppose the one to the other. While they build the kingdom of God, they invariably labor at the same time to improve man's earthly condition. And it should be stated very firmly that the gentle message of the gospel has never, in the Church's experience, been regarded by the poor or oppressed as an affront.... The spreaders of the good news bring to every people (with due loyalty to the patrimony of the teaching of Christ and due respect for their various cultures) what they believe to be "the only, the true, the highest interpretation of human life in time, and beyond time: the Christian interpretation."[5] They indeed believe that "Christ, who died and was raised up for all, can through His Spirit offer man the light and the strength to measure up to his supreme destiny."[6] Evangelization, which responds to man's noblest aspirations, thus becomes a leaven of development.

Thus, we see the perennial need to preach the gospel, in order to offer man the ultimate reasons for his efforts towards development: "the acknowledgement by man of supreme values, and of God their source and finality... faith, a gift of God accepted by the good will of man, and unity in the charity of Christ, who calls us all to share as sons in the life of the living God, the Father of all men."[7]
—Pope Paul VI, message for Mission Sunday, 6-25-71.

Can there be a greater or more urgent duty than to preach the unsearchable riches of Christ (Eph 3:8) to the men of our time? Can there be anything nobler than to unfurl the "Ensign of the King" before those who have followed and still follow a false standard, and to win back to the victorious banner of the cross those who have abandoned it? What heart is not inflamed, is not swept forward to help at the sight of so many brothers and sisters who, misled by error, passion, temptation and prejudice, have strayed away from faith in the true God and have lost contact with the joyful and life-giving message of Christ? —SP.

Our thought takes wing to those who, giving up their father's house and their beloved homeland, enduring serious hardship and overcoming difficulties, have gone to foreign countries. At the present time they toil in far distant fields in order that the pagan peoples may be brought up according to the truth of the gospel and Christian virtue and in order that among all "the word of the Lord may run its course triumphantly" (2 Thes 3:1).

Great indeed is the task entrusted to them, to the execution and the extension of which all who are reckoned Christians or boast of that name must contribute their support, either by their prayers or by an offering according to their means. No undertaking, perhaps, is so pleasing to God as this, for it is intimately linked with that duty which binds all—the spreading of God's kingdom.

For these heralds of the gospel make a complete dedication of their lives to God, so that the light of Jesus Christ may enlighten every man who comes into this world (cf. Jn 1:8); so that His divine grace may flow through and bring warmth to all souls; so that, with a view to their salvation, all may be encouraged to a good, noble and Christian way of life.

These seek not what is their own, but what is Jesus Christ's (cf. Phil 2:21), and giving a generous hearing to the invitation of the divine Redeemer, they can make their own those words of the Apostle of the Gentiles: "We are Christ's ambassadors" (2 Cor 5:20), and "though we walk in the flesh, we do not make war according to the flesh" (2 Cor 10:3). —APC 35, 36.

1. On this synthetic idea, see the teaching of St. Irenaeus, *De Recapitulatione.* Cf. also Hippolytus, *De Antichristo,* 3: "Wishing all, and desiring to save all, wishing all the excellence of God's children and calling all the saints in one perfect man..." (PG 10, 732; GCS Hippolytus I 2, p. 6); Benedictiones Iacob, 7 (T.U., 38-1, p. 18, 1 in 4ff.); Origen, *In Ioann.* Tom. I, n. 16: "Then there will be one action of knowing God on the part of all those who have attained to God, under the leadership of the Word who is with God, that thus all sons may be correctly instructed in the knowledge of the Father, as now only the Son knows the Father" (PG 14, 49; GCS Orig. IV 20); St. Augustine, *De Sermone Domini in monte,* I 41; "Let us love what can lead us to that kingdom where no one says, 'My Father,' but all say to the one God: 'Our Father'" (PL 34, 1250);

St. Cyril Alex., *In Joann*. I: "For we are all in Christ, and the common person of humanity comes back to life in Him. That is why He is also called the New Adam.... For He dwelt among us, who by nature is the Son of God; and therefore in His Spirit we cry out: Abba, Father! But the Word dwells in all, in one temple, namely, that which He assumed for us and from us, that having us, all in Himself, He might say, as Paul says, reconcile all in one body to the Father" (PG 73, 161-164).

2. Cf. LG 28.

3. Cf. Pius XI, *Rerum Ecclesiae* (AAS, 1926, 72).

4. AG 5.

5. Address to the Parliament of Uganda, 8-1-69, AAS LXI (1969), p. 852.

6. GS 10.

7. PP 21.

Works favoring vocations, whether diocesan or national, are highly recommended to the consideration of priests.[1] In sermons, in catechetical instructions, in written articles, priests should set forth the needs of the Church both locally and universally, putting into vivid light the nature and excellence of the priestly ministry, which consoles heavy burdens with great joys, and in which in a special way, as the Fathers of the Church point out, the greatest love of Christ can be shown.[2] —PO 11.

Building Up the Ranks

LET YOUR PRIESTHOOD SHINE FORTH
DEDICATION DRAWS

LET YOUR PRIESTHOOD SHINE FORTH

Our Lord Jesus Christ did not hesitate to confide the formidable task of evangelizing the world, as it was then known, to a handful of men to all appearances lacking in number and quality. He bade this "little flock" not to lose heart (Lk 12:32), for, thanks to His constant assistance (Mt 28:20), through Him and with Him, they would overcome the world (Jn 16:33). Jesus had taught us also that the kingdom of God has an intrinsic and unobservable dynamism which enables it to grow without man's awareness of it (Mk 4:26-29).

The harvest of God's kingdom is great, but the laborers, as in the beginning, are few. Actually, they have never been as numerous as human standards would have judged sufficient. But the Lord of the kingdom demands prayers, that it may be He, the Lord of the harvest, who will send out laborers into His harvest (Mt 9:37-38). The counsels and prudence of man cannot supercede the hidden wisdom of Him who, in the history of salvation, has challenged man's wisdom and power by His own foolishness and weakness (1 Cor 1:20-31). — SCl 47.

The Shepherd and Bishop of our souls (cf. 1 Pt 2:25) so constituted His Church that the people whom He chose and acquired by His blood (cf. Acts 20:28) would have its priests to the end of time, and that Christians would never be like sheep without a shepherd (cf. Mt 9:36). Recognizing Christ's desire, and at the inspiration of the Holy Spirit, the apostles considered it their duty to select men "who will be capable of teaching others" (2 Tm 2:2). This duty, then, is a part of the priestly mission by which every priest becomes a sharer in the care of the whole Church, lest ministers be ever lacking for the People of God on earth. Since, however, there is common cause between the captain of a ship and the sailors,[3] let all Christian people be taught that it is their duty to cooperate in one way or another, by constant prayer and other means at their disposal,[4] that the Church will always have a sufficient number of priests to carry out her divine mission.

In the first place, therefore, it is the duty of priests, by the ministry of the word and by the example of their own lives, showing forth the spirit of service and true paschal joy to demonstrate to the faithful the excellence and necessity of the priesthood; then they should see to it that young men and adults whom they judge worthy of such ministry should be called by their bishops to ordination, sparing no effort or inconvenience in helping them to prepare for this call, always saving their internal and external freedom of action. In this effort, diligent and prudent spiritual direction is of the greatest value.

Parents and teachers and all who are engaged in any way in the education of boys and young men should so prepare them that they will recognize the solicitude of our Lord for His flock, will consider the needs of the Church, and will be prepared to respond generously to our Lord when He calls, saying: "Here I am, Lord, send me" (Is 6:8). This voice of the Lord calling, however, is never to be expected as something which in an extraordinary manner will be heard by the ears of the future priest. It is rather to be known and understood in the manner in which the will of God is daily made known to prudent Christians. These indications should be carefully noted by priests.[5]

Works favoring vocations, therefore, whether diocesan or national, are highly recommended to the consideration of priests.[6] In sermons, in catechetical instructions, in written articles, priests should set forth the needs of the Church both locally and universally, putting into vivid light the nature and excellence of the priestly ministry, which consoles heavy burdens with great joys, and in which in a special way, as the Fathers of the Church point out, the greatest love of Christ can be shown.[7] —PO 11.

Vocation today means renunciation. It means unpopularity, it means sacrifice. It means preferring the inner to the external life, it means choosing an austere and constant perfection instead of comfortable and insignificant mediocrity. It means the capacity to heed the imploring voices of the world of innocent souls, of those who suffer, who have no peace, no comfort, no guidance, no love: and to still the flattering, soft voices of pleasure and selfishness. It means to understand the hard but stupendous mission of the Church, now more than ever engaged in teaching man his true nature, his end, his fate and in revealing to faithful souls the immense, the ineffable riches of the charity of Christ.

It means, young men, to be young, to have a clear eye and a big heart. It means accepting the imitation of Christ as a program for life, His heroism, His sanctity, His mission of goodness and salvation. No other prospect of life offers an ideal more true, more generous, more human, more holy than the humble and faithful vocation to the priesthood of Christ. —Pope Paul VI, address on seminaries and vocations.

The Holy Spirit imposes upon us the duty to activate all the pastoral resources capable of awakening young men to the priestly vocation, to help them recognize the call of the Lord and the needs of the Church, to guide and encourage them in the midst of difficulties, to teach them how to overcome these difficulties with a spirit of faith, hope and greater love.

...Need We stress the fact that priests themselves should make the priesthood shine forth with a light that renders it desirable? Wherever a priest leads a truly evangelical life, drawing love, courage and joy from a ministry exercised in deep union with Christ, then such a testimony cannot remain for long without fruit for vocations. Who does not see this?

The collapse of the priestly ideal, hesitation concerning this ideal, as well as mediocrity of life and dissension within the clergy inevitably dries up the source of this ideal. Is this not one of the dramas of the present crisis at which so many lay Christians assist with sorrow? Yet We are firmly convinced that with God's help, with the support of so many generous priests and with the prayers of so many faithful and consecrated souls, this crisis will be overcome. — Pope Paul VI, to directors of vocations, 5-13-71.

The problem is very grave. It is a problem of men who will devote themselves in the priesthood, heart and soul, chiefly and properly to the sacred ministry,[8] after having been consecrated "to preach the gospel, to be the pastors of the faithful, to celebrate divine worship, as true priests of the New Testament who, according to their grade in the ministry, are sharers in the function of the sole Mediator, Christ."[9] The Ecumenical Council Vatican II clearly entrusted consecration of the world to the mature responsibility of the Catholic laity,[10] but it also reconfirmed the guidance of bishops and of their collaborators, the priests, because only they "ought...to preach the message of Christ in order that all earthly activities of the faithful may be imbued with the light of the gospel."[11] — Pope Paul VI, message for day of vocations, 4-24-69.

1. Cf. OT 2.
2. The Fathers teach this in their explanations of Christ's words to Peter: "Do you love me?... Feed my sheep" (Jn 21:17); thus St. John

Chrysostom, *On the Priesthood*, II, 1-2 (PG 47-48, 633); St. Gregory the Great, *Reg. Past. Liber*, P.I. c. 5 (PL 77, 19a).

3. Roman Pontifical on the Ordination of a Priest.

4. Cf. OT 2.

5. Pope Paul VI, allocution of 5-5-65, *L'Osservatore Romano* (5-6-65), p. 1.

6. Cf. OT 2.   7. See footnote 2 above.

8. LG 31.   9. Cf. *ibid.*, 28.

10. Cf. *ibid.*, 34.   11. GS 43.

DEDICATION DRAWS

The mystery of vocations pertains solely to God, and we cannot have any doubt at all that God will provide for the good of His Church, to which He promised His presence and assistance until the end of the world.

The cause of the present situation of vocations in the world is therefore to be sought in ourselves.

In ourselves, not in the souls of the young. Their generosity today is no less than before. Even though their attitude toward contemporary society often takes the form of rejection or violent rebellion, We have faith in the youth of our time. They are open to great ideals, they are hungry for authenticity, and they are ready to devote themselves to their fellows.

We therefore think that there are still numerous youthful souls who are capable of responding with greatness of soul and with loyalty to a call from God. In any case, the very quality of the vocations which are appearing in the Church today demonstrates the continuity of the divine work and brings out the deep reasons for Our hope.

The grace of a vocation placed in a soul by God is fundamentally nothing else but a more abundant provision of divine charity, destined for the Church and for the building up of God's kingdom on earth. In the times in which we live it often happens that this grace does not attain its goal. In order that it may do so, favorable conditions must be created, in the minds of the young in a particular way, in the family environment, in the Christian community and in places of training for the priestly and religious life.

In the minds of the young above all. In order that they may accept the gift of the divine vocation with enthusiasm, it is necessary that its true reality be put before them, together with all its severe demands, such as total gift of self to the love of Christ (cf. Mt 12:29), and irrevocable consecration to the exclusive service of the gospel.

In this respect considerable, indeed preponderant, weight is borne by the testimony provided by an exemplary priestly life and the value possessed by a religious life, given concrete expression in the various institutions recognized by the Church. Christ's invitation, "Come, follow me" to a future minister is conveyed through a priest, and something similar occurs in a vocation to the religious life. It is true that grave difficulties exist for the priest himself, yet he will find a new source of courage in the awareness of his responsibilities in regard to the Church's future. More than ever before, people are calling for those who will announce Jesus Christ to them. "But," says St. Paul, "how shall they hear if there be no one to preach to them?" (Rom 10:15) —Pope Paul VI, on World Day of Prayer for Vocations, 3-15-70.

We do not resign Ourself to the thought that our field of pastoral labor is barren of youthful and adult souls capable of understanding the call to the heroic service of the kingdom of God. We think that the scarcity of vocations in big cities does indeed depend to a large degree on family and social conditions, which make the consciences of new generations unresponsive to the urging of Christ's voice; but We also trust that a priest will have the virtue, rather the grace in him to light in other souls the flame which burns in his own, the fire of love for Christ the Lord, and that he will be able to do this if he be a true priest, neither sanctimonious, nor worldly, but a priest living his priesthood with intense wisdom and sacrifice in contact with the community, especially the young.

We believe that greater attraction to embrace the ecclesiastical state will be exercised by presenting the priestly life through living it in full dedication, together with the sacred celibacy which it entails, to the sole and total love of Jesus the Master and Lord, the High Priest and sole redeeming Lamb, together with the complete and exclusive following of Him in pastoral service to God's People. All this will have greater effect than a more natural and apparently easier formula, from the human point of view, in which dedication to Christ and self-sacrifice are no longer perfectly and sublimely linked together.

It is all a matter of understanding. This is the charism which conditions the life. Shall we doubt that the Holy Spirit will grant it to the more generous spirits in the new generation? Moral fortitude, gift of self, sacred and superhuman love for Christ, most true, most vital, and most sweet love (cf. Mt 19:29), in a word, the cross, accepted for one's own and others' salvation, have greater and more effective influence upon the human heart than has an invitation to take on a priesthood which has been eased by combining natural with supernatural love.

Even though there is a pressing need for vocations to the Church, We believe that transfigured and transfiguring celibacy is a better incentive to qualitative and quantitative recruitment than an easing of the canon law which prescribes celibacy firm and entire, and sets it as a seal on the loyalty and love for the kingdom and ascetic and mystic struggle of our Latin Church. You know this, and with Us you also wish it, sons and brothers. — Pope Paul VI, to Lenten preachers, 2-9-70.

MARIAN DIMENSION

Let priests love and venerate with filial devotion and veneration this Mother of the eternal High Priest, Queen of Apostles and Protectress of their own ministry. — PO 18.

Mary: Path to Christ

NEAR TO CHRIST

THE IMMACULATE ONE

QUEEN OF APOSTLES

NEAR TO CHRIST

With his mind raised to heaven and sharing in the communion of saints, the priest should very often turn to Mary the Mother of God, who received the Word of God with perfect faith, and daily ask her for the grace of conforming himself to her Son. — Ministerial Priesthood, Nov. 1971, Synod Document.

...**Mary remains** ever the path that leads to Christ. Every encounter with her can only result in an encounter with Christ Himself. For what other reason do we continually turn to Mary than to seek for the Christ she holds in her arms — to seek in her, through her and with her the Savior to whom men, in the perplexities and dangers of life here below, must of necessity have recourse, and to whom they feel the ever-recurring need of turning as to a haven of safety and an all-surpassing source of life?

And if the grave faults of men weigh heavy in the scales of God's justice and provoke its just punishments, we also know that the Lord is "the Father of mercies and the God of all comfort" (2 Cor 1:3), and that Mary most holy is His appointed steward and the generous bestower of the treasures of His mercy. — Pope Paul VI, The Month of May, 4-30-65.

...**This is** a moment in which, reflecting on our vocation to belong to Christ's Mystical Body, which is the Church, we are invited to be mindful of and to venerate her who was the Blessed Mother of the physical body of the Son of God, who became the Son of Man.[1]

It can happen on occasion that, all intent on justifying the honor which Catholics owe to Mary, even we who are invested with Christ's priesthood, when involved in controversy and apologetics against those who attack its lawfulness or attenuate its grounds, are solicitous about bringing forward the biblical, theological, traditional and devotional titles which give form to devotion to the Blessed Virgin, while to some extent we allow to languish the filial expression in our lives of our piety toward her. Perhaps it is that today we find it less easy than before to hold pious, heartfelt conversation with Mary, who, because of being Christ's Mother according to the flesh, is also spiritually our Mother, Mother of the Church.

...We have continued to discuss the Church, its essence of hierarchical communion, the fact and the mystery of the generative power conferred on some chosen ministers of the People of God. And, this time too, We have noticed the relationship between Mary and the Church, especially that between those who have the particular functions in the Church of expressing the word of God by the ministry of the word, of pouring forth the life-giving and sanctifying Spirit by means of the sacraments, and of authoritatively exercising the service of pastoral guidance of the faithful in their temporal and eschatological pilgrimage—that is to say, between us, who are priests and pastors, and the most holy Mary. It is because of that relationship that we are gathered here....

It is a relationship of analogy. Mary is the Mother of Christ; the Church is the Mother of us Christians. The more this aspect of the Church is made evident, the more the mystery of the Incarnation, from the moment of its revelation at Bethlehem, finds reflection in its historical extension, in every local Church, in this Church of Rome, and especially in this basilica which has been called "the Bethlehem of Rome" (Grisar), the easier then and the more obligatory becomes the placing side by side, the comparison, and the kinship between Mary and the Church. Let us all at this point recall a basic consideration of theology and Marian devotion. It is an ancient one, but the Council has reminded us of it.[2] It is that of St. Ambrose, who defines Mary as the "type of the Church,"[3] and again as the "figure of the Church."[4] St. Augustine echoes it: "She (Mary) showed forth in herself the figure of the Holy Church."[5] The reason is that the virginal generation of Jesus is mystically reproduced in the maternal and supernatural generation of the faithful by the Church. This is a parallel that brings us even closer to Mary: all that fullness of grace that made Mary all beautiful, most holy, immaculate — does it not find a certain reflection in the richness of grace that has been poured upon us when sacred ordination made us like to Christ in the charisms of holiness and ministerial power? It will always be a fine thing if we make Mary our priestly mirror, the "Mirror of Justice." — Pope Paul VI, to synod bishops, 11-6-69.

We must think and model our existence in an intensified way. Even though it be good in itself, we cannot have an exterior action of ministry, of speech, of charity, of apostolate which is truly priestly, if it does not arise from and does not return to its source and interior font. Our devotion to Mary educates us to this indispensable act of reflection in a dual way: because it leads us to the gospels, which inspire us and can be our gauge, and because we meet the Madonna in this identical attitude, meditating over the events of her life: "she considered in her mind what sort of greeting this might be"

(Lk 1:29); "pondering them in her heart" (Lk 2:19); "his mother kept all these things in her heart" (Lk 2:51). Mary discovered a mystery in everything that pertained to her; and it could not be otherwise for her, who was so near to Christ. Can it be any different for us who are so near to Christ that we are authorized to be "stewards of God's mysteries" (cf. 1 Cor 4:1), and to celebrate them "in the person of Christ"?

...Introduced into this path of research into the example of Mary, our whole life finds its "form" (cf. Phil 2:7), the spiritual, the moral, and especially the ascetic. Is not Mary's life entirely permeated with faith? "Blessed is she who believed!" (Lk 1:45) is Elizabeth's greeting; and one can give no higher praise to her, whose life is entirely encircled by faith. The Council has acknowledged this.[6] And does not our priestly life perhaps have the same plan; must it not be a life that derives its very existence, its qualification, its final hope, from faith?

Mary is our model in her absolute obedience which places her in the divine design: "Behold the handmaid of the Lord..." (Lk 1:38); in her humility, her poverty, her service to Christ. Everything in Mary is an example for us.

Her magnanimous courage is superior to that of all other classic figures of moral heroism. She was "beside the cross of Jesus" (Jn 19:25), to remind us that as sharers in the one priesthood of Christ, we must also share in His mission of redemption, that is, be victims with Him, wholly consecrated and offered to the service and salvation of men.

We can meditate in this way on the prophecy that weighed on Mary's heart during her whole life — the impending, mysterious sword of the passion of our Lord (cf. Lk 2:35) — and we can in this way apply to ourselves the words of the Apostle: "In my flesh I complete what is lacking in Christ's afflictions for the sake of his body, that is, the Church, of which I became a minister" (Col 1:24).

It then becomes easy, sweet, and strengthening, to repeat the beautiful ejaculatory prayer: "Mary, my Mother, my trust," today and always in our priestly lives. — Pope Paul VI, to Lenten preachers, 2-20-71.

1. Cf. St. Augustine, PL 40, 399.

2. LG 63.

3. PL 15, 1555.

4. PL 16, 326.

5. PL 40, 661.

6. Cf. LG 53, 58, 61, 63, etc.

THE IMMACULATE ONE

Christ wished to be born of a Virgin, and what a Virgin! The Immaculate One! Does this mean nothing, this drawing near to the Immaculate Virgin in our choice of the ecclesiastical state, which should be, not repressed, but exalted, transfigured, and strengthened by holy celibacy? Today we hear the negative side criticized, to the point of calling it inhuman and impossible: that is, the renouncing of sensual love and of the marriage bond, which is a normal, very worthy and holy expression of human love.

Drawing near to Mary we are aware of the triple and superior, positive value of celibacy, which so well becomes the priesthood: first, the perfect and religious mastery of self (remember St. Paul: "I chastise my body and subdue it..."? [1 Cor 9:27]), an indispensable domination for those dealing with the things of God and who become teachers and doctors of souls, and a luminous sign of direction to Christians, and to worldly people, showing the way which leads to God's kingdom. Second, ecclesiastical celibacy guarantees that the priest will be completely available for the pastoral ministry — this is obvious. Third,

a unique love, sacrificial, incomparable and inextinguish-
able for Christ our Lord, who from the cross entrusted His
Mother to the care of the disciple John, who according to
tradition remained a virgin: "Behold your son; behold
your mother..." (Jn 19:26-27). —Pope Paul VI, to Lenten
preachers, 2-20-71.

We invite you, with a soul
responsive to Christ's great love, to turn your eyes and
heart with renewed confidence and filial hope to the most
loving Mother of Jesus and Mother of the Church, and to
invoke for the Catholic priesthood her powerful and
maternal intercession. In her the People of God admire and
venerate the image of the Church, and model of faith,
charity and perfect union with Him. May Mary, Virgin and
Mother, obtain for the Church, which also is hailed as
virgin and mother,[1] to rejoice always, though with due
humility, in the faithfulness of her priests to the sublime
gift they have received of holy virginity, and to see it
flourishing and appreciated ever more and more in every
walk of life, so that the army of those who follow the
divine Lamb wherever He goes (cf. Rev 14:4) may increase throughout the earth. —SCl 98.

Let Mary's life be for you
like the portrayal of virginity, for from her, as though from
a mirror, is reflected the beauty of chastity and the ideal of
virtue. See in her the pattern of your life, for in her, as
though in a model, manifest teachings of goodness show
what you should correct, what you should copy and what
preserve.... She is the image of virginity. For such was
Mary that her life alone suffices for the instruction of all....[2]
Therefore let holy Mary guide your way of life.[3] "Her grace
was so great that it not only preserved in her the grace of
virginity, but bestowed the grace of chastity upon those
upon whom she gazed."[4] How true is the saying of Ambrose, "Oh the richness of the virginity of Mary!"[5] —SV.

Above all, we ask for ourselves that love which coming down to us is called grace, and which, rising again from us as a "fiat," echoing that of Mary, is our offering and is that charity which we hope will never go out during the years of our earthly life, so that it may burn for ever in the life immortal. Mary, we ask for love, love for Christ, unique love, highest love, love which is a gift, a sacrifice. Teach us what we already know and already humbly and faithfully profess: to be immaculate as you are; to be chaste with that tremendous and sublime commitment which is our sacred celibacy — something so much discussed by many today, and not understood by some. We know what it is: more than a state, it is a continuous act, an ever burning flame. It is a superhuman virtue, which therefore needs supernatural support. You, Mary ever Virgin, make us understand the paradoxical essence of this state, which belongs to the Latin priesthood and, for the episcopal order and the religious state, to the Churches of the East as well. And make us also understand its worth: its heroism, beauty, joy and strength; the strength and honor of a ministry without reservation, wholly directed toward dedication and immolation in the service of men; the crucifixion of the flesh (Gal 5:24), the unconditional soldiering for the kingdom of God. Mary, help us to understand: to understand once more that mysterious calling to an inseparable following of Christ (cf. Mt 19:12). Help us to love like this. — Pope Paul VI, to synod bishops, 11-6-69.

1. St. Ambrose, *De virginibus,* lib. 11, c. 2, n. 6, 15.
2. *Ibid.,* c. 3, n; P.L. XVI, 211.
3. St. Ambrose, *De institut. Virginis,* c. 7, n. 50; P.L. XVI, 319.
4. *Ibid.,* c. 13, n. 81; P.L. XVI, 339.
5. LG 63, 64.

QUEEN OF APOSTLES

Mary is the model of the Church.[1] She "possesses in an eminent degree all the graces and all the perfections" of the Church (Olier), the graces and perfections that we should and would possess. Mary is a teacher. She is a teacher for us who have the task of being, by our teaching and example, teachers of the People of God. What does Mary teach us? We know it well: the whole of the gospel!

But for us, especially? Today?

Study becomes prayer. Mary teaches us love. Mary obtains love, Mary, who conceived Christ through the power of the Holy Spirit, the Living Love which is God. She presides over the birth of the Church at Pentecost, when the same Holy Spirit takes possession of the group of the disciples, the first among them being the apostles. And she vivifies in unity and charity the historical Mystical Body of Christians, a redeemed mankind.

We have come here to implore, through Mary's intercession, the never-ending continuance of the same miracle, which can be obtained through her as from a spring, a new outpouring of the Holy Spirit. For we have discovered once again ecclesial communion, which at the apostolic level we call collegiality, that is, an intercommunion of charity and apostolic effectiveness which, at this prophetic age of the world and the Church, we wish to honor and to render more effective in sentiment and action, through love: that Love that granted Mary the power to generate Christ, and which we beg for ourselves that we may be able to carry out our mission of generating Christ in the world. —Pope Paul VI, to synod bishops, 11-6-69.

We may hope that those who meditate upon the glorious example Mary offers us may be more and more convinced of the value of a human life

entirely devoted to carrying out the heavenly Father's
will and to bringing good to others. —MD 42.

Raised above Peter, the Vicar
of Christ on earth, the Mother of our Lord Jesus shares
with Peter, in a manner which is entirely her own, a dignity, an authority, a *magisterium* which associates her in
everything with the apostolic college. Because she loved
Jesus more than Peter did it was to her that Jesus confided
in the person of John, beneath the world's redemptive
cross, all men to be her sons: the sheep and the lambs of
the flock, in the fold and outside it, making of her in some
sort a divine guardian, the common and universal Mother
of all the believers, and making her like to Peter who is
the common and universal father and the earthly shepherd.

She is the august Sovereign of the Church militant,
suffering, and triumphant; the Queen of Saints, the teacher
of every virtue, of love, of fear, of knowledge, and of holy
hope.

...If Peter holds the keys of heaven, Mary has the
keys of the heart of God. If Peter binds and looses, Mary
binds also with the chains of love. She also looses, by the
art of forgiveness. If Peter is the guardian and minister of
indulgence, Mary is the prudent and generous Treasurer
of divine favors, and "to desire grace without recourse to
her, is to desire to fly without wings."[2] —Pope Pius XII,
allocution to pilgrims of Genoa, 4-21-40.

We have noted how the
pages of the Council dedicated to you, Virgin most faithful, recognize in you one primary virtue, the first virtue
that unites us to God: faith. A person who penetrates deeply into the diagnosis of the needs of this stormy hour in
society, and, by reflection, in the Church of God, sees that
what the Church most needs in order to be united with

Christ—and therefore with God and men—is, before all else, faith: supernatural faith, faith which is simple, full and strong, sincere faith, drawn from its true source, the word of God, and from its indefectible channel, the magisterium set up and guaranteed by Christ, living faith. Do you, "blessed...who believed" (Lk 1:45), strengthen us with your example, obtain for us this charism. How could we be followers of Christ, if doubt and denial were to deaden our certainty? (cf. Jn 6:67) How could we be witnesses, as apostles, if the truth of faith became dark in our spirits?

And then, Mary, we shall ask from your example and intercession for hope. "Hail, our hope!" We also need hope—and how much hope! You, Mary, as the Council says at the end of its great lesson on the Church of God,[3] are the image and first flowering of the Church as she is to be perfected in the world to come. Likewise you shine forth on earth as a sign of sure hope and solace for the People of God, O Mother of the Church! —Pope Paul VI, to synod bishops, 11-6-69.

1. Cf. LG 52.
2. Dante, *Parad.*, XXXIII, 13-15.
3. LG 68.

Topic Index

Daughters of St. Paul

In Massachusetts
50 St. Paul's Avenue, *Boston*, Mass. 02130
172 Tremont Street, *Boston*, Mass. 02111

In New York
78 Fort Place, *Staten Island*, N.Y. 10301
625 East 187th Street, *Bronx*, N.Y. 10458
525 Main Street, *Buffalo*, N.Y. 14203

In Connecticut
202 Fairfield Avenue, *Bridgeport*, Conn. 06603

In Ohio
2105 Ontario St. (at Prospect Ave.), *Cleveland*, Ohio 44115

In Pennsylvania
1127 South Broad Street, *Philadelphia*, Pa. 19147

In Florida
2700 Biscayne Blvd., *Miami*, Florida 33137

In Louisiana
4403 Veterans Memorial Blvd., Metairie,
New Orleans, La. 70002
86 Bolton Avenue, *Alexandria*, La. 71301

In Missouri
203 Tenth St. (at Pine), *St. Louis*, Mo. 63101

In Texas
114 East Main Plaza, *San Antonio*, Texas 78205

In California
1570 Fifth Avenue, *San Diego*, Calif. 92101
278 17th Street, *Oakland*, Calif. 94612
46 Geary Street, *San Francisco*, Calif. 94108

In Canada
3022 Dufferin Street, *Toronto* 395, Ontario, Canada

In England
57, Kensington Church Street, *London* W. 8, England

In Australia
58, Abbotsford Rd., Homebush, N.S.W., *Sydney* 2140,
Australia